AF540103

THEORY OF PUBLIC ADMINISTRATION

THEORY
OF
PUBLIC ADMINISTRATION

Compiled & Edited
By
Dr. R.K. Pruthi

DISCOVERY PUBLISHING HOUSE
NEW DELHI-110002

First Published – 2005

Reprinted – 2025

ISBN: 978-81-7141-999-9

Theory of Public Administration

Published by:

DISCOVERY PUBLISHING HOUSE
4383/4B, Ansari Road, Darya Ganj
New Delhi-110 002 (India)
Phone: +91-11-23279245; 23253475; 43596065
Mobile: +91 9811179893 / +91 9871656464
E-mail: discoverybooksindia@gmail.com
orderdphbooks@gmail.com
namitwasan9@gmail.com
web: www.discoverypublishinggroup.com

Printed at:
Infinity Imaging Systems
Delhi (INDIA)

Preface

Aim of this book is to describe the character and scope of public administration. What is its theoretical and practical role in the contemporary society? How public administration is related to other social sciences? Which are its various stages of evolution? The meaning, nature and scope of comparative and development administration. It also deals with the concept significance and relevance of the new public administration.

Attempts has been made to select the material in accordance with the course contents of the subject, keeping in view latest innovations and developments. Some critical essays by the authorities on the subject have been included to facilitate further research on the subject.

We record our indebtness and acknowledgements to the authorities on the subject.

Librarians and their staff members have been kind and helpful. We thank them all.

Hard work and cooperation of my publisher and his staff members have been immense. They deserve my readers love and patronage.

R.K. Pruthi

Contents

Introduction

Administrative Theory, aims at introducing the discipline of Public Administration to you. It explains the meaning and characteristics of the discipline of Public Administration, as an aspect of governmental activity is very old. It is as old as human history. In European languages, the term Public Administration began to creep in during the seventeenth century to separate the absolute monarch's administration of public affairs from his management of his private household. It was a period when the church was separated from the state and the government was superimposed on all other societal institutions within a definite territory. In every society there are some activities like maintenance of law and order and defence which have to be undertaken in public interest. Public Administration as a system of organisation is mainly concerned with the performance of these activities. Political decision makers set the goals for the political system. It is the business of Public Administration to work for the realisation of these goals. At the present stage of man's evolution, Public Administration has proved to be indispensable. The scope of Public Administration has expanded with the rise of the modern administration state. Its growing importance in the conduct of human affairs is evident in the birth of numerous public laws, growth of public profession, accumulation of huge arms and increasing coverage of taxes and public expenditure. The domain of sate functions is almost all-comprehensive in socialist countries. Even the capitalist states have expanded their functions under compulsions of welfare considerations. The post-colonial 'third-world' countries have embarked upon Development Administration to speedily bring about state sponsored socio-economic reconstruction.

Specificity of Administration

It terms of activity, Public Administration is an aspect of a more generic concept of Public Administration. Administration has been defined as a cooperative effort towards achieving some common goals. Thus defined, administration can be found in various institutional settings such as a business firm, a hospital, a university, a government department etc. As an aspect of this more generic concept Public Administration is that species of administration which operates within a specific political setting. It is an instrument for translating political decisions into reality, it is the action part of government, the means by which the purposes and goals of government are realised". Nigro and Nigro (1980) have identified the following five important characteristics of Public Administration.

- It is a cooperative group effort in a public setting.
- It covers all three branches—legislative, executive and judicial—and their inter relationships.
- It has an important role in the formulation of public policy, and is thus a part of the political process.,
- It is different in significant ways from private administration.
- It is closely associated with numerous private groups and individuals in providing services to the community.

Public Administration Defined

Public Administration is a specialised field. It essentially deals with the machinery and procedures of government activities. Administration has been defined as a cooperative human effort towards achieving some common goals. Thus defined, administration can be found in various institutional settings such as a business firm, a hospital. a university, a government department and so on. As an aspect of this more generic concept. Public Administration is that species of administration which operates within a specific political setting. It is a means by which the policy decisions made by the political decision makers are carried out. Public Administration is decision making, planning the work to be done, formulating objectives and goals, working with the legislature and citizen organisations to gain public support and funds for government programmes, establishing and revising organisation, directing and supervising employees, providing leadership, communicating and receiving communications, determining work methods and procedures appraising performance, exercising controls and other functions performed by government executives and supervisors. It is the action part of the government, the means by which the purposes and goals of the government are realised.

Some well known definitions of Public Administration are:

- Public Administration is detailed and systematic execution of public law. Every particular application of law is an act of administration"— L.D. White.
- Public Administration is "the art and science of management applied to the affairs of the State"—D. Waldo.
- "By Public Administration is meant in common usage the activities of the executive branches of the National, State and Local Governments"—H. Simon.

The 'Public' aspect of Public Administration gives the discipline a special character. It can be looked at formerly to mean 'government'. So, Public Administration is government administration, the focus being specifically on public bureaucracy. This is the meaning commonly used in discussing Public Administration. Public Administration in a wider sense, has sought to expand its ambit by including any administration that has considerable impact on the public. From this standpoint, a private electricity undertaking like the Calcutta Electric Supply Corporation can be considered a fit subject of discussion under Public

Administration. It is, however, in the first sense that Public Administration is usually considered.

The Domain

Public Administration is the complex of government activities that are undertaken in public interest at different levels such as the central, state or provincial (in a federal set-up) and local levels. The Discipline of Public Administration aims at a systematic study of these activities. Government, as political authority, is the major regulator of social life. With the emergence of democracy, and the concept of welfare state, the governmental activities have increased by leaps and bounds. The historical movement has thus been from regulation to service and welfare. The police state has gradually given place to popular governance in the interest of widest possible public welfare in close association with the people themselves. Expanding governmental activities have resulted in expansion of the bureaucracy, creation of different forms of public and semipublic organisation, raising public expenditure, and overall control over public life. Since government has come to have such widespread influence and control over public life, its organisation, basis of authority, functions, finances and impact on society have been subjected to intellectual examination.

The area chosen by Public Administration has generally been "executive action" or the activities of the executive organ of the government. This means really a study of the bureaucracy: its structure, functions and behaviour. But, the other organs of government such as the Legislature and the judiciary have also been found useful in Public Administration analysis. The policy-forming impetus comes from the legislature, and the legislative committees very often undertake important vigilance and control function. The Estimates Committee, the Public Accounts Committee, Committee on Public Undertakings etc. could be mentioned as examples of such Committees.

Similarly, the judiciary often adjudicates on quasi-judicial issues and passes important judgements affecting executive operations. Judicial administration itself forms a major component of Public Administration. Thus, the study of Public Administration is basically focused on the 'executive' no doubt; but an adequate undertaking of Public Administration is not possible without taking into account the legislative and the judicial administration as well.

The Scope

It is widely acknowledged that the scope of the discipline of Public Administration has to be wide enough to respond to the complex social realities of today. Major concerns of the discipline are:

Promoting 'Publicness': In a democratic society, Public Administration has to be explicitly 'public' in terms of democratic values, power-sharing and openness. This calls for a new climate in the bureaucracy. Public Administration in practice, has to absorb the principles of democracy as an overarching form of the government.

Policy Sensitivity: As governments are called upon to play increasingly active roles in times of rapid changes and social crisis, innovative and timely policy formulation becomes a prime necessity in the government. This would necessitate a new preparedness within the administrative set-up that has hardly any precedence in the past.

Implementation Capability: Effective policy implementation is going to test the coping capacity of the governments in today's complex situations. Goals have to be clearly set; planning, programming and projections have to be followed step by step; and project management in all its ramifications has to have top priority in government. The strength of administration and the legitimacy of the government itself would depend more and more on the administrations capacity to deliver the goods in time and in response to the demands of the citizens.

Shared Understanding of Social Reality: The capacity to cope with social and administrative complexity can be enhanced by a deliberate policy of organisational openness. The underlying assumption here is the administration needs to understand the diverse interests and influences. In today's complex administrative world, construction of administrative reality has to be based on the shared understanding of its actors such as the men at the top, the middle managers, the employees and the citizens. The centralised, insular bureaucracy does not fit in with the contemporaneous socio-administrative reality.

Administration as a Learning Experience: Shifting social reality and complex environmental conditions impose certain rigorous on Public Administration today. Rusted 'principles' of the past or the administrative receipts of bureaucratic routine are no longer appropriate tools for analysis and problem solving. Public Administration in modern times has to be proactive, innovative, risk-taking, and often adventurous. This new, entrepreneurial zeal is expected to transform 'bureaucracy' into a new kind of learning organisation, more adaptable to changes, more open to new insights and innovations, and more accessible to the clientele.

These are the major concerns of government in all democratic countries. In the developing countries, these have added significance, as Public Administration has a pivotal role to play in the socio-economic reconstruction of post-colonial societies. The discipline of Public Administration cannot live in isolation. It has to develop in close association with the dynamic social changes. As a body of knowledge, it must develop explanatory strength to analyse socio economic complexity and assist in the ushering in of a new society free of exploitation and human misery, poverty and deprivation of the past era.

Character

The discipline of Public Administration has been evolving over the years under the impact of changing social conditions, and new developments in the allied Social Sciences. The original disciplinary interest was to improve Governmental performance: This led to its separation from is parent discipline of Political Science. In its enthusiasm to 'reform' government and make the administration agencies more business-like and productive. Public Administration as a discipline has titled markedly toward the "management sciences". The accent is on administration and managerial tools and principles such as budgeting management techniques, application of operations research methods, computer technology, etc. Such heavy management orientation has tended to rob the discipline of its social science character. It has necessarily parted company with Political Science and almost merged itself into management education. The discipline has gradually come to assume a vocational character, the objective being to produce public managers much in the same fashion as the management institutes produce a cadre of managers for the business world.

This shift of disciplinary focus has been questioned by many. While acknowledging the importance of borrowing knowledge from allied disciplines, it has been argued that Public Administration is essentially concerned with nation-building, social regulation and public service activities. Management science orientation and application of management techniques to Public Administration need not be a blind emulation of private management practices. The evaluative techniques of non-profit public organisations have to be significantly different and the basic orientation and sensitivity of public organisations to public interest brings in certain necessary constraints in governmental decision-making and bureaucratic behaviour. Functioning under the compulsions of public law and under the glare of open public and legislative criticism, the bureaucracy has willy-nilly to follow certain administrative norms that have hardly any parallel in private management. A certain sensitivity to politics and a readiness to appreciate the citizens demands and multiple interests of the clientele are desirable qualities in a bureaucrat. The private manager, by contrast, may afford to be inward-looking and secretive, but not the public servant.

Golembiewski has posed this dilemma of Public Administration as a discipline in terms of choice of 'locus' and 'focus'. 'Locus' stands for the institutional 'where' of the field, while 'focus' is the specialised 'what' of the field. As an academic discipline, for a long time, the place (locus) of Public Administration was, in most cases, with Political Science and at times with subjects like History, Economics, etc. So far, the question of 'focus' is concerned, in recent years, there has been an increasing tendency to lay emphasis on administrative techniques and not so much on public policy.

As Golembiewski has observed, the shifting paradigms (substantive concerns) of Public Administration may be understood in terms of 'locus' or 'focus', while one has been sharply defined, the other has been conceptually ignored in academic circles in turns. Depending on the definition of the substantive concerns of the discipline, Public Administration can exist within the broader field of Political Science or, move away from the mother discipline in a search for a more free floating professional career in the company of business management or the management sciences.

It may be said that since the 'New Public Administration movement of the late sixties there has been an increasing awareness of the basically social science character of the discipline of Public Administration. The vocational orientation of the discipline has been found to be somewhat misguided and supportive of status quo. In turbulent times when social problems cry out for innovative social analysis, a conservative, management oriented discipline might be inadvertently reinforcing the forces of repression and social regression.

Distinction Between Public and Business Administration

As earlier observed, the 'management' euphoria at one stage led to a blurring of distinction between public and private administration.

The distinction between the public and the private sector is however, greatly influenced by the political philosophy of each nation. In the USA, for instance, the private sector plays a very important role in the American economy and society. The public sector is in many ways dependent on the private sector for the supply of goods and services. Hence, the tendency in that country is toward a blurring of lines rather than a distinct bifurcation of responsibilities. In India, by contrast, the public sector is slowly emerging as the dominant sector in the context of mixed economy. The steady expansion of the public sector in India, if it continues unabated, is expected to draw a sharper distinction between the public and private management.

Consideration of general welfare should be the common concern of both public and business administration. Private management can ignore the larger public interest only at its peril. At the other end, Public Administration can hardly ignore the needs of efficient management. Yet, the two types are basically different, as discussed below:

(i) The major purpose of Public Administration is to serve the public; hence general welfare and, in specific cases, public satisfaction are the ends that Public Administration must serve. By contrast, business administration is basically oriented toward earning profit for the business proprietors. Inability to earn profit will soon drive a private enterprise out of business.

(ii) Public Administration has to operate strictly according to law, rules and regulations. Adherence to law brings in a degree of rigidity of operation in the public sector. There is always the fear of audit or accountability that acts as a constraint on performance. On the contrary business administration is relatively free from such constraints of law and regulations. There are of course general laws regulating business, but individual business firms have considerable flexibility to adapt their operations to changing situations. This is possible because of their relative freedom from specific laws and rules that abound in Public Administration.

(iii) The actions of Public Administration are much more exposed to the public gaze. An achievement rarely gets publicity, but a little fault hits the newspaper headline. Organisations like the police have to be on their toes to make sure that their operations do not incur the public wrath. The wide publicity is not to be found in business administration, nor is it so very closely watched by the public and the media.

(iv) In Public Administration, any show of discrimination of partiality will evoke public census or legislative commotion. Hence, the administrators are to be very consistent and impartial in their dealings with the public. In business administration, discrimination is

freely practised due to competitive demands. In the choice of products and in fixing prices, business administration overtly practises discrimination which is almost a part of business culture.

(v) Public Administration, especially at higher levels of government, is exceedingly complex. There are many pulls and pressures, many minds have to meet and discuss, consultations go on in several rounds of meetings before decisions are taken. Activities is one department have ramifications that spread over several other departments. By contrast, business administration is, generally speaking, much more well-knit and single-minded in operation. There is much less complexity in organisation and operations. The pressures are certainly almost non-existent.

(vi) Public Administration as organisation is thus much more complex, compared to business or private organisation. Any unit of government administration is tied up with a network of allied public organisations and has to work in close interaction with them. A private organisation by contrast, has more compactness, insularity and autonomy of action.

(vii) Public Administration has overarching responsibilities in terms of nation-building, and shaping the future society. It is, therefore, much more value oriented. Business organisations have to follow the guidelines laid down by the public authorities.

All societies have their political systems and economic systems, so also they have their Public Administrative Systems. In contemporary societies, Public Administration has proved to be indispensable. Its scope is very wide. It includes all the activities undertaken by the government in public interest. Business Administration and Public Administration have much in common through their are several points of differences as well.

2

Definition of Administration

Administration is that part of the activity of a body or group of men which is concerned with the management of the affairs of that body or group. It consists of the acts or series of acts committed on behalf of that body or group and which bear on the strength and fortunes of that body. That group may be a family or a club, a business company or a religious corporation, a State or a union of States. When the father of a family arranges the time-table of the life of the family or punishes a child for playing truant at school or coming home late at night, or a mother gives instructions to the cook about the food for the day or the secretary of a club arranges for a whist drive, or the General Manager of a railway company issues alterations to the time-table or passenger-fares, they are said to administer the affairs of the body or group to which they belong. When administration has to do with the affairs of a State or minor political institutions like Municipal or Country Council, or District Board, it is called Public Administration. All the acts of the officials of a Government from the people in a remote office to the Head of a State at the capital constitute public administration. These acts must be committed by them in their capacity of officials of the State. A people posting a letter to his mother inquiring after her health is not doing an act of public administration but he would, if he were posting a letter in which the Government granted leave to the Magistrate of a district.

Administration, an Art and a Science—But an Art more than a Science

As administration, private or public, consists of acts or a series of acts, the doing of things, it is an art. Whether a member of an administration called for short, an official, speaks or writers, or tours on duty he does a thing which has some practical end, the collection of revenue for the State, or the building of a road for a village, or the keeping out yellow fever from the country by means of quarantine rules. As administration consists of deeds and acts with a practical end in view, it is an art. But like all arts to be perfected or developed to all possible perfection it must be based on science, that is a knowledge of all that will make for good administration. Just as a painter, to be a great artist and not a mere user of colours must know the laws of composition, of perspective, of the decomposition of light, and of the harmony of colours, so the successful administrator must possess knowledge of political economy which is the science of the wealth of nations—in fact, the first considerable work in political economy was called by its author Adam Smith, the *Wealth of Nations*—some knowledge of psychology, especially the psychology of the crowd, as administration has to manage men not only "in singles but in battalions", some knowledge of the general principles of science, as science has been put at the service of human welfare in modern times, some knowledge of the general principles of government, as administration is a section of government—all this and other kind of knowledge would be useful and even necessary, to the administrator. For modern government is a complex and complicated machine, it has to do so many things for the people, it is faced by so numerous and so difficult problems that are mixed up with so many other branches of modern life, that the administration of a modern State, becomes difficult if not impossible if the administrator especially in the higher ranges of administration is not equipped with knowledge.. Science, therefore,—and what is science but systematised knowledge, the study and classification, of a body of facts coming within its range and getting them into one ordered whole—forms the foundation of administration as of every other art.

It is not only to this extent that administration is a science. It is a science also in the sense of an organised and systematised body of knowledge on the art of administration. Administration of some sort has existed from the beginning of the history of human government. The patriarchal Sheikh, in his tent ordering the movements of his pastoral tribe, the feudal noble in his castle whether in Normandy or in Rajasthan counting the levies to be furnished by his vassals, the enlightened despot of the age of Louis XIV, of France, or Frederick the Great of Prussia, or Peter the Great of Russia, organizing his army for conquest, or creating Ministries of industry and commerce, or a modern ruler in the manner of Napoleon stimulating administrative reform on rational and utilitarian lines, or the makers and rulers of the modern Welfare State, intervening even in the private lives of people for their good have in the course of history accumulated a large and extensive volume of knowledge in this business of administration. That knowledge gathered and systematised in books on administration such as this, forms the science of administration.

It was the conviction of a great administrator, that there is a science of administration. Lord Haldane, described by Lord Haig, Commander-in-Chief of the British Army, in the first World War of 1914-1918 as the greatest war minister since Pitt, giving evidence before the Royal Commission on coal in 1919 spoke of the science of administration and when he was asked if it was something that can be taught and not merely got up "in the act of actual administration" he answered "Certainly, taught exactly as a university professor teaches his students." Another great administrator, Lord Milner, conservative though he was in politics, was of the opinion that "the empirical method is out of date". The condition which according to an academic authority is, necessary to build up a separate science of administration, requiring primarily a subject-matter which could be distinguished from other subject-matter for particular study but forming part of the processes of nature and of life is fulfilled in the case of administration. Any great administrative act or proceeding requires a mass of knowledge to initiate it and perfect it. When a Finance Minister who is framing a Budget for the next financial year and wishes to remit certain old taxes or impose new ones requires so much information both on the nature of these taxes, the persons or things they affect, the incidence of the taxes, the economic consequences of these taxes, that his act unjustified and unsupported by the necessary information would mean disaster to the finances and the economic welfare of the country. A great British administrator was of the opinion that, if France and Germany had had as efficient and well-organised a system and department of Inland Revenue of England has the problem of raising as income tax in those countries would have been easier and the failure of the French Income Tax came through the failure of the French Finance Department to know how such a tax should be raised and what returns could reasonably be expected from it. The Government of a colony or the administration of an Education or an Insurance Act requires the collection and classification of a mass of facts gathered without reference to the use to be made of them.

This volume of knowledge in administration, as the science of administration has reached such proportions that schools of public administration, are to be found in England and American Universities. The Institute of Public Administration in England with its Journal of Public Administration, the French Review of Administrative Sciences, and the International Conference on Administrative Sciences further show that knowledge of public administration is being organised and systematised, in other words it is becoming a science. Public Administration has also attained respectability in India, it has become the subject of study at universities. In India administration has a great historic tradition—it has filled a much larger place in government than the Legislature or even the Judiciary. Kautilya's *Arthasastra* which is more a manual of administration than a treatise on political philosophy the *Akbar Namah* of Mugal times and the Daftar of the Mahrattas and the Records and Reports and Blue Books of the British period contain records of administrative experience which few countries can match.

But when all that is said and done about the science of public administration, administration persists in being an art. For administration when it begins to operate, issues in an act or series of acts. It is the doing of things, preceded, no doubt, by knowledge information, science. All the science of public administration will not get things done in administration. It may help to good action but it is no substitute for action. In the beginning of administration there must be thought but in th end there must be action and action is art.

The Place of Administration in Government

To gain a clearer notion of what administration is, we might compare and contrast it with other branches of government. How does Administration stand to the other chief powers in the State?

One thing is certain, and that is that the administration must be in keeping with the other institutions of government. Despotic or aristocratic or democratic systems of government require different kinds of administration. The general principles of a government must inform and govern its administration. As Burke observed "if a system of administration is attempted entirely repugnant to the genius of the people and not conformable to the plan of their government everything must necessarily be disordered for a time until this system destroys the constitution or the constitution gets the better of this system."

Thus the administrative system of any State must be in keeping with its legislature. As Burke again insisted "every sort of government ought to have its administration correspondent to its legislature." A legislature constituted on the aristocratic principle will have its chief administrative offices filled by scions of the nobility. A democratic legislature must have the administrative services filled with persons representative of every class of the people. Popular election in the one will require election to the great administrative offices and even to the smaller administrative offices as in the United States of America. If popular election causes inefficiency and corruption, selection by impersonal methods like free and open competitive examination making possible careers open to talent must be used.

According to modern constitutional theory the Administration is supposed to be the subordinative of the Legislature. But this is true only to the extent that the latter is also at the same time the national representative assembly of the people. This does not mean that the Administration is the servant of the Legislature, that its business is only to carry out the laws and other directions of the

Legislature. If the Administration had to wait for its work and activity on the laws and directions of the Legislature it would have to mark time for long periods. In fact, in all matters not legislated for, the Administration has its own jurisdiction and exercises its own discretion. Daily, departments of administration and officials issue directions, take decisions, make arrangements for which extant laws make no provision. Not every contingency or circumstance can be provided for by a legislature, however active and fecund it may be. And legislatures have vacationus whereas the Administration has to be in constant and continuos session. The Administration has a right to exist and work independent of any support given to it by a legislature. Administration cannot be the slave of the Legislature. An Administration bound hand and foot to a Legislature cannot do justice to its work. Responsible, administration is to a Legislature under the modern system of constitutional government. But subordinate, it is not, as a servant is to a master. It is the instrument of the Legislature. It has been called the legislature in action. But just as a workman cannot do with his tools or instruments what he likes but must follow the rules and laws of his work—the laws of mechanics or the laws of resistance—so a legislature has to respect the law and rules by which administration works. The nature of things political give it a right to exist and act according the laws of its being.

The Judiciary being entrusted with the guardianship of the laws of the country has and exercises jurisdiction over the acts of the administration. For, officials high and low in the execution of their duties may contravene the laws of their country or venture beyond the lawful exercise of their discretion. For instance, a police officer in putting down a riot or minor disturbance may, in the exercise of his common law right and duty to put down force by force, use more force than was necessary to disperse the people that were creating the riot or the disturbance. A court of law, if it is moved by one or those that were injured by the police officer's use of force may pronounce judgement on the act of the officer and have sentence of punishment passed on him. This is possible in a free state where the rule of law prevails. Since in a free state everyone from the highest to the lowest is bound by law, officers of the administration especially with the vast powers they wield in the modern State should be kept on the straight path of law and justice. In certain countries like France, officials are subject to the jurisdiction of a special system of law called *droit administrative* or administrative law and special administrative courts. But it is law and courts of law all the same. In England the ordinary courts of law have jurisdiction over the official for his public as his private acts, as the ordinary citizen. The difference between the two systems is due to differences of historical experience and political tradition. Administrative law is a body of statutory and codified law and is as free from arbitrary addition or substitution as the general law of the land and is not made at the discretion of officials. The administrative courts are as independent of the administration as the English Courts of law. In fact they have some advantage over the English system which we shall examine when we come to deal will the system of administrative tribunals and administrative law.

But the submission of administration to law and law courts does not mean that the administration is subordinate to the judiciary. It does not mean that everyone of its acts is subject to the scrutiny and review of courts of law. The acts of the administration so far as they interfere with the rights of the citizen should be subject to the jurisdiction of courts of law. The citizen should be able to challenge points of law involved in administrative action, he should be able to show that such action is *ultra vires* of the law. He should also be permitted to attack an administrative act on the ground that the manner of its exercise is improper according to the rules of natural justice. But the courts may not review the act of the administrator in regard to purely technical acts of administration, for instance deciding whether a house is fit for human habitation or not, as courts of law are ill-equipped for performing such administrative work. The autonomy of administration is to be asserted as much against the Judiciary as against the Legislature. Each has its own sphere of activity. And the State is well governed where Legislature, Judiciary and Administration, each keeps within its sphere and rights, and respects the boundaries and rights of the other.

Administration and Allied Subjects of Study

The study of public administration would gain not only from a consideration of the distinction between the administrative and the other parts of government, but from a consideration of the distinction between administration and other studies allied to it. Administration must be distinguished from Politics, Law, Economics, Sociology. Politics is the study of the State and Government in general, whereas Administration is a study of a part of the executive government of a State. Administration, therefore, does not concern itself with the kinds of government or the ends of government. It is an instrument of government and therefore common to all forms of government. Administration is to be distinguished from Constitutional Law which is concerned with the several institutions of government and their relations. Neglect of the distinction accounts for many books on Indian Administration which deal with the several institutions of government like the Legislature and the judiciary and their relations whereas Administration deals with one part of one institution of government, namely the executive in action. Although administrators must be familiar with Economics, they have to apply the teachings of Economics in their activities so far as government affects or is affected by the economic life and ideals of the people. And while all that Sociology or social science has to teach the administrator may be useful he uses it and is not dominated by it. The study of administration would benefit by the definition and limitation of its scope and range. Here, as it many other human activities, restraint is the condition of efficiency.

Administration and the People

More than the other parts of government, Administration comes close to the "business and bosoms" of the people. In is the branch of government that touches more directly and more strikingly than any other lives of the people. The Legislature may pass laws for the people, but they remain on the statute book till the administration applies them and brings them home, and so to speak, to the doors of the people. It is the administration through its Ration Shops, its Ration Officers, its Ration cards, that puts the system of rationing through. The Judiciary may sit in judgement over the acts of the Administration and even bring officers of the administration to book for offences committed by them in the course of the performance of their official duties. But the judges have to wait till case and offenders are brought before them. It is the Administration that discovers cases of offence against the law and sends them to the courts. It is the police, an important department of the administration, that looks out and detects such cases, takes hold of the offenders and produces them before the courts for trial. In other and countless ways the administration comes into contact with the people. Through its tax-collectors it collects the money of the people for the service of the State. Through the land-revenue system in India the revenue officials from the Collector of the District to the village headman and Karnam brings Government and people into direct contact with each other. The postman bringing letters to one's home or office brings one into touch with the department of government that runs the postal system of the country. Through the schools and colleges, and hospitals and agricultural farms, other departments of government bring the work of government for the people to their notice. In fact, not a day passes in the lives of the people without one or other activity of one or other department of government being placed before the eyes of the people.

As the benefits, so the evils of administration are felt by the people from the centre to the circumference of the State and in between. Especially, the poor suffer poignantly from the wrong doings of officials. If a policeman takes to brow-beating, it is the poor that he brow-beats. If the revenue officer takes bribes, it is the poor ryot that pays through his nose. If the clerk in the registration office delays registering deeds it is the poor man that suffers most from the delay. It is the poor that the peon at the office door shoos away from interview with his officer. It is the common people that benefit most from good administration and suffer most from bad administration. Good administration is therefore a popular interest.

Importance of Administration

One can, therefore, understand the importance of administration in the life of a people. It is this part of the government of a country which carries on the day to day management of the affairs of a State. It is the Administration that defends through the Defence Department and Defence Services, the State against enemies from without. It is the Administration that through the Police Department preserves internal security and order. It is the Administration that through the Finance Department collects the revenue of the State and authorizes expenditure for the purpose of government. It is through other departments that the State performs the services that the modern State renders to its people. In the promotion of the education, the health, and the economic prosperiety of the people it is through Administration that the modern State serves the people. In fact it would be no exaggeration to say that administration is the indispensable part of the government of a State, that part without which the State would break down. It is possible for a State to exist without a legislature in fact States have existed without legislatures; India in the days before British Rule was one such country. A State may exist without an independent judiciary as in Nazi Germany or other totalitarian States. But no State can exist without administration. And it has lasted whatever changes may take place in the other parts of the government or in the life of the people. Systems of government may have their day and cease to be, constitutions may come and go, but Administration goes on for ever. "Constitute government how you please" and Burke, "infinitely the greater part of it must depend on the exercise of the powers which are left at large to the ministers of State" and he was also of the opinion that the due arrangement of men in the active part of the State, far from being foreign to the purposes of a wise government, ought to be among its very first and dearest objects "for otherwise" Burke adjoured "your commonwealth is no better than a scheme on paper; and not a living, active, effective constitution."

Administration survives even revolution. Throughout the cataclysm of the French Revolution, even in the time of the Terror, the administration of the ancient regime persisted. The Napoleonic reforms have survived down to the time of the Fourth Republic of France. The Russian bureaucracy has been utilised and developed by the Soviet in Russia. The Congress Party and Government in India have not repudiated the administrative system of the British.

Especially, must a democracy realise the importance of administration, for the ideals of a democracy, especially the protection and progress of the common man, can be realised chiefly through administration. Bu if administration is to serve democracy, it must be left to operate according to its nature and using the methods and instruments peculiar to it, and enjoying that freedom and autonomy under the law and the constitution which is necessary to the efficient functioning of every institution. "But the new democracies" a great student and teacher of politics who also had wide acquaintance with administration said "suffer from an insufficient appreciation of the need in modern States of legislative and administrative knowledge and skill." But this insufficient appreciation does not prevent them from claiming the right of interference in the details of administration. Such undue intervention of democracy or its representative in administration would only tend to impair the efficiency of administration. And democracy would lose the services of an effective instrument for the realisation of its ideals.

3

Nature, Scope and Importance of Public Administration

Meaning of 'Administration'

The word, administer, is derived from a combination of two latin words, *viz 'ad* and '*ministiare'* which means 'to serve'. In other words, administration is the management or proper ordering to the collective activities of human beings. And as most of the human activities are collective and cooperative, "administration is a general process" which is discernible in every group activity, whether private or public, large or small. "It is" as Prof. John A. Vieg puts it, "the systematised ordering of affairs and the calculated use of resources, aimed at making those things happen which we want to happen and simultaneously preventing developments that fail to square with or intentions". Pfiffner defines it "as the organisation and direction of human and materiel resources to achieve desired ends.". Herbert A. Simon defines it as "the activities of group cooperating to accomplish common goals"

We are well aware of the marvels of modern science and technology. We look at the working of a power plant or an automobile and wonder at the mind of the scientist who invented it. But very few of us are conscious of the social technology (*i.e.* cooperation) which lies behind this invention, that is, the technology of the 'invention' of inventions. Could Stephenson invent an engine in solitude? Or for the matter of that, can any scientist invent by remaining outside the society? In other words, can any technological research or invention take place in a social vacuum? Behind the invention of an automobile, the running of a factory or the carrying on of a business there lies an intricate web of human cooperation and coordination. Without such a cooperation no mill or factory can work. Usually we take this cooperation for granted. But we seldom realize the time and energy, both mental and physical, which this development of human relationship has taken and is still taking. When the first atomic bomb fell upon Hiroshima, every one wondered upon the mind of the scientist who invented it. But did anybody think of the vast and intricate human organisation that made the bomb travel safe from an obscure place in the United States and to explode according to plan over that beautiful but unfortunate eity? Had there been any defect in this machinery of human organisation, could the bomb explode over Hiroshima at that fateful hour of 6th August, 1945?

Ordinarily we are not conscious of the intricacies of these human relationship because they have mostly got institutionalised and have become a part of our nature. But there is no gainsaying the fact that there is a technology of social relationships just as there is technology of physical sciences. Where men live together, they have to work together and where they work together they have to be so put to their jobs and to each other as to create a harmonious combination of men and material. The technology of this harmonious combination of men and material is called 'administration'.

We described administration as a collective activity directed towards the attainment of a common goal. That means it is a rational action—that is, an endeavour to maximize one's goal achievement by rationally relating means to ends. For example, for the rolling of a stone to a fixed place, persons are put to the stone, (*i.e.* organised) in such a relationship as to maximize their efforts in a certain given direction. Now, this arrangement of the persons in relation to the stone (*i.e.* the job) is called 'organisation' and the act of arranging the relationship is called 'management'. These two factors—namely organisation and management—are a special feature of the administrative activity. Every collective activity cannot be called administration. When two school boys are dragging a class-room furniture in two opposite directions, then it is no administration. When two thieves, engaged in breaking open an iron safe, incidentally hit at the alarm-bell fixed to the lock of the safe and thus awake the owners, they perform no administrative activity. Administration is only that type of collective activity which involves rational organisation and management of men and material.

Meaning of Public Administration

Now, a rational activity involving organisation and management of men and material may be found in any group, big or small. It is found in a club, a society and an association, a school and a university, and in corporations and states. So there is administration in all these and innumerable other like them. But when the term refers to the activities of a club, association and company or corporation, it is called Private Administration; and when it refers to those of the State, Central, regional or local, it is called Public Administration.

In political science, the term, public administration, is used in two senses—in a broader sense and in a narrow one. In its broader sense, it denotes the work involved in the actual conduct of governmental affairs regardless of the particular branch of government concerned. Thus we speak of administration of justice or administration of the legislative affairs. In its narrow sense, it denotes the operation of the administrative branch only. Although the traditional classification of government is made into legislative, executive and judicial branches, yet there arose during the nineteenth century a custom—due to reasons we shall study later on when we come to the growth of the study of Public Administration—of dividing government into policy-determining or political branch and administrative branch. The function of the former was to lay down public policy through statute, executive order or judicial decree and that of the latter to enforce this policy. There, thus, arose a dichotomy of politics and administration. And this give rise to the development of Public Administration as a separate and distinct subject of study. It won't be out of place to mention here that there are writers and thinkers, specially in our country, who use the term as covering the whole-field of government. Books have been published which purport to deal with public administration (*e.g.* Palande's Indian Administration) but actually deal with all the activities of the government, executive, legislative and judicial. Such writers confuse between Principles of Government and Principles of Public Administration. Now, while conceding that public administration may sometimes be called upon to exercise, in a subsidiary way, the legislative and adjudicative activities, it is mainly confined to purely administrative activities of the government, or to be more exact, with the administrative activities of the non-military, civil departments, commissions and corporations of the government.

Growth of Public Administration

The administrative activity, as distinct from the governing activity, beings to develop very early in the history of civilisation. It is a normal product of division of labour and specialisation of functions. Although not so discernible in the age of primitive cave dwellers, it is quite developed when human life gets organised into households, each with a Pater Familia. And while in the Pater Familia, there appears no distinction between private and public administration, with the development of village communities this differentiation is well-marked. Perhaps the earliest public administrator was the tax-collector who, usually a member of the Royal Households, was sent by the King with orders to collect his fee of peace from other households. The early Vedic Age is a fine example in question.

This process continues and with the growth of civilisation we find another kind of differentiation of administration, namely, regionalisation of administration—a differentiation of central and local administration. With the growth of complexities in social life, the King finds himself overburdened with public activities. Hence he begins to delegate the less important of them to his Ministers, usually to members of the Royal Households, who, on their part, further delegate them to their assistants. These "assistants" may be called the Fathers of the modern Civil Service. Their task might have been partly mental and partly clerical.

The growth of autocratic monarchies in Egypt, China and India gave a great impetus to public administration. In China, specially, the art of administration made rapid strides, as the political axioms of Confucius show. She developed in the Third century B.C. a Civil Service which resembled in many respects the modern Civil Service. The urban civilisation of Rome gave administration a legal form. The growth of feudalism during the Middle Ages checked its growth. But the emergence of the autocratic national monarchies in the Renaissance period set the sail again and it grew very rapidly to its present formidable place. The Prussian and the French Monarchies have made the largest contribution to its development and their systems have left indelible marks upon its form and structure. The growth of liberal democracy in the wake of the Industrial Revolution has given the greatest impetus to its development. It has not only given it a new form but also a new content. The formal organisation of government posts into pyramidal hierarchies, the transformation of 'Civil Services' into 'Public Services', the growth of the Budgetary system and the system of internal and external controls are some of the most conspicuous contributions of this period. In recent years, the growth to international organisations like the U.N.O. the UNESCO, the I.L.O. and the Public Corporations, like the B.B.C. the TVA and the DVC, have added much to its complexion and character.

Definition, Scope and Importance of Public Administration

No study can be called systematic unless its terms have well-defined meanings and its subject-matter has well-defined principles. Hence attempts were made quite early to provide Public Administration with a set terminology and principles. The earliest attempt at definition of Public Administration was made by Hamiltion in the Federalist. But it was more a description than a definition. The most acceptable definition produced in the Nineteenth Century was that of Prof. Woodrow Wilson who defined it as "detailed and systematic execution of public law." Modern writers have tried to improve this definition in their own ways.

According to Dr. Leonard D. White, "Public Administration consists of all those operations having for their purpose the fulfilment and enforcement of public policy as declared by competent authorities." Prof. Pfiffner defines it "as the coordination of collective efforts to implement public policy." Harvey Walker defines it thus: "The work which the government does to give effect to a law is called administration." According to Willoughby, "administrative function is the function of actually administering the law as declared by the Legislative and interpreted by the judicial branches of the government." A comprehensive though a lengthy, definition is given by Marshal E. Dimock. According to him, "Administration is concerned with the "what" and "how" of Government. The "what" is the subject-matter, the technical knowledge of a field which enables an administrator to perform his task. The "how" is the technique of management, the principles, the principles according to which comprehensive programmes are carried through a success."

Taking another set of definitions, Waldo defines Public Administration as "the art and science of management as applied to affairs of state." According to Luther Gulick, "Public Administration is that part of the science of administration which has to do with government and thus concerns itself primarily with the executive branch where the work of the government is done.

While some of these definitions are good epigrammatically, they hardly make the meaning of the term clear. In order to explain one abstract term, they have introduced many others like "Management", 'Public Policy' or "Public Affairs", Principles and "Art" and "Science" of Administration. Instead of clearing the sense, they confuse the mind. We, therefore, start with an analysis of the term and would pass on to its scope and subject-matter.

The term, Public Administration, is a combination of two words, *viz.*, "Public" and "administration". We saw above that administration is a collective rational activity. An activity is collective when it cannot be performed by a person singly and it is rational when directed to desired ends. Now, administration presupposes a particular type of cooperation. A crowd performance is no administration. Human cooperation in terms of administration involves an authoritative and habitual personal relationship, called, 'organisation' in administrative terminology. It gives a set pattern to cooperation. Rationality involves conscious, calculated effort of relating means to ends. This is called 'Management' in the administrative terminology. So administration is the organisation and management of human efforts for the achievement of some objects.

When the objects to be thus achieved are "Public", then it is called public administration and when they are "Private", then it is called private administration.

But what is public and what is private? In actual practice it is very difficult to draw a line of demarcation. Usually we say that all governments activities are public administration and all non-governments activities are private administration. But there are so many private activities which governments perform and which are not studied in Public Administration. Another distinction which is usually made between public and private is that activities leading to public or common good are public and those leading to private good are private. But there are lot of public welfare activities carried on by private organisation, such as, Charitable Trusts, Philanthropist Societies and so on and yet we do not include these organisations in the study of Public Administration. Another distinction that is pointed out is that profit making is the chief motive of private administration, while public service is that of public administration. But there are in the government business concerns which do make profit and, on the other hand, there are, in private life, organisations which are not at all run on profit motive but are run public service. Yet another distinction made between public and private administration is that the former is clothed with coercive authority while that latter is not. But Dr. Charles E. Merriam has shown "the Poverty of Power" in the so called sovereign States. This 'Poverty of Power,' he says, "may in certain cases reveal in a lightening flash the weakness of those who seem to be invincible". No doubt, the state has a military and a police force which other groups do not have. But society is not sustained at force. "The Church, or the industry, or the labour union may protest effectively without the sword or even in extreme cases against the sword". Then, public and private administrations are also distinguished on grounds of public responsibility and accountability and a system of bureaucratic organisation. But these features are now no less visible in private administration than in public.

So all the generalisations which distinguish public administration from private administration "by special care for equality of treatment, legal authorisation of and responsibility for action, public justification or justifiability of decisions, financial probity and meticulousness and so forth" are, as Prof. Waldo says only of "very limited applicability." What basically distinguishes public administration from private administration are the cultural values which a community might cherish at a particular age. To put it in Prof. Waldo's words, "the concept of culture—plus knowledge about the actual culture—enables us to see administration in any particular society in relation to all factors which surround and condition it, political theories, educational system, class and caste distinctions, economic technology and so forth. And enabling us to see administration in terms of its environment, it enables us to understand differences in administration between different societies which would be inexplicable if men were limited to viewing administration analytically in terms of the universals of administration itself. For as the constituent parts of culture vary within a society, or between societies, so does administration vary as a system of rational cooperative action in that society, or between societies."

Scope of Public Administration

Broadly speaking, Public Administration embraces all the area and activity under the jurisdiction of public policy—public policy considered in terms of the cultural values of the community. But by established usage, the term "has come to signify primarily the organisation, personnel, practices and procedures essential to effective performance of the civilian functions entrusted to the executive branch of government." The first point which needs clarification is that Public Administration is concerned with the performance of only the civilian part of public policy. The definitions given above seem to confuse tnis point. Public

Administration does not include the study of Military, Police. Judicial or Legislative administrations, although they too share in the implementation of public policy.

From the functional point of view, Public Administration covers everything the civilian agencies of the government do, or could do, to help the body politic attain its purpose. After all, Administration is only a means to the attainment of the objects of the state. Therefore, 'the ends of administration are the ultimate objects of the state itself—the maintenance of peace and order, the progressive achievement of justice, the instruction of the young, protection against disease and insecurity, the adjustment and compromise of conflicting groups and interests—in short, the attainment of good life." The last clause in the above sentence better explain the point, than the whole sentence, because the ends of the state change from time to time and society to society. In ancient time, they included every aspect of human life—their religion, social and cultural life and their all. During the Medieval period, they remained mainly undefined During the Eighteenth and Nineteenth centuries, they were limited to only military and police activities. And now since the spread of the concept of Welfare State, they embrace innumerable social, cultural and economic activities but totally exclude the religious activities. So the scope of Public Administration varies with the people's conception of good life.

Although not completely ignoring the individual problems and activities of the various civilian agencies of the government, Public Administration centres its concern mainly in matters of organisation, management, procedure, and methods and technique common to all or most of these agencies. It is not so much concerned with the particular activities of, say, the health department in this government or that, but with those problems and conditions which are general to all or most of the departments and to which certain general principles may be uniformly applicable. The general problems comprise the Elements of Public Administration which are as follows:

1. *Organisation:* Which means "the structuring of individuals and functions into productive relationship."

It represents the state pattern of administration. We may call it the "Anatomy" of administration .

2. *Management of Personnel*: Which is "concerned with the direction of these individuals and functions to achieve ends previously determined." It represents the dynamic aspect of administration and may be called its "Physiology."

3. *Method and Procedure:* Which is the technique of administering, the process of working, *i.e.*, the 'how' of administration.

4. *Material and Supply:* These are the tools with whose help the administrative work is carried. For example, a form cannot be filled without a pen and ink; files cannot be kept without cabin or cardboard and a tag, office work cannot be done without furniture and so on.

5. *Public Finance:* This is a part of material, without which personnel cannot be employed and work cannot be performed. But it is more than material. It is the chief determining factor in Public Administration; in fact, is the whole of government, as the efficiency and prestige of administration depend upon it; and

6. *Administrative Accountability:* Both in terms of internal control as well as external responsibility to Law-courts. Legislature and the People.

Thus we may conclude with Prof. Pfiffner that "Public Administration, in sum, includes the totality of government activity, encompassing expertise of endless variety and the techniques of organisation and management whereby order and social purpose are given to the efforts of vast numbers."

Viewed from the jurisdictional point of view, the sphere of Public Administration includes the Central government of the state, its regional and local authorities and also the public corporations which, though moulded on the lines of private concerns, are nevertheless, closely controlled and largely owned by the State and which serve the community or part of it in general.

Then, there is a sphere of international administration which is a sort of top-layer administration operating outside the national sphere. Since the end of the First Great War, it is expanding very fast and is likely to go on expanding with the gradual integration of the whole world community. Although this administration also is 'Public' in the sense that it professes of serve the humanity at large rather than any particular class or section to the exclusion of others, yet it does not part of Public Administration which is essentially a study of administration in the national sphere.

The following diagram illustrates the spheres of the different types of administration:

Importance of Public Administration

Public Administration has a very important place in the life of people. It is the organ which carries on the day-to-day administration of the country. Howsoever lofty may be the ideals of a state and howsoever attractive its programme, it cannot adequately serve its ends without a well-organised body of efficient and trusted officials. And organisation and management are the two basic elements of public administration. The function of organisation is to channalize the "irrational" patterns of human behaviour, which may be source of danger to any sort of government, and to achieve standardisation and stability. Emphasizing the importance of organisation, Edmund Burk had said long ago, "Constitute government how you please, infinitely the greater part of it will depend on exercise of the powers which are left at large to the ministers of state." The second element of public administration *viz.*, management, is equally important. It provides leadership in administration, coordinates individual and group activities, and maintain employee morale. Without proper management "your commonwealth is not better than a scheme on paper and not a living, active, effective constitution" as Burke puts it.

Further, administration is a "vital social process, charged with implementing great end". It is the part of the economic, social and

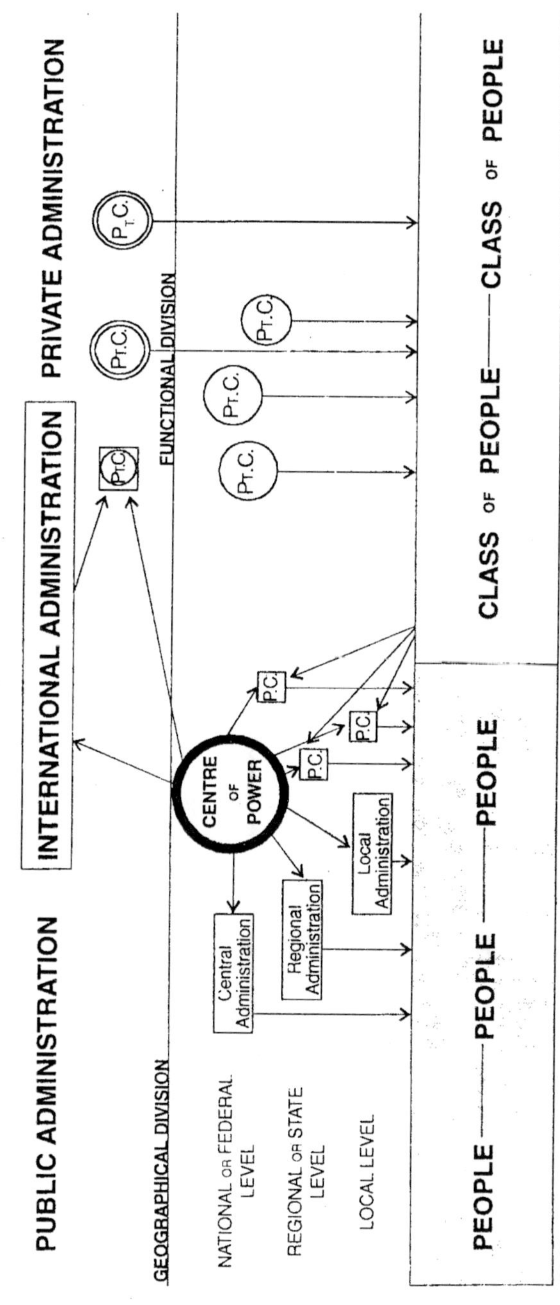

P.C. Represents Public Corporations.

P.C. Represents International organisations which do not represent the people but represents states and are responsible to them, e.g. International Bank.

P.C. Represents Associations at the National level.

P.C. Represents International Private associations.

cultural life of a nation and is a permanent forces in her life. While governments may come and go, ministries may rise and fall, administration of the country goes on for ever. No upheaval can uproot it and no revolution can change it. This, of course, does not mean that it will always follow the old ruts. Quite the contrary, public administration is a dynamic force often following the will of the people but sometimes even leading it and giving it a definite, positive turn, as it did, for example, during the Viceroyalty of Lord William Bentinck in India. In the words of Proft. Waldo, it is a "part of the cultural complex; and it not only is acted upon, it acts." The administration of a country reflects the genious of its people and embodies all their qualities and flaws, wishes and aspirations. It is a great creative force in their hands. It was not the Royal Force which held the vast British Empire for over three centuries but the British Civil Service. And it was not the 'steel' army of Bismarck that welded the forty and odd kingdoms and principalities of Germany into a mighty nation but the Prussian Civil Service. Lack of a sound administration may bring even the mightiest empire to pieces as it did in case of the ancient Roman Empire.

According to Paul Pigors public administration is a great stabilizing force in the society. It "insures the continuance of the existing order with a minimum of effort and risk. Its fundamental aim is to 'carry on' rather than to venture along new and untried paths. Administrators are, therefore, the stabilizers of society and the guardians to Tradition." Similarly Brooks Adams, a great American historian, says, "administration is the capacity of coordinating many, and often conflicting, social energies in a single organisms, so adroitly that they shall operate as a unity."

Until the end of the Nineteenth Century, the functions of the state were mainly protective and regulatory but since the idea of 'welfare' state has gained ground in politics, the province of state action is expanding by leaps and bounds. It has, since, entered into economic, commercial, social and even cultural fields. Therefore, public administration today not only protects us from external and internal dangers but also protects us from disease and insecurity, feeds our children, runs our transport, manufactures goods for our daily use, provides us education and maintains parks and other means of entertainment for us. All this increases the importance of a sound system of administration . In the words of Prof. Beard. "The future of civilised government, and even, I think, of civilisation itself, rests upon our ability to develop a science and a philosophy and a practice of administration competent to discharge the public functions of civilised society.

Although technically public administration is concerned only with carrying on public policy and has nothing to do with policy-formulation. But in practice, it plays a great role even in this sphere and its role will go on increasing (despite all cries of 'New Despotism' and 'Tyranny of Bureaucracy) with the increase in the volume and complexity of state activity. Sir Josiah Stamp has rightly said that 'the official must be the mainspring of the new society, suggesting, promoting, advising at every stage". The question of the role of public official will be fully discussed later on in Part III. Suffice it to say here that his position has greatly increased vis-a-vis the legislature due to two facts, *viz.*, one, that administrative problems are day-by-day becoming more and more intricate and complex and, two, that, legislators and ministers are only amateurs who cannot understand these intricacies and have, more and more, to depend upon the permanent officials who, with their special training and long experience in, and technical knowledge of, the subject, exercise far greater influence in policy-formulation than what is permitted to them in theory.

Characteristics of Public Administration

In order to understand the proper nature of Public Administration, let us summarize some of its chief characteristics. This will further clear the distinction between public and private administration. This, however does not mean that all the characteristics given below are exclusive to the public field. Some of them are common to both.

1. *The Urgency of State Services:* Public Administration does not perform all the human activities. But we cannot say, even after looking into the whole course of human history, which activities are exclusively state and which individual. During the ancient period, state

managed almost every walk of human life; during the medieval period, it left overmany important activities but continued its hold over religion; during the 18th and 19th centuries it confined itself only to police activities, and today again state is engulfing most of the individuals activities but with a marked exception of the religious activities.

Is there any criterion on which this question can be determined? Yes—the principle of urgency. In all the state services there is a quality of urgency—an urgency which takes its tone from the publicly accepted philosophy of the time. This urgency may arise due to a desire, on the part of the people, for having higher standard of living, or due to their sense of public duty or moral need or national prestige and so on. The people begin to feel that such and such activities are very urgent and they cannot be left over to individual caprice. So they are handed over to public administration.

2. *Large-scale Organisation:* We have seen above that only such activities are handed over to the state which, the people feel, can be best performed by the state and the state alone. Hence public administration develops a tendency of centralised activity based on large-scale organisation. This avoids duplicity of personnel and activity and thus gives economy, unity of purpose and activity, and centralizesd initiative and management. Therefore, much administration is accomplished, not by personal contact, but by writing, reporting and recording, and proper analysis. Thus public administrative activity becomes mainly impersonal.

3. *Monopoly:* Monopoly is one of the main features which distinguishes public administration from private administration: The state renounces, almost entirely, to charge any price from the consumer. It treats all its clients alike. No person can threaten to find a competitive service of supply. In fact, its service cannot be judged by the results attained in like

industries outside the state control, because its purpose is not to earn profit but to provide equal service to all its citizens.

Mosy of the other characteristics of public administration flow from this characteristic.

4. *Consciousness of Community Service:* This characteristic issues from the previous ones. State performs those activities which have a quality of social urgency and in those activities, the state is given complete monopoly. Hence the aim of public service is, not profit but public service.

5. *Equality of Treatment.* For the same reason as given above, public officials must give equal treatment to all the citizens irrespective of caste, creed or political affiliations, otherwise public administration defeats its own purpose. That is why, every democratic constitution lays down the principle of equality before law.

There must be in the officials a high sense of social service.

6. *Public Accountability.* The profit incentive lacking and the personal factor being minimum, public administration cannot maintain a high tone of efficiency and integrity if an effective system of public accountability is not exercised upon public officials. So every democratic constitution has devised means to hold the official accountable. This is done by means of judicial review of administrative acts, by means of a budget system and through legislative committees, and also in some countries by a system of recall and impeachment.

7. *Hierarchy:* Due to the rather inflexible determination of the nature and scope of state activity and also due to its impersonal nature, public administration builds up its personnel establishments into, "a carefully graded hierarchy and number of posts with duties and

salaries to match." The profit motive missing and the personal contact being minimum, public administration has to hold out to its employees an incentive of permanent career, better salary and a sound system of promotion and has also be bind them in an inflexible system of discipline. All these factors need a hierarchical organisation which is an indispensable element of public administration.

Study of Public Administration

Though the art of administration was being practised since the very beginning of human civilisation, yet its systematic study as an academic discipline began only recently. It was military administration which first became the subject of scientific analysis and study. Public Administration followed it much later. The term, public administration, came into use in the Seventeenth Century and was employed in its contemporary sense by the Federalists in America towards the close of the Eighteenth Century. Hamilton defined its subject-matter in No. 72 of the Federalist Paper. A comprehensive treatise on the subject appeared for the first time in 1812 in France—"Principles *d'* Administration Publique" by Charles—Jean Bounin. A number of other political thinkers dealt with various aspects of the subject. Woodrow Wilson's essay entitled. "The study of Administration" published in the Political Science Quarterly in 1887 is a remarkable piece among such astray studies. But on the whole, the study of the subject remained only scattered and topical.

It was since the beginning of the Twentieth Century that a systematic, and comprehensive study of Public Administration began. To put in Prof. Waldo's words, "In the late nineteenth and early twentieth centuries important developments took place in the study of administration. These developments have tremendously changed the perspective, the scope and the content of administrative study, so much that it is no exaggeration to say that collectively they constitute a revolution or mutation in human culture." A number of factors have contributed to this rapid growth in the study of Public administration.

The most important factor was the spectacular development of modern physical science and technology. We saw above how social technology helps the development of physical technology. But physical technology in its turn creates far more complex problems in social cooperation, which unless met in time, may cause the ruin of the whole society. The Industrial Revolution caused tremendous problems of labour organisation, employer-employee relationships, market and company organisation and ultimately of government organisation. Concentration of population in industrial centres, large scale unemployment, tense employer-employee relations and many other similar problems threw a challenge to human intelligence. Man had to lend his mind to the solution of these problems that arose in private as well as public organisations.

The Scientific Management Movement, which arose in America in the last quarter of the last century, gave to this trend of study of public administration not only a great impetus but supplied it with a new methodology and a new vision. This movement is associated with the name of Frederick W. Taylor who first discovered 'One Best Way' of steel-cutting and then engaged in discovering One Best Way to perform complex human operations. The movement soon spread throughout the whole Western World and even in Russia and affected Private as well as Public Administration equally.

The third factor which has helped in this process is the growth of the concept of welfare State which arose in the thirties of this century. The welfare movement has not only extended the dimensions of state activity but has also depended its roots. State is no longer the maintainer of public peace and guard of our property but is the very expression of our culture. Hence its administration is a phase of our cultural life. An International Society of Scientific Management was established. A number of other societies of Public and Business Administration arose in different countries. Special mention may be made of the New York Bureau of Municipal Research and the Royal Institute of Public Administration which did pioneering work in U.S.A. and the United Kingdom respectively. Graduate and postgraduate courses in Public

Administration were started in various universities and at places, universities and professional societies organised Research and Training Institutes in Public and/or Private Administration.

Lastly, the new trends in political and other social sciences are in a way, made the study of administration a central theme to study of Social Sciences. Without attempting to summarize trends here, it would be sufficient to say that studies in the various social sciences are no longer pursued in isolation but are studied in an integral whole, with the result that one helps the growth of other. There is much give and take amongst these sciences. The greatest contribution is being made by Sociology, Social Psychology and Anthropology. This tendency has not only helped in the study of Public Administration but has given it a new horizon and new content. The change that has occurred in the study of public administration is so revolutionary that the pioneering books of the Nineteen-twenties have either become out-of-date or have changed in all but their title. In order to understand the significance of this change, it would be useful to copare the features of the study of Public Administration as made until the Nineteen forties and as made thereafter.

The first main feature of early Public Administration was the dichotomy of politics and administration. It was, then, very much emphasised that there are two separate and independent branches of government, the policy-making branch and the policy-enforcing branch. The first was political and hence was associated with chicanery and passion, while the latter was administrative and was characterised by proper professional and legal standards and procedures. The emphasis was on the legal and constitutional aspects of administration.

The second feature which arose in the wake of the Scientific Management Movement was that Public Administration's claim to being a science was very emphatically asserted by its protagonists. In fact, there used to rage a very acute controversy between its supporters and critics. The students and teachers of Public Administration used to assert very boldly that administration, if divorced from the passion and chance of politics, and put to the cool, calculating and rational spirit of science, would yield the same result as physical science does. The academic approach of the previous decade was modified by the scientific approach. The dichotomy of politics and administration was still maintained but the scientists now turned their attention from legal forms to techniques of administration under the limited criteria of economy and efficiency. Work flow studies, time and motion studies and other objective studies of human relationships were undertaken. Man was viewed as an automation subject to the same control as any other production unit.

The third feature was a strenuous effort on the part of its protagonists to discover "Principles" of Public Administration, through objective scientific analysis, which could be a universal application. The Scientific Management movement gave them a scientific methodology and through it they built up principles or laws of public administration so that it may squarely rank with physical sciences.

The fourth feature was their belief that economy and efficiency the sole goals of administrative study. The sole object of building up a science of public administration, and discovering the one best Way of organisation and Management was to secure economy and efficiency in administration. Administration being a mechanical organisation, could produce only mechanical results.

All these doctrines have been eclipsed by the recent trends of public administration. The separation of politics and administration no longer holds good. On the contrary it is asserted that "the administrative process is the decision-making, action part of the larger process of governance, deriving from it and flowing into it." Therefore, the students of Public Administration are no longer contended with the study of the mechanism of organisation and management but also probe into the process of policy formulation and leadership—what they calls the Dynamics of Administration.

Secondly, the controversy over the scientific nature of Public Administration has come to be taken as sterile, scholiast and hence to be avoided." Public Administration is now considered both a science as well as an art, both an academic discipline as well as a process or activity. There are, at present, academic courses providing graduate, post-graduate and doctorate degree as well as professional training Institutes imparting training to internees in public and economic administrations.

Thirdly, the doctrine that there are principles of Public Administration has been completely left over. At present, the accepted goals of administration are—"(i) the understanding how people in organisation behave and how organisations operate, and (ii) how organisations can be most effectively organised, that is, to discover a sound theory of human behaviour in organisation. Thus modern administrative scientists affirm that the job of a scientist is "fact-analysis" not "value-analysis" and that the older "Principles" were no more than "naturalistic fallacies."

Lastly, the "efficiency and economy" goals are considered by modern administrative scholars as "too narrow, negative, mechanical." The idea of efficiency to physical dexterity and per-man-hour costs have given place to that of "broad social efficiency". Urgency of need is seen to justify waste. Public Administration is now conceived as a part of the cultural complex, which is permeated by the political and social values of the community. This has made it possible to make a pragmatic study of Public Administration, that is, administration as it is and not administration as it ought to be.

The pioneering works in this direction are Prof. Herbert A Simon's Administrative Behaviour and his Public Administration written in collaboration with Messers. Donald W. Smithburg and Victory A. Thompson, Dwight Waldo's Administrative State. Chester I Bernard's 'Functions of the Executive and Paul H. Appley's Morality and Administration.

Study of Public Administration in India

In India, the study of Public Administration is still in its early stages and the subject is studied as a part of the general study of Political Science. At the Intermediate and Degree stages there is no separate subject of Public Administration, although some universities include some elements of Public Administration in the study of Political Science and Economics. Some Universities, however, provide a full paper for the B.A. (Hons) degree as part of Political Science or Economics or Sociology. At the post-graduate level, Nagpur and Lucknow Universities provide for a special and independent course of instructions in Master's degree in Public Administration. The Universities of Lucknow, Patna, Madras, Nagpur and Osmania have provided for a Diploma Course in Public Administration. Most of the other Universities have made provision for one optional paper, on Public Administration as part of the M.A. Political Science course. Besides, some Universities also provide for a degree or diploma course in other specialised branches of Administration. The Delhi School of Economics Officers a course of instructions in Business Administration. The Sydenham College of Commerce and Economics provides for a Diploma Course in Public and Business Administration. The Government of India has recently started the Indian Administrative Staff College in Hyderabad for higher education and research in Business Administration. The Nagpur and Allahabad Universities offer a Diploma Course in Local Self-Government. The Agra University's Institute of Social Sciences, the Patna University and the Baroda University provide a degree course in Social and Labour Welfare Administration. The Kashi Vidya Peeth offers a degree course in Labour Welfare.

Indian Institute of Public Administration

The need of intensive study of the problems of administrative reforms and for specialisation and research was stressed both by the Gorwala Report of 1951 and the Appleby Report of 1953. Hence in March. 1954 the Government of India established, with the help of the Ford Foundation, an Indian Institute of Public Administration at New Delhi under the Presidentship of Pt. Jawahar Lal Nehru. The Institute has drawn an ambitious plan to lay the foundation of administrative reform and at the same time to give Public Administration both a professional and practical basic. For this purpose the Institute proposes to start by 1958 a School of Public Administration. which, jointly with the Institute. would maintain a library of basic reference books and documents on the subject and impart trainignt to internees and public servants. The Institute also proposes to guide and direct a basic research programme in Public Administration and the Government of India's administrative practices and to help develop teaching materials for Government Personnel. The Institute has Regional and Local branches at important places like Patna, Jaipur, Calcutta, Bombay and Bangalore which act as discussion forum and a focal point in stimulating, outside the Government and inside it, interest in and action toward a continually improved public service. The Institute also maintains a professional journal entitled 'Indian Journal of Public Administration' which has proved as a very informative and stimulating sources of knowledge on Indian Administration. The programme also includes in-service training within the Indian Government for officials having common responsibilities and problems.

Methodology

Different methods should be adopted for the study of a subject to have logical and dependable conclusions. This has its own limitations and those who apply these should try to overcome these. This can become possible only when one is conscious of these. Each method is always complementary to the other. The study of public administration is closely related to all other social sciences such as history, economics, political science, law, philosophy or psychology. In spite of close relationship, public administration has maintained its own separate entity. It continues to be studied seriously and exhaustively. As it has emerged as a separate social science subject, usually all those methods which are applied to the study of social science subjects can also be applied to it.

Methods of Public Administration

Scientific Method: It is the most common method applied for the study of social sciences for arriving at safe conclusions. It is applied for the study of political science from which Public Administration has been separated only very recently. In order to have safe conclusions, certain basic principles are accepted and adopted in it like those of the natural sciences, e.g., deciding about staffing, time to be taken in disposing of pending cases, space to be allotted to each officer, analysing the task, watching the movement and the work of individuals etc. There are decided on certain basic and well established and recognised principles on more or less uniform basis'. Scientific method has been criticised largely, because, it is believed that it cannot be safely and accurately applied to social sciences. H. Bernstein has criticised the application of this method to Public Administration, as in it the techniques have been given more attention than real activities. It has taken certain things for granted without appreciating their limitations.

Experimental Method: It is mainly applied in natural sciences where available material does not change with environments and circumstances. In this method, articles are picked up and certain experiments are carried out on these. If these are certain doubts either at the experimental or conclusion stages, such experiments are carried again. Such an experiment can be made in any part of the world because the articles or committees on which experiment is done e.g., copper, wood, iron, glass etc. have universal character. It is difficult to apply this method to public administration but this method is being used. Its difficulty arises as public administration deals with human beings having different habits, customs, qualities and behaving differently under different situations, conditions and environments. This method is applied in public administration in a limited way. For a student of public administrators this vast world is as big laboratory and human begins are the objects on which experiment is being carried on. Each law, each act of administrator and each administrative policy is in itself an experiment. The causes of its failure and success are carefully watched by public administrators in all parts of the world. Again, every new institution is set up on an experimental basis. No act or policy is taken or accepted as final till it has been fully experimented and its results have been carefully watched. There is, however, little doubt that since our objects are not of a uniform character and quality, the results too cannot be uniform. It is difficult to overcome this serious limitation.

Legal Method: Countries, like France, have administrative laws, as against the rule of law. Administrative law primarily deals with public servants, in their capacity as administrators or part of the administration. Each government sets up administration tribunals and courts of adjudication which go into the behaviour of public servants, and also investigate their charges of omission and commission in their capacity as public servants. Having legal standing and status these bodies provide useful information about powers and responsibilities of public servants and the way in which they behaved and should have behaved. This method throws light on the legal foundations of administrative authorities and administrative processes. In a Welfare State the Government is taking more burden upon itself and the concept of Welfare State is getting more and more deeper roots. Therefore, the system of delegated legislation is becoming unavoidable. It has considerably increased the importance of public administration and its study through legal method is bound to become very important.

Case Study Method: Largely the contribution of Americans to public administration, it is a method under which a particular representative case is picked up and studied thoroughly in all respects. It is presumed that the findings of this case will be applicable to the wider studies as well. According to the supporters of this method, a public administrator can arrive at reasonably sound and rational conclusions provided he studies previous cases of more or less similar nature. He shall know and appreciate the method of recording facts, limitations and powers to be used as well as methods to be adopted in arriving at conclusions.

Case Study method has serious limitations. As the government might not co-operate to the desired extent, the administrator might arrive at conclusions on the basis of incomplete data. Again, administrator too has his own ideas and viewpoint about the cases before him. Thus he would try to mould the conclusions of the case under study to suit his own viewpoint. He may become subjective rather than becoming objective. While dealing with the case, formalities might get prominence posing a serious threat to the problem under study. This method is, however, being put in greater sue both in India, U.S.A. and many other countries of the world. In 1961 F.M.G. Wilson brought out a book entitled '*Administrators in Action—British Case Studies*'. Indian Institute of Public Administration has brought out '*Cases in Indian Administration*'. Andre Molitor rather rightly said, The account as a whole is, in fact intended to reconstruct and explain with reference to the greatest number of identifiable factors, the initiation, procedure and conclusion of the operation considered and, more especially, the process for formulating the Administration decision.

The Historical Method: It has very recently been applied for the study of public administration. At every stage of political and human development there has been a type of administration dealing with public and the problems of law and order. The administrative arrangements suited the conditions and people of those times. But these are now providing a very useful data particularly for assessing development and growth of public administration. Many eminent authors have produced useful documents about administrative arrangements of the past.

Under historical method the basic data is collected from historical sources. It is said that history is a good lesson for our present public administrators. They learn several lessons from past successes and failures. Thus sufficient time and resources are saved which otherwise would have been wasted in experimenting.

But historical method has its own limitations. In the past, administration was not tedious and the task of administration was not complex, as it is today. Administrative problems of those days and their methods of solutions were different and these cannot be applied to the Contemporary situations. There is no reason to believe that what has been narrated in the history books is a true and dependable account. Usually the accounts overestimate or underestimate events. Whereas in the past the social system was run and managed on authoritarian basis, today it is based on democratic principles. This has altogether changed the role of public administrator, what it used to be in the past and what it is at present.

Biographical Method: It is a method for the study of public administration which is becoming more popular these days. Administrators are now supposed to write their opinions about important administrative problems. Churchill's *War Memoirs',* V.P. Menon's *'Integration of Indian States'*. Dr. Rajendra Prasad's *'India Undivided'* and Maulana Azad's *'India Wins Freedom'* are important and useful autobiographies. Many important politicians and public administrators and now inclined to write their autobiographies, providing useful material for the successors. Biographical method, however, is very subjective. The conclusions drawn from biographies can be accepted only after throughout consideration and pondering.

Psychological Method: Miss M.P. Follet is the chief exponent of this method. Public administration cannot be separated from other human relations. It is observed that human psychology and mass behaviour, community sentiments and trade union feelings always influence decision-making process. Individual's favours and prejudices also considerably influence decision-making process and the implementation of the decision arrived at. In industry 'industrial psychology' has come to stay as a separate subject.

Quantitative Method: It has been very successfully applied in pure sciences where the quantity produced is the only criteria for deciding success and failure of an experiment. However, it cannot be applied in administration to that extent because here both quality and quantity matter. The number of scholars produced in a country or comparatively low fees charged in schools are not the indications of success or failure of a system unless the scholars leaving the institutions are of high standard and calibre. But this method can be applied to public administration in many ways e.g. the number of people who are satisfied or dissatisfied with a type of administrator or administration can be decided by this method. Routine functions of repetitive nature e.g. allocation of typing work, filing of papers, preparing of files etc. can be decided by this method.

Behaviour Method: Some of the thinkers have tried to establish that the behaviour method has no utility in the study of public administration. But on the whole it has proved its utility for the study of this subject. Its main object is that the behaviour of individual should be judged in society before any consideration is given to his decision. A public administrator is not supposed to blindly implement policies but to discover facts about human behaviour. Legal theory of sovereignty has out-lived its utility and as such it is essential to analyse the behaviour under which a public administrator obeys the commands. As the need and necessity of informal communications is considerably increasing, no successful administrator can exclusively depend on commands issued by him from his office. He is now supposed to carefully watch the reaction and behaviour of the people about his commands and orders.

Institutional Method: As long as it was believed that the task of an administrator is to carry out the wishes of political executives and to produce set of facts without building theories, this method worked quite well. Since the nature, functions and character of public administration has now considerably changed, the utility of this method has considerably reduced.

Public administration is as yet an unexplored subject. Extensive research is yet to be carried out. Important facts are yet to come to light and are to be linked with other social sciences. Therefore, all these methods should be collcctively studied. Each method should complement and not contradict the other. Each method has its own utility and usefulness. To underestimate any one of them will be doing injustice to the subject under study as a whole.

Questions for Exercise

1. What are the various method for the study of Public Administration?
2. Discuss principal approaches to the study of Public Administration. Evaluate the merits and limitations of historical method of study.
3. Briefly discuss the following methods for the study of public administration:
   (i) Biographical Method; *(ii)* The Psychological Method:
   (iii) Quantitative Method; *(iv)* Behaviour Method;
   (v) Institutional Method.

5

Basic Principles of Public Administration

Public administration as a subject has certain basic principles around which it is developing and growing. Though its process of development is slow and gradual, yet it has certain objectives and aims for promoting specific administrative ends. Its study as well as scientific analysis of its basic principles has been a useful addition to the study of administrative problems.

Today there is a no proper and universally acceptable definition of Public Administration and differences exist about its scope. Therefore, there is uncertainty about the principles which govern it. Warner has gone to the extent of saying that, "We cannot say quite clearly what administrative principles are, and what they are not." It has also been said that the principles of public administration are nothing more than naturalistic fallacies. There has so far been no unanimity about principles of public administration. All the attempts made in this direction in England, America and India have failed.

Principles of Public Administration

However it is wrong to presume that these principles cannot be broadly laid down or these are mere improbabilities or natural fallacies. Though the task ahead is very difficult and requires patience and research, one can be optimistic about possibility of having commonly acceptable principles and that too not in the distant future. In the meanwhile following principles govern public administration and have wide, if not universal, acceptance.

Authority: Ours is a very complex social, economic and political setup. The political executive is obliged to be satisfied with giving broad guidelines and directions leaving the details of the job to the care of the public administrator. He has a difficult responsibility to discharge and is supposed to handle every situation with great care so that it does not become explosive or uncontrollable. He can, however, be a success only when he has sufficient authority and is given considerable freedom and liberty to exercise it. Obviously, he cannot discharge his legal and constitutional obligations, unless he has sufficient authority. Therefore, the principle of authority has come to stay in public administration.

Political Direction: Both in a Parliamentary and Presidential form of Government, there is a popularly elected body, enjoying the confidence of people on the basis of an election manifesto which contains policies and programmes of the political party. Taking election manifesto into consideration the people vote in favour of the party. After returning to power every effort is made by the political executive to implement those policies and programmes. It is, therefore, a principle in public administration that a public administrator must carry out the directions of the political executive honestly and obediently. A public administrator should never have any political affiliations. He should serve with the lofty idea of serving the others, within a framework given to him by his political executive. He should neither take such initiatives, nor implement policies in a way which may annoy or irritate the political executive. Civil servant neutrality is one of the most essential and basic principles of public administration. He is supposed to be above politics. He should know the aims and objectives of all political parties, particularly the political party in power so that he can conveniently mould himself according to the situation.

Discipline: A public administrator should obey and enforce discipline. He should tune his mind in a way that he is most willing to obey the commands of his superiors, more particularly, the political executive. He is at liberty to place his cards on the table of his political boss, but once he has been commanded to implement a decision, as a disciplined public administrator, he should carry out the same. He should be capable and competent enough to keep his subordinates under discipline. He should see to it that his administrative orders are carried out effectively and that all parties working under him are disciplined. Neither public nor private machinery can function smoothly and give the desired results without discipline.

Span of Control: A senior officer's work should be so organised that maximum number of subordinates can approach him and he has sufficient time to supervise the work of his subordinates. This number cannot be fixed and it must vary from one organisation to the other. it is related to the nature of work and quality of persons employed. But no organisation should feel that a senior person can control indefinite number of employees.

Responsibility: Authority and responsibility go hand in hand. An unbridled and uncontrolled authority is likely to make public administrator not only irresponsible but also corrupt. A public administrator is, therefore, supposed is follow the principle of responsibility. He should work with the idea that he is by and large responsible to the tax-payer. He should hold himself fully responsible for the execution of his policies. He is supposed to be willing to shoulder consequences for all the acts of omission and commission. He should also realise that all his activities are being seriously and consciously watched by the public. He should not shirk his responsibility towards the superiors and also to the public. His political executive can ask him for giving detailed information about his department. It is the foremost duty of a public administrator to give most reliable and authentic information so that he can take some decision on that. He should not avoid taking initiative due to the fear that it would involve more responsibilities. He should willingly take additional responsibilities.

Social Necessity: Richard Warner has enunciated the principle of social necessity. He is of the view that today public administration is an integral part of whole social system. Each State has undertaken so many responsibilities upon itself that the politicians alone cannot discharge those social obligations. Public administrators play a big role in implementing social policies and programmes. The principle of social necessity has come to stay on these considerations.

Efficiency: Efficiency is rather the sole standard of judging the success or failure of an institution. Public administration is not an exception to the rule. Efficient public administration is most essential for the development of the growing complex social, political and economic set-up. Public administrator should work with more and ore efficiency brought about in many ways. It is essential that the targets fixed for achievement should be rational and achievable with available resources. Neither religion nor sex but ability of a persons should be the sole criteria for making all public appointments. Staffing should be on scientific lines. Division of labour should be on very sound footings. There should not be frequent administrative and policy changes. These should be made when absolutely necessary. There should not be too much of rigidity. The employees should be given reasonable and proper promotion opportunities. Initiative should be encouraged and properly rewarded. There should be courses and in-service training facilities for the employees so that public administrator is fully well informed about the latest administrative techniques and methods.

Unity of Command: According to some thinkers if the work is to be completed smoothly and efficiently each one should be responsible to one superior in the organisation. The others, however, argue that in our modern systems there are many activities which fall outside the hierarchical line. Though the controversy is going on yet, by and large, unity of command is a good principle in public administration.

Coordination: Each organisation is divided into various departments and sub-departments. Each individual, high or low, is loaded with certain responsibilities. Each has been given certain power to discharge his responsibilities and obligations efficiently. He has certain duties towards his superiors and subordinates. There is bound to be inefficiency resulting in disorder and dislocation of work if all this is not properly and rationally co-ordained. It may lead to corruption and put the public to great inconvenience. Therefore, it is very essential that a public administrator should devote his time and attention to coordination so that many departments of the same organisation do not go on performing the same types of functions and much of man power is saved. This will avoid duplication of labour and save manual and monetary resources.

Economy: Today developing countries are faced with several economic problems. There is demand and desire by the tax-payers that minimum amount should be spent in running the administrative machinery and that maximum should be spent for productive purposes. Administrative charges should be kept as low as possible. It is very much imperative that an administrative officer should introduce economy though not at the cost of efficiency. There should be no wastage. Efficiency should not be scarified for want of finances or in the name of economy. A good public administrator should work with thus both economy and efficiency.

Division of Labour: Since the days of Montesquieu, the desirability of separation of powers has been widely appreciated. It is being increasingly realised that there should be no concentration of power in any department of the government to weed out inefficiency and corruption. Division of labour brings efficiency and avoids corruption. Functions should be clearly divided as far as possible so that one department or individual may not retard progress due to his own lethargy or any other similar reasons.

Delegation of Authority: In every organisation senior persons exercise some power and authority. Too much concentration of authority results in neglect of a lot of work and can at times result in serious dislocation of work when the person concerned is not available. Some authority must be gradually delegated to subordinate officers and their work over viewed. Delegation, however, does not mean freedom from responsibility. It means that some subordinate person does the work on behalf of his seniors.

Public Relationship: A public administrator should have close relationship with the public. He must realise that success of democracy very much depends on properly appreciating the sentiments and feelings of the public. He should realize that he is not living in a Police State but in a Welfare State. There cannot be much difference between policy and its execution. If one fails to keep pace with his political executive, which has close public relations, he is bound to be a failure. He should always informally try to get the views of important leaders of various sections of society about the results of execution of his policies. He might adopt the method of inviting them for discussions. He can even constitute committees which render him informal advice on all important matters. If he fails to realize the necessity of maintaining relations with the people whom he is to serve, he cannot reasonably discharge his social and legal obligations. Maintaining right relations is likely to considerably end strikes, lock-outs and many other similar methods which reduce production and profits.

Hierarchy: According to Prof. Marx, Hierarchy means grouping of units into a large unit for direction and control of activities. It is the method whereby the efforts of different type of individuals are coordinated. Hierarchy is another indispensable feature of large scale enterprise. No large organisation can successfully work without proper hierarchy in which some receive commands from their superiors while other give orders to their subordinates. The subordinates are expected to faithfully carry out the instructions of the seniors and superiors. Though equality may be an attractive slogan, yet in practice, in a department there must be persons of different grades and cadres. Hierarchy is an accepted principle in public administration. It is essential that it should be logically strengthened for free flow of information, upward as well as downward, as an essential channel of command and communication.

Organisation: In every organisation there is problem of avoiding overlapping. A good public administrator should have scientific organisation which should have needed expertise and knowledge of subject with which it deals. Richard Warner is of the opinion that this principle of public administration has come to stay.

Evaluation: Though not qualitatively but quantitatively one can measure national progress and also evaluate it to some extent. One of the principles of public administration is that from time to time progress made in different directions should be evaluated by scientific method. In the past the State did not bother about that, as there was not much of anti-thesis between the individual and the State. The State measured national prosperity in terms of revenues collected for the treasury. But today individual and State are supposed to pull on together. Both should be complementary rather than contradictory and harmonious rather than inharmonious to each other. Public administration should thus promote harmony and a spirit of intelligent cooperation rather than disintegration. Periodical reviews of production and productivity are the accepted principles of public administration.

Research: Research is most essential for all physical and social sciences, otherwise these become out-dated and stagnant. A regular and continuous research work is accordingly being carried out in the public administration to enable a public administrator to keep pace with rapid social, economic and political changes. Research helps in systematic study and evolution of new methods. It promotes both advancement and enrichment of knowledge. Without this laboratory process, the study of public administration will be useful for none.

Confidence: At whatsoever level he might be working, a public administrator, should inspire the confidence of those who come in contact with him. His subordinates must have faith in his sense of justice and fair play. Similarly, as a junior officer, his superiors and senior officers should have confidence in him. They should be sure that he will honestly and faithfully discharge duties assigned to him.

Questions for Exercise

1. Discuss the significant principles of Public Administration.

2. "We cannot say quite clearly what administrative principles are what they are not." (Warner). Discuss.

6

The Principles of Administration

Like every other art, administration has its own laws or principles according to which it is conducted. Just as a painter, or an architect or a sculptor has to follow certain laws of draftsmanship, or construction or carving determined by the requirements of his art and the nature of the material on which he has to work and the peculiarities of the instruments which he uses, so the administrator has to follow certain laws, or principles, or rules determined by the nature of the work he has to do, the nature of the material he has to work on and the instruments that he has to use. Just as the laws and rules that the painter, or the architect, or the sculptor has to follow have been discovered by generations of painters, or architects or sculptors in many countries, so that principles and laws or chief rules of administration have been discovered by the actual experience of generations of men, in many countries, that have practised this art. It is from the vast and varied experience of men that have administered the public affairs of several countries in the course of history that the principles of administration have been gathered. Sumer and Akkad and Egypt and Persia and India and Peru and China and Japan and Greece and Rome, the States of Asia and Europe and America have all contributed their quota to this treasure-house of administrative experience. Some have given more than others, Egypt more than China, India more than Persia, Peru more than Japan, Rome more than Greece, Germany more than England, France more than Italy. But the sum of this great experience has left the deposit of the chief principles of administration which govern the political life of the progressive peoples of the world. It is not a theorist but an experienced administrator who says "All efficient systems of administration conform to ascertainable principles. Such principles are independent alike of forms of government, of the nature of undertakings and of the extent of the monetary transactions involved. They are eternal; their violation inevitably entrails disorganisation inefficiency and waste."

First among the principles of administration—is The Principle of Authority.

Administration is done by persons who do certain things. To do these things they have to be clothed with certain powers or attributes. The first of these attributes is the attributive of authority.

Authority is the right of the power of a person commanding other people to do things and in general of getting work done by them. It is one of the results of organised like and activity which gives some people the right to issue orders, to others the duty to obey these orders. It results from the position of superiority or ascendancy occupied by some people over others. For every business whether in government or in industry or in social life must have a chief or head. "A chief is necessary everywhere in all matters" said Napoleon. Whether he is called master or captain of industry, or director of a company, on him depends ultimately the success of the business. His is the head which plans, directs, commands and countermands, his is the eye which sees, supervises, watches, the course of the action which he has ordered.

The authority which a superior exercises is of three sorts, one legal or statutory, which follows from the function he performs or the office he holds, and the other from the nature of the position he holds and the third from his own personality. The exercise of this authority is possible not only by reason of the sanctions in the form of punishment provided by the rules and regulations of the administration but by the natural relation between a superior and a subordinate. Not all the things which a subordinate has to do on the orders of his superior can be stated in the rules and regulations governing the work of the administration but conditions and circumstances may arise not contemplated in the rules and regulations which may call for command on the one side and obedience on the other. Provided these unexpected and unprovided conditions and circumstances are connected with public affairs over which the person in authority has jurisdiction, the natural relation between superior and subordinate calls for orders on the one side and compliance on the other. The third source of the superior's authority is the personality of the superior due to his intelligence, his knowledge, his experience, the moral value of his personality, the gift of command he possesses, the services he has rendered. This obedience is a willing obedience, because nobody compels the subordinate to place himself in his position. But having placed himself in that position he is expected to obey not only all lawful, but all legitimate orders of his superior, i.e., not only all orders supported by rules and regulations but all orders natural and justifiable by the relations between superior and subordinate, if the ends of that relationship in the field of administration are to be achieved. Authority and its counterpart obedience keep an administration in order and ordered action. But the commands of a person in authority recommend themselves to the subordinate by certain notes or marks they possess. There must be (1) unity of command, (2) stability or continuity of command, (3) independence of command to make authority operate or function.

Unity of Command

Nothing destroys the prestige and power of a superior whether he is a commander of an army in a battle, or the captain of a ship on the high seas, or the head of a department of government or of a district, as the multiplicity of voices of command bringing about confusion and doubt and perplexity in the minds of those to whom the commands are issued, giving them an opportunity to discuss them or a temptation to break them. Plurality of voices of command is a negation of command. There may be wisdom in multiplicity of council, but not in multiplicity of command. A superior may seek counsel from others, may surround himself with boards of advisers, may consult all and everybody before issuing his commands. But when the commands are issued there must be only one voice issuing them. Even when the superior is not a single person but a body of persons like a Board, or a Cabinet, or a Council, the voice that issues the command on behalf of that Board or Cabinet or Council must be one. The practical rule to ensure unity of command is that for any action, an agent or subordinate should receive orders from one head or chief speaking one voice.

Unity of direction is a corollary of unity of command. The practical rule to ensure this is that there should be only one chief and only one set of operations to achieve any one end. It is this unity of direction as of command that will ensure unity of action co-ordination of forces, and the convergence of all efforts necessary to achieve certainly and effectively the end of that action.

Stability and Continuity of Command

If the commands of a superior are to receive respect and compliance from a subordinate, there must be certainty that they will not be changed or qualified soon after they are issued or at short intervals. Then only will the subordinate be compelled to obey them instantly. Otherwise, he might wait to see if the orders are going to be changed, and he will be tempted to use his own judgement as to the time he will take to carry them out or whether he will carry them out at all. Nothing is calculated to promote slackness and insubordination among subordinates as this instability and discontinuity of command.

Independence of Command

Within his own sphere and jurisdiction limited by the constitution of the country the administrator is entitled, as we have already argued to independence in action. And the persons in authority are entitled to this autonomy and independence. Provided they are acting within the law and the constitution they must be allowed free scope for action. They should not be subject to constant nagging and interference by those placed in authority over them by the law and constitution of the country, like Ministers, the legislature or even those set in administrative authority over them. Ultimate authority of these latter bodies must not be interpreted so as to include ordinary and daily exercise of that authority. Otherwise, the subordinate finds it difficult to obey a superior, who, he knows is liable to be countermanded by somebody above him. That ready obedience cannot be expected of subordinates if they knew that the superior who commands them is constantly looking to those above him for approval or confirmation.

There is another condition—an external condition for the successful operation of authority. And that is the consideration shown to it by the subordinate. But this esteem of the subordinate for person in authority, these must earn. They can earn it only by the superiority of their intelligence and character which must show itself in the actual acts of administration performed by the superior. In the exercise of his functions he must exhibit an extent of knowledge, a liberality of outlook, proofs of the utility of his suggestions and orders that will carry conviction of confidence to the subordinates. The superior must be in competence superior to the subordinate. Any manifest superiority of the subordinate to his superior in knowledge or competence would be disastrous to authority.

A more external, but nonetheless necessary, condition for the successful operations of authority is public esteem. Authority which has the esteem and confidence of the people is confident and sure of success.

The Principle of Obedience and Discipline

Corollary and consequence of the principle of authority is the principle of Obedience and Discipline. Authority becomes real and realised only when its exercise is followed by obedience. Persons in authority must obtain obedience from those to whom the commands of authority are issued. Discipline is absolutely necessary for the success of any enterprise—an army in the field, or a school, or a factory. Any military manual would contain these sentences: discipline is the chief strength of armies, discipline is what makes a chief. But it is authority that makes discipline; it is the manner in which persons in authority make use of their powers that promotes or destroys discipline. A chief that is weak, that does not know his mind, that issues contradictory orders, that a partial and unjust, breaks up the discipline of the body of persons over whom he is placed in authority—whether that body be a troop of soldiers, or a school of children or workman in a workshop. But there must be a reason for the command of the chief. The highest form of obedience or the highest form of authority is that based on the dictates of reason. And therefore when obedience and discipline is expected the people from whom it is expected must be convinced of the reasonableness of these commands. Men are rational beings, not dumb-driven cattle, and gladly and, therefore, efficiently carry out the commands of which they can see the reason. But men are not always reasonable, and therefore, authority and obedience or discipline are supported by sanctions. The fear of punishment, enforces the reasonableness of authority, ensures the maintenance of continuous obedience and discipline.

The Principle of Duty and Interest

Among the powerful motives and incentives to administrative action, so powerful that they constitute a principle, is the motive and incentive of duty and of interest. An administrator by the mere fact that he is an administrator does not cease to be a man. The sense of duty impels him to action. He must get the approval of his conscience on the manner and the extent of the performance of his duties. Not only the fear of the law, his obligation to carry out the operations indicated by rules and regulations or by the orders of his superior, or the needs of the moment, not only the fear of punishment, but a sense of duty to his office, to his government, to the State, and his country animates the good administrator and calls him to perform not merely the minimum requried of him but the most and the best he is capable of even to the point of sacrifice and heroism. We can expect the highest and the best of an administration when every member of it does his work from a sense of duty and with a view to getting the approval of his conscience.

But administrators are men and the ordinary motives for conduct of men move them. Interest, self-interest included, has done much to increase the wealth of individuals, to ensure the contentment of the poor, to promote the health and sanitary progress of a community. It has played and has a part to play in administration with a view to its progress and prosperity. Make it the interest of member of the administration, clerk, or inspector, or director to do his work efficiently and he will do it to the best of his power. Prove to him that he will benefit from work well done and he will try to do it well. That idea has inspired all the movements, ancient and modern for improving the material lot of the workers in administration. The improvements in rates of salaries or allowance, the bonuses, provident funds, commissions for extraordinary good works, overtime wages, piece-wages, gratuities, pensions are all calculated to make it materially worthwhile for the worker to do his work well. Interest, even self-interest, is powerful enough to be treated as a principle of administration.

But there is one condition on which alone it can be given a free field in administration. And that is, the interest of the administrator must be made to coincide with that of the Government or the State. The interest of the individual administrator must be subordinated to the interest of the public. Any benefits that are offered to him to encourage and stimulate him towards efficiency, by way of salary or allowances, or bonuses or gratuities, or leave, or prospects of promotion must not be at the expense or to the detriment.of the interests of the State or the people. As our own interests are nearer to us and therefore appear more important to us than the interests of the State or the people, the temptation always besets us of preferring our interests to those of the State or the country. An administrator who takes a bribe for a service rendered to a citizen is sacrificing the interests of the State, for only citizens, who can afford to pay bribes can get the service which the State professedly offers to all citizens. It is not to the interest of the State that only those that can pay bribes should be entitled to the services of is officials—it would lead to popular discontentment, imperil the peace of the State, and, if the system is practised on a large scale, will end in the destruction of the State. Whereas, bonuses or commissions or rapid promotion openly offered by the government for extraordinarily good work openly done and open to all that are entitled to it serves the interests of the State at the same time. As it has been well put the personal interest of the administrator must be made a satellite of the collective interest and therefore must be given less importance.

The Principle of Responsibility

From the two principles of Authority and Duty and Interest follows the third important principles of administration—the principles of Responsibility.

Responsibility is the obligation to stand by and answer for and take the consequences of one's acts. It has been called the counterpart and corollary of Authority and Duty or Interest. It makes the administrator do the best things to achieve his end, to choose the best means for achieving that end, to make use of the best materials to build, as it were, the edifice of his administrative action. It also forces him to avoid all that will frustrate his end, bad means, bad material and bad personnel. Responsibility on account of the consequences which its exercise involves can stimulate action, it can also paralyse action. Strong men are encouraged to action sometimes even daring action by it; weak men are frightened and benumbed by it. Responsibility frightens men much more than the danger of cannon, said Theirs, a great French statesman and administrator. But the fear of the consequences of responsibility may lead to wise action. It obliges a man who has this sense of responsibility to acquire all the information that may be necessary to weigh the arguments for and against any suggested action, to think and reflect on the possible consequences of a proposed course of action, to look at the matter from all standpoints, especially the standpoint of the general principles of administration. Study, thought and deliberation are made to precede decision. And after decision, it forces the administrator to follow and watch the consequences of the action, to find out how far the anticipated consequences have come off and to withdraw from persistence in the course of an action that has been found detrimental to the interests of administration.

Responsibility is possible only if there is scope for its exercise. That presupposes one condition—the man who is called upon to exercise responsibility must have the power of initiative. It also presupposes independence within the limits of his duties and his work. That initiative or independence varies in direct ratio to the grade in administration of the one who exercises it. The supreme chief of the administration, whose forces are extensive has a larges scope for initiative and independent action than the head of a department or the head of a district or a village. Responsibility is measured by power; the greater the power the greater the responsibility because the scope for initiative and independence is greater.

The Principle of Co-ordination

Administration as a whole consists of many parts—as we shall see in detail later. There are many sections of work, many seats of authority, many sets of subordinates. If the administrative system which is composed of them is to work well, these parts must be made to work in harmony with one another, in subordination one to the other whenever that is necessary, parallel but not contradictory one to the other for that would cause friction and therefore loss of energy and spoilt work. Co-ordination of the work of all the parts of administration is absolutely necessary to make the administrative system work. It is the cement which binds together the several portions of the administrative structure together. This principle of co-ordination applies to the administrators as well as to acts of administration. Administrators have to be kept working with and for one another and not at or against one another. Combination, co-operation, consultation are important in modern administration. Administrative acts have to be kept in agreement with one another, the natural cause or consequence of one another, in natural sequence and harmony not clashing with and spoiling the effect of one another. Administrators whether acting at the same time or at different times, in quick succession or at long intervals, must not be allowed to distract or detract from one another's work but must follow up and supplement the work of one another. Administrative acts co-ordinated with one another, directed towards one end or result must follow one another up so as to complete the whole of which they are parts and must not become parts not serving the cause or purpose of the whole and therefore not helping to achieve the result which was the object of those acts. By means of frequent communication with one another, by way of speech or writing, administrators working for a common end must keep touch with one another so that they do not contradict one another, so that they work with and not against one another and break up and destroy each other's work and the work of that part of the administration entrusted to them.

That is why in every section or part of the administrative system there is a chief or head who keeps the men in his part or section working with one another, in co-operation with one another, in agreement with one another; he is there to co-ordinate them and their work.

The Principle of Division of Labour

The administration of a State is a many-sided business because the duties of a State and its Government are manifold. The Government of a State has to see to the defence of the territory of the State against external enemies, as well as the defence of the peace and order of the State within, it has to look after the sanitation and health and education of the people, it has to take measures to promote the economic prosperity of the people or at any rate to remove the obstacles to their moral and material progress. Each of these duties must have a section of the administration to carry it out. These sections are called the Departments of the Government. It is not only convenient to have such a division of the administration into Departments, but to ensure efficiency of the administration, it is necessary to have this specialisation in the administration. Having one particular duty or one particular set of duties to perform, each Department would be encouraged to acquire the knowledge and the *expertise* required for the efficient performance of the duty. And it is good for everyone concerned with the administration to know which Department is responsible for the performance of which duty. Not only the Head of the State, or the Head of the Government, but the other institutions in the State, the National Assembly and Legislature, the Judiciary should know which duty is performed by which department, so that the relations of those powers with the administration may be certain and established. But the public also, the general body of citizens who are most interested in the administration of the State, ought to have this certainty of knowledge. Who administer what, how does he administer it, how much of it does he administer—these are questions that every-body interested in the administration asks for, especially the general public which has most to benefit or suffer from the results of administrative action. And the division of the labour of administration, the division into the Departments of administration makes the answering of these important questions possible. The fixing of responsibility for the acts of administration is made easy.

The Principle of Separation or Speciality

As it is desirable to create or maintain connection between acts of administration or administrators related to or connected with one another working for one end or result, so it is desirable to keep certain sets of acts or groups of administrators apart from one another. There are certain sections of the administration which it is desirable to keep separate from the others in the interests of the administration as a whole. Just as in a free and constitutional system of government, the legislative, executive, and judicial powers should be kept separate from each other in the interests of political liberty, so in the interests of good and efficient administration certain parts or sections of the administration must be kept separate from each other. There are two important necessaries of administration—material and money. A modern government has in its possession large quantities of material of different kinds—paper, ink, pens, pencils, etc., required for its work. And no government can do without money. And the departments of administration which are in charge of the money and the material or stores of government are important. And their importance is of an extraordinary kind. The money of the State with which the whole work of government is carried on is of such great quantity that it must be used with care for it is collected from the people, and it has to be issued from time to time to the several departments of the State, that the department in charge of the money of the State must be a special department and must be kept separate from the other departments. As the expenditure of the several departments must be controlled and checked by this department it must be kept separate and independent of the other departments. Otherwise waste or improper use of the money of the State will ensue. Similarly the department in charge of the material or stores of the State would have to exercise check and control of the use of such material and stores by the several departments of the administration. For these reasons, the Finance and Stores or Supplies Departments must be kept separate and independent of the other departments. Otherwise, they cannot exercise their important and highly necessary functions of check and control. And the material and money of the State may be wasted or misused or lost to the detriment of the State.

The Principle of Hierarchy

When there are a number of persons or bodies of persons acting together towards a common end, the question who is superior and who is inferior, who is master, and who is subordinate, arises. Otherwise, there is bound to be confusion and clash and the ends of the common action are bound to be prevented. Among the departments of the administration and the members of the administration within each department the question has to be settled which of them is superior and which is inferior, which is leader and which is follower. In all well-organised departments of administration there is a regular grade of persons, one person, or body of persons placed over the other from the head down to the last subordinate. There is a regular chain of office with many links making it. It is a road leading from the top to the bottom, from the centre to the circumference of the administration along which are sent the orders of the superior to the subordinate and along which information and reports and other communications from the subordinate to the superior, from the circumference to the centre travels the other way.

And, among the Departments there must be one supreme department which is on the whole and ultimately responsible for the administration. Administration requires hierarchy, and hierarchy connotes leadership and the best and most effective leadership is that of the single leader. Although the principle of separation and speciality allows a large measure of autonomy, this practice of autonomy must be modified and controlled by the principle of hierarchy. Centralisation or concentration of authority is necessary in an efficient or successful system of administration. Only this must not be excessive—otherwise it kills that other principle of administration—the principle of responsibility.

The Principle of Equity

Administration is not a material machine. It is composed of living persons. And whenever or wherever persons are brought into contact or relation with one another their relations if they are to be peaceful and fruitful, must be governed by the idea and the practice of equity and justice. A superior can get the best out of his subordinates only if the latter feels he is getting justice from the other. All the persons in the administration, subordinate as well as superiors must act towards one another in equity and justice.

Methods and Instruments of Administration

Every work done by man has its own particular tool or instrument with which he does that work. The farmer works with plough or hoe to cultivate his land and makes it grow grain or vegetables or fruit, the blacksmith has his hammer and anvil and tongs in his smithy, the carpenter works with saw and chisel and plane. The administrator has his own special tools or instruments to work with. And as in every other kind of work the tools and instruments used are determined by the nature of the work.

Words

As administration consists largely of commands, or directions, or orders issued by one person or set of persons to another, first among the tools or instruments of administration are words—words of command, or order or direction. In the early ages of society when the ruler and his servants and subjects were in direct contact with one another, words filled a larger place in administration then in later times when the chain of administration has become elongated and the ruler, chief or subaltern, is separated from his subordinates and the people ruled by long distances. The patriarchal ruler of the nomadic tribe, the commander of a small army all under his eyes or the captain of a sailing vessel could do most of their administration by word of mouth. But as soon as the State and its government become more complex, and the centres of government and administration were multiplied not only at the centre or headquarters of government but at the circumference the words of command or order or direction directly given and taken cease to be as frequent as before. But, as we shall see later even now in order to improve the pace and progress of administration, it is necessary to make use of the direct communication of superior to subordinate, and spoken words are beginning to recover their importance. And modern means of communication like the telephone, the wireless have brought spoken words into their own in administration.

The Written Word

As soon as writing came to be known and used among people the written word came to drive the spoken word into the background of administration. There were reasons for this development. Administration is no longer simple and straightforward as it was in patriarchal times. The centres of administration have increased at the centre and at the circumference of the State and in between. It is no longer possible to communicate the commands or directions or orders of the superior to the subordinate by word of mouth. So the commands and orders and directions of the superior have to be communicated by the written word. This written word takes different forms. Simple orders, take not more than a few words. The Dispatch is much longer and consists of arguments and other *pieces justificatives*. The issue of the order or despatch is preceded by all kinds of writing—the Statement, Memorandum, Note, the Minute—in which the information of facts and figures is canvassed—the whole constituting the File of the case. These in the form of the file constitute what may be called the study of the case which is preliminary to any action. This study looks before and after, the history of the case (including the precedents) the present situation of the case, i.e., the actual state of all the facts, the resources, the needs of the action contemplated, it includes also a forecast of the probable future of the action, the political, economic, social consequences, And after the action from the other side of the administration, from the circumference, whether of the State or any smaller unit, like district, or town or village come information by way or Returns, Reports, Letters which form the elements of the traffic to headquarters. The reports of subordinates to their superiors occur at every stage and they are daily, weekly, monthly or annual. These reports are a forceful means of control of the action taken, its consequence and its efficiency. The report is at one end the counterpart of the programme of work at the other. Together they ensure responsibility in administration. Just as without programme there is no policy, so without the report or the return there is no checking of programme by performance. Hence irresponsibility at either end of the administration.

All this writing goes to form the records of administration stacked in the Record Room of every administrative office. This instrument of writing is used to an extreme extent in certain systems of administration. Not only the necessities of the case, but inertia and laziness also account for the amount of writing in modern administration. When administration is so complex and complicated, when it requires intellectual effort and alertness to dispose of cases expeditiously, the second-rate administrator is tempted to postpone decision and what better way is there for postponing decision in administrative business than to sit on the file asking for further information or elucidation or framing new doubts and difficulties—and sending the file once again on its rounds to superior and subordinate.

For the making of the written word in administration many kinds of tools are requried, paper, pen (formerly quill, hence the description of clerks as quill drivers, and now steel), ink have to be bought and kept in large quantities in any modern public office. The Stationery Department of an office whether at the centre or at the circumference is a costly item of public expenditure. The Government of India has been called government by stationery. Files, trays of papers and despatch boxes which circulate within a department and from department to department loom large in the daily life of the public office. The Government of India was once described by a brilliant partner in its administration as "government by despatch box tampered by an occasional loss of keys". The red tape used to bind papers and dockets and files together has become the symbol of routine and precedent in administration.

Modern inventions have brought new tools into Government offices. The printing press has made administrative records more prominent and encouraged their multiplication. No modern public office can do without typewriters and typists. No longer is the neat-handwriting that Lord Palmerton used to insist on at the British Foreign office requried. The telegraph has become a frequent means of communication. When Napoleon used the first semaphore he realised the importance of this means of communication and promptly nationalised the telegraph. His comment on the discovery was "nobody knows what they mean to mankind"—now we know. The telephone is another great time-saver, it reduces the volume and frequency of the written work and in fact brings back the spoken word and direct contact between superior and subordinate and equal into its old importance. Shorthand writing is another great time-saver, so is the Dictaphone. To save labour and time, a number of mechanical instruments have been adopted for business offices like the adding and calculating machine, the registering machine for the issue of receipts, the Hollerith machine for cost accounts. Photography is not without its uses in a public office. The photostat method of copying the documents in a registration office is an easy and reliable method of reproducing such documents.

Documentation in administration has come to fill such a large place that the International Congress of Administrative Sciences at its second sessions in 1923 devoted a whole section to the study of documentation. There, an administrative document was defined as anything which serves to register, transmit, or preserve the record of "anything useful for and in administration and which presents that thing in a form suitable for study". Documents in administration would include books, reviews, journals, letters, reports, notes, maps, charts, plans, statistics, tables, photographs, diagrams, graphs—also specimen models, patterns as in the technical departments of engineering or geology.

The following are considered to be the chief classes of documents requried in the administration of a State.

1. Books, reports, etc., giving general and particular information about the State including its history, its

geography, its constitution, its laws, its social, and economic life and organisation.

2. Tables of administration showing the organisation of the administration at a glance and in one picture—this gives a better view of the administrative structure than any verbal description, defects and lecunae in the administrative organisation are more easily detected such as overlapping, functions without functionaries, and functionaries without functions.

3. Programmes and Plans of Departments.

4. Collections of Instructions, decisions, orders.

5. Reports of Conferences of Chiefs of Departments or departmental and interdepartmental and other conferences.

6. Reports of activities of departments or of their officials.

7. Indexed books of information about officials, their work, their activities.

8. Records of original documents used in the departments.

9. Records of the achievements of the departments and the documents pertaining thereto, e.g., those connected with, say the digging of a canal or the construction of a building.

Documentation has been described "the crystallisation of thought in administration". The keeping of these records is an important part of documentation. Loose leaf ledgers, card-indexes, strip indexes, manifolding, visible indexes which allow the cards to be arranged in such a way that the titles are displayed and the card wanted mav be selected without fingering the others have been adopted from business offices. The Record or Document Room is the tool-room of administration.

The life of a document consists in its writing, its registration and classification, cataloguing, analysis and extracts, placing and preservation, consultation and use, recording, transmission or destruction.

The tools of administration are not so important as all that. Men like to be governed by men in the manner of men. The spoken word is not altogether eliminated from administrative intercourse. In fact the evils and abuses of the written word—voluminous writing, circulation, *paperasserie* are corrected by resource to the spoken word. Interviews, conferences, consultations shorten the rounds of administration.

Statistics in Administration

Statistics is information conveyed in fitures. It has been described as "the science of social facts expressed in number." It is derived from the word State itself and originally was held to include enquiries respecting the population, the political circumstances, the production of a country and other matters of state. Its importance was realised as early as the 17th century in Germany when Leibniz the famous philosopher and statesman, urged the value of organised and systematic information on the social and economic life of the people as a means to good government. These State-Tables, as he called them, are, he said, to the administration what charts are to the captain of the ship and books and book-keeping to the merchant. The statesman, the administrator, the economist, the publicist have to take care to study on and off and to express in figures the results of a law or regulation or activity. Was it not Lord Kelvin, the famous physicist, who said nobody could be sure of anything in the world of matter till it was expressed in figures? The regularity or irregularity, the prominence or intermittence of facts or events in social life, knowledge of which is so useful to the administration, can be studied only by means of statistics. Facts and figures relating to population, agriculture, industry, commerce, educational and charitable institutions, prison, disease are, if collected accurately and systematically, useful for the framing of policy and programmes of work in the department concerned. Some departments furnish such information automatically by their very activity like the Customs, the Land Revenue and the Income Tax Departments. But the statistics of agriculture and industry are more difficult to get. The Agriculture Department would have to collect facts on the nature and production of the soil, the quality and extent of the land, cultivated, the value of the crops, the number of cattle in each and every part of the country. Statistics have to be collected for each year and for periods of years,—generally decades. Not all collections of statistics need be paid for. In the census, patriotism and public spirit ought to enlist the services of volunteers. Paid and permanent officials and unpaid volunteers would supplement and help each other. Preliminary and provisional publication of statistics might be submitted with profit to public scrutiny at the several stages of the departmental enquiry. In France it used to be said in the middle of the last century that the whole of France worked on statistics and check and control appeared at every step in the administration.

Hard things have been said against Statistics and the use to which they are put. Nothing, it has been said, is so deceitful as facts except, perhaps, figures. These unfortunate figures, a French writer has said, which look at first sight so rigid, so intractable are on the contrary of a docility and of an elasticity truly marvellous. Statistics is an art, according to him, fantastic and perfidious which people have long learnt to distrust. The disrespect which follows the abuse of statistics can be avoided by the observation of the following rules and precautions:

1. Exactitude and accuracy in the collection and arrangement of facts—obstacles in the way of securing this are:
    1. insufficiency of means and sources of information;
    2. imperfection of methods of collection which have to contend with the sensitiveness and ignorance of those questioned;
    3. the extreme fluidity of facts or events to be recorded;
    4. the prejudice and preconceived notions of the collectors of facts which make them look for

confirmation of those prejudices and notions in the facts they are after;

5. comparative statistics, which seeks to compare facts and figures on a given subject in different centres has to contend against the additional obstacle of differing standards of accuracy, organisation, education, degree of civilisation and culture.

2. Classification and sub-division of the heads of subjects of information kept within limits—otherwise too much trouble and time would be spent on what would be of little use.

3. Simplicity of the questionnaire issued to collectors of information—rules for their guidance must be short and simple.

4. Check and control must be exercised in the collection and study of statistical information.

Two functions of statistics have been distinguished:

(i) Information and intelligence.

(ii) Combination, and interpretation of this information.

An Administrative Department has not only to collect facts and figures relative to its department but to formulate conclusions with a view to the formulation of policy which these facts and figures demand.

Methods of Administration

Questions of method, according to the famous saying of Descartes, predominate over the others in any human endeavour. Method determines the course of administration as of every other business. The best laid plans of Governments "gang of tagley" for faults in the execution. Tactics put strategy into effect and there is a tactic of civil administration as there is in military effort. Bentham wrote a book on the Tactics of Assemblies; there is also a Tactic of administration. And this Tactic of administration consists in organising methodical discussion and decision with a view to arriving at a fruitful expression of the will of the government or of the head of the administration and loyal perseverance in the avoidance of faults of evils that retard action, the chief of them being inaction, indecision, useless discussion, waste of time, conflicts between different sets of authorities, surprise of precipitate action, variation in decision, decision vitiated in form or in substance.

Money the Determining Factor

Administration is the art of managing the affairs of the State. But as in every other art its practice is dependent or is controlled by the material, the instruments and the sources with which it is practised. Just as the painter's art is controlled by the resources of the painter in canvass, in colours and in pen or pencil or brush, so the practice of the art of the administrator is controlled by the resources placed at his disposal. The administrator practices his art with the aid of money. The work of an administrator, the nature and number of the functions he performs, the methods he uses are determined by the amount of money he can command. And the methods he employs must be those that will give the best results with the limited amount of money that is at its disposal. Money is, therefore, the determinant of the methods as of the functions of administration.

Programmes of Action

"To govern is to foresee" was one of the maxims of a modern French Statesman. If it is not the whole of the art of administration it is a good part of it. Foreseeing is to estimate what can be done in the future (not in the distant future, for the business of an administrator is to serve his time and not distant times) and to prepare to achieve it. Foreseeing, therefore, consists not merely in thought or conception but in action. Foresight involves, therefore, preparing a programme of action. This programme should include all the steps that must be taken, the means that must be employed to reach the end. The programme of action taken by any administrative unit would depend on:

1. the resources available (the money, the material, the personnel),

2. the nature and importance of the operation.

3. the possible changes of the near future.

The preparation of a programme of action is one of the most important as it is one of the most difficult of administrative acts. It requires initiative, knowledge, power of co-ordination, length of vision and breadth of outlook and finally a high grade of administrative capacity.

A programme of action is to be distinguished from Planning. Planning is the business of the Government as a whole. Planning has general objectives, it aims at the orderly development and exploitation of all the resources, human and material, of a country by means of comprehensive, long term policies and programmes. Strictly speaking we can attribute true, i.e., complete planning only to the totalitarian State. There are various degrees of planning from the restrained, piece-meal planning of the New Deal of President Roosevelt in a free democratic State to the thorough planning of a Communist State. However, that may be, Planning is the work of the Government as a whole supported by its Legislature and public opinion. Whether a Government shall indulge in Planning or not is a question to be considered and determined as a matter of high policy by the Ministry with due regard to its monetary resources, the personnel available, the temper of the people. The humbler role of a programme of action for a year or two is that cast for an administrative department. It is the business of each of the departments of Government. Within the amount of money annually appropriated to it, with the fixing of which it must have had much to do before the amount was fixed if it knows its business, it must frame its programme of action.

General Characteristics of a Good Programme of Action

1. *Unity of programme*—there must be only one programme to achieve one administrative result; two or three programmes lead to confusion, cross-purposes—therefore to no action; this unity must govern the several sections or parts of a programme which may have an economic side, a financial side, a

technical side. A programme may also have to be split into smaller parts of bits for easier and quicker realisation, but all these smaller sections and parts are dominated by the idea of the main programme to the realisation of which they must contribute.

2. *Continuity of programme*—parts or sections of a programme must follow one another, otherwise the chain of activity may be broken and the result frustrated, and when the main programme has been put through it must be followed by another; a department cannot be left without some programme, that is a thought out, planned course of action to occupy its time and attention and energy; otherwise it would waste its time in unnecessary or bootless work.

3. *Time fixed for it*—fixing a period of time for the realisation of the programme is absolutely necessary as such as fixing of time would concentrate the activity and energy of the department and the officials of the department on the achievement of the objective: the usual time for most programmes of action in administrative departments is one year, the official year; but large projects like Irrigation and Hydro-electric projects require 5-10 years for their completion. But these decennial programmes must be precise, take count of fluctuating circumstances from time to time.

4. *Suppleness of the programme*—Every useful programme of action must be capable of modification during its course on account of change of the conditions and circumstances in which the programme is to be put through.

5. *Precision*—This cannot be absolute in the conduct of human affairs in which men are the actors; in administration we have to deal not with machines but with men with individual weaknesses, idiosyncrasies

and wills of their own; unforeseen circumstances and facts and events may happen which would impose changes and modifications of the programme.

Practical Rules for Promoting the Efficiency or Programmes of Action

1. Previous study of resources, possibilities and the means to be employed.
2. Periodical reports must be made and checked on the progress of the programme during the period fixed.
3. Periodical conferences of the chiefs of the departments and sections of departments concerned with the programme.
4. Stability of the personnel entrusted with the realisation of the programme—frequent changes of personnel will interfere with the progress of the programme.
5. Among the directing personnel are required—
    1. the act of management of men,
    2. constant activity,
    3. moral courage,
    4. professional competence and administrative capacity,
    5. experience of affairs in general, if possible of business affairs.

Initiative and Direction

After provision and formulation of a programme of action comes action itself. The first step in that action is Initiative. Here again, money is the determining factor. With the amount of money placed at his disposal the Head of a department of administration has to take the initiative and pursue the successive acts necessary to carry the programme of action into effect.

After Initiative comes Direction. No enterprise can progress without proper direction. Any enterprise badly directed in doomed to failure. The importance of direction increases with the magnitude of the enterprise. Direction consists in preparatory action, in overseeing the execution, and in verifying the results. To prepare the action is to plan and to organise; to oversee it, is to command and co-ordinate; to verify the results is to control the action.

Two ways of Administration

There are two ways of conceiving the administrative process—the pyramidal way and the fan-likeway. The pyramidal way of effecting a programme of action is for the head of a department to issue the programme and for the programme to descend to and through the several layers till it reaches the layer of those of the administration who have to give the final push to the act or acts. The very picture of the pyramid shows that the action cannot be quick, it might be delayed on one stage or the other, and the money get lost or spread out and frittered or untraceable.

The pyramidal way of administrative action may produce solidity (amounting to stolidity), certainty and security; but it does not lead to quick action and effective results and especially to sound use of the money available.

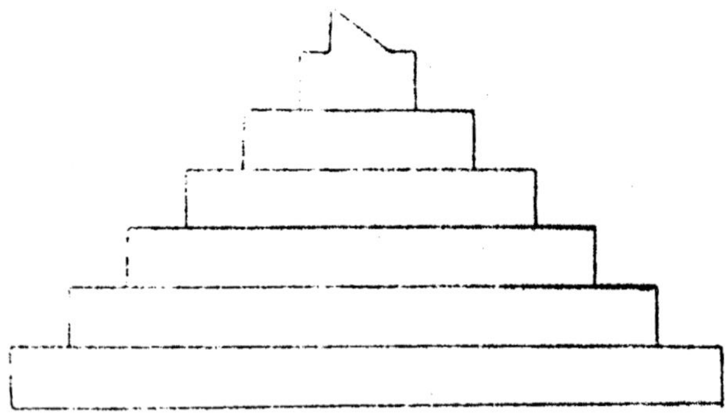

The Fan way on the other hand ensures quick actions, results controlled activity and financial accountability.

As the head of the department issues the programme; in its several parts it is split up to B_1 B_2 B_3 and B_1 B_2 B_3 B_4 split up the order they have received into more divisible parts according to the nature and parts of the programme of action; and at each

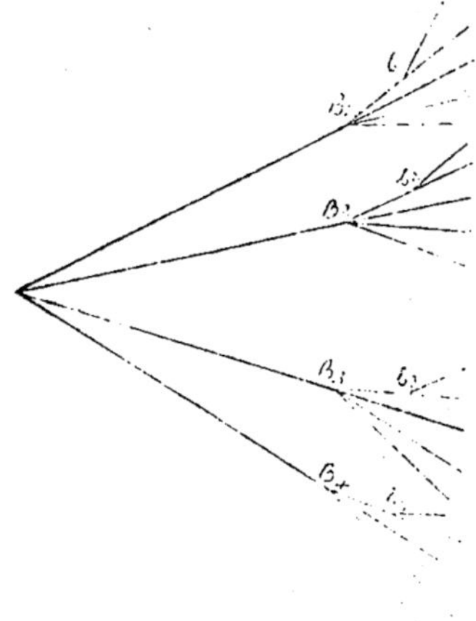

stage B_1, B_2, B_3, B_4, or again at b_1, b_2, b_3, b_4, the action can be checked and especially the expenditure of money set apart for the programme checked and controlled. This way makes it possible not only for the programme to be split up into a definite number of parts, but the money allotted to each part so that check and control not only of each part of the administrative act but of the money allotted for each part are possible. This method gives to the head of the department the initiative in regard to the framing of the programme and the allotment of money and to the officials at each stage the powers to direct and control the activities of those immediately in front of them.

The essence of this fan method of administration is the splitting up of the money or credits (to make use of the official expression) at the disposal of the head of a department among the several sections of his department.

The very picture of the fan way shows direction, rapidity of action, command and control of action, a straightforward and pointed attack.

Reserves

The danger to avoid in this distribution of money is not to give any section more than it needs; for this may mean that other sections get less than they need; or, if it is not so, then the first section having more than it needs may be tempted to waste it on unnecessary expenditure. The credit allowed to a section ought to be slightly lower than its demand requires so that it may be incited to economy. The credit allotted to any department or section of it cannot be determined or precise. But past experience can make it reach an approximation. Variations and corrections will be anticipated by the experienced administrator. If sections of departments are allotted credits slightly lower than their needs require, the heads of departments would have at their disposal reserves which would allow them to meet excess expenditure required in the course of the execution. This device of reserves is intended to compel administrative authorities to reduce the amount of their expenditure.

Or a section of a department in the course of the execution of its work, especially midway, may make known to the head of the department or the authority immediately above it the percentage of proportion of the amount still left at its disposal. The idea behind this midway or latter half report is again to keep a strict check and control over the expenditure. Combined with the method of reserves this method of coefficients as it has been called in French, helps to preserve economy in expenditure. The difference between the method of reserves and the method of coefficients is that with the method of reserves, the attention of the administrative authorities is called to the possibility of exceeding credits only in the latter part of the work, when it would be necessary to resort to the reserves; with the method of coefficients, attention is called to the commencement of the second half of the execution of the work and subsequently when there is time to restrict the expenditure.

Other methods of keeping control and check over expenditure in each department is for the head of the department to see that the total credit allowed for the department is not exceeded; he also has to see to it that by building sufficient reserve out of the total of his credits he is able to come to the help of this or that section as the need may arise. It is his business to see that consumption (say of paper and ink) is reduced to a minimum and that materials (furniture) needed for his department are bought cheap. It is he that must suppress waste and abuse, he must try to satisfy the needs of his department with the minimum of resources, buying in the cheapest market, making sections or offices at the circumferences buy cheap in the local markets. It is his business to see that the amount of his departmental credits is not exceeded. But this financial responsibility of the head of each department requires financial decentralisation and leaving to each departmental authority the role of initiative and responsibility; it ensures the efficiency of administration in that department. The supreme Executive should in its turn see to it that the total credits of each department are not exceeded.

But decentralisation to be effective must go down all along the line and levels of administration. Ultimately and eventually every administrative act must be done by an individual. And to get the best work out of an individual, self-interest ought to be brought to play on his activity. And with regard to this business of economy in administration, the individual administrator, must feel that it is to his interest to keep down the cost of administration. He must individually benefit from every practice of, and made to pay for, every act of extravagance. The system of wages, salaries, allowances, pension, awards, and other kinds of remuneration paid to the individual for the services he renders comes under the category of incentives which make his self-interest give his best to the work allotted to him.

Execution

After Initiative and Direction comes Execution. The organisation of the execution of a programme of action consists in the following chief processes:

1. watching the execution of the programme,
2. establishing a single, competent, and vigorous direction.
3. procuring a competent personnel, defining its powers, and activities;
4. formulating decisive, clear, exact, precise directions,

5. unifying and co-ordination actions and efforts,
6. encouraging initiative and responsibility in subordinates,
7. rewarding adequately efficient service,
8. watching to see that individual interests are subordinate to the interests of the work or action.
9. ensuring discipline, preventing faults and errors,
10. eliminating the abuses of the methods of work in administration.

Activity is the note of a sound administration. The activity in ensured in four essential forms:

1. generality—the administration has to watch over all the interests entrusted to it in every part of the country and among every section of the people;
2. continuity—this watchfulness must be continuous and connected without passing from feverish activity to sterile repose.
3. promptitude—slowness of administrative process is a sign of the weakness of a government.
4. energy—a soft government is deprived of the moral right to exist and to operate. Energy in the execution, said Hamilton, recommending a federal constitution to the people of the future U.S.A. is a leading character in the definition of good government. A feeble government is a lost government for it cannot command the respect of the people.

The Method of Control

Administration and administrative acts can have no effect if care is not taken that instructions issued by superiors are obeyed by subordinate; and if they are not, responsibility must be fixed on them. Verification that orders or instructions issued are obeyed is an essential function of this control. To control is to make sure that at every step and every moment everything happens according to the programme of action adopted, to the orders given and to the principles inspiring the action. Control consists in comparing, discussing and criticizing, it tends to stimulate foresight, to simplify and strengthen the administration to increase the efficiency of direction and facilitate co-ordination. This control to be effective must be exercised not only at the place at which orders are issued but at the place where they are to be executed. For these reasons it is necessary that this control should be distant from and outside the unit of administration to be controlled and should be dependent only on the head of the administration or the head of the administrative department. The controlling personnel ought, in order to perform its function, be independent of the persons or units to be controlled. It ought, therefore, to be special and permanent. Next to independence, competence should be requried of the controlling personnel. This competence ought to be at least equal to that of those to be controlled. To attain the maximum of efficiency the controlling personnel should be at the circumference as well as at the centre—it ought to be local as well as central. It should not be continuous, as then the control might be a hindrance rather than a help—it need only be intermittent. And the controlling authority should ever remember that its business is not actual administration but only control, and the control ought to be orderly and balanced. The object of the control is not to retard but to help administration.

And, as Finance is the core of administration, the control is of two kinds—Financial beside Administrative.

This principle and practice of control will help towards the elimination of all that is useless or parasitic. It will help towards the perfection of the administrative organisation. For its application will necessitate study and thought which are necessary for all human progress.

Division of Labour as Method of Work—Horizontal Division of Labour

Administration, like industrial work and progress, requires division of labour. On account of the size of the modern State as of every large State this division of administrative labour has to be horizontal as well as vertical. The administrative labour at the capital or centre of government has to be divided according to the functions or duties of government. As administration becomes more and more complex with the growth of the State and in the number of the duties of the State, its work has to be divided among a number of departments. As the number of functions of the State increases the number of the departments of government must also increase. The history of the State from the primitive patriarchal times to the times of the modern Welfare State shows how and at what rate these departments have increased. The object of this division of administrative labour as of labour in the economic sphere is to produce the largest amount of administrative good or effect. Specialisation of functions and the consequent specialisation of work leads to greater efficiency. Like the individual workman who works at the same job day after day, the administrative workman who works at the same job day after day become more and more efficient. He acquires a certain skill, precision and confidence which lead to better and better results. Division of labour also reduces the number of objects on which the attention of the worker has to concentrate. The division of labour in administration as in industry has its limits. It cannot be extended *ad infinitum*. And every form of divided labour has its maximum of results—the *ne plus ultra* beyond which efficiency cannot go. The law of diminishing returns applies to administration as to industrial division of labour.

Vertical Division or Labour

And as it is found difficult if not impossible to govern a large State from one centre, some power or functions or duties are either wholly or in part devolved on authorities at the circumference. And in free states, as the practice of freedom must be widely distributed, an additional motive is found for developing power on local units of government.

Territorial Division of Labour

The obvious line of demarcation between the jurisdiction of the central and of local units of govern meant is that affairs which concern the country as a whole must be the business of the central government and affairs which can be looked after conveniently by the people in the local units had best be administered by them. Thus the defence of the State and the maintenance of peace and order must be the business of the central government. Relations with other countries, Foreign Affairs as it has been called, must be administered from the centre. Similarly the administration of the railways, the highways, the post-office, the currency and exchange, the trade and commerce of the State within or abroad must be the business of the central government as for all these things the country must be taken and treated as a whole. Instead of each province or other unit of a State having its own Postal or railway system with its own Postal and Railway offices it would be chapter and more efficient to have a single unified centralised railway or postal administration. Similarly, the administration of law and justice controlled from one centre would conduce to uniformity of law and unity of the life lived in law and according to law by the people. The maintenance of the internal peace and order of the State must be controlled from the centre as the promoters of disorder can run from place to place and may have accomplices in many parts of the country and the police must be able to pursue them without let or hindrance. On the other hand, village roads could not be built from the centre—nor village school houses nor village wells. Nor need cinema houses and other places of entertainment be supervised from the centre. And even in the case of subjects that are administered from the capital it would be useful and convenient for the State to have part of the administration in the free and loosely controlled hands of people in local units. Thus in most free countries a militia as part of the army of a State is recruited and controlled by local authorities like the States in the U.S.A. and although the police is best centrally administered, to rouse interests in the maintenance of peace and order, the village police under village authorities may be allowed to take the detection of crime and the punishment of at least small crimes. To promote interest in the administration it is sound policy to devolve power on the people at the circumference. The balance must be kept between centralisation and decentralisation.

The territorial division of labour in administration—or administrative decentralisation as it may be called is necessary for efficiency in administration. The history of administration and the experience of administration bear out the truth of this maxim. The history of army administration in England for instance shows how the army has benefited from the gradual decentralisation of administration from the year 1870 when regimental indents for things like barracks furniture or cooking utensils passed all the way up through the Brigade and Division to the Commander-in-Chief and the War Office till 1902 when branches of the War Office Finance Departments were posted at the headquarters of military commands to examine accounts and to act as financial advisers to the generals in command though not under their orders and expenditure on building services was decentralised as far as maintenance and new services were concerned; and then in 1922 government departments were allowed to pay the Post Office for telegrams sent by them and Lord Wolsley's complaints that as Commander-in-Chief he was buried in silly little papers on silly little subjects was no longer possible and the Navy like the Army has its own Ordnance Department. And the case for decentralisation has been put on the grounds borne out by actual administrative experience:

1. that decentralisation is a necessary evil,
2. the central point of view is not right in every case just because it is central,
3. discretion of the man at the circumference and in between the circumference and the centre must be encouraged if we are to get initiative and responsibility from him.

A powerful argument for decentralisation is put forward in a recent Report on Administration of a Committee set up by the late President Roosevelt, as lessening the insensitivity of administration to public opinion and that decentralisation would bring the persons that actually administer in detail into touch with the people whom they serve in their own local units. Especially in the administration of democracy is this administrative decentralisation necessary for the safeguarding of the citizen from a dictatorial and unresponsive administration, dictatorial and unresponsive on account of its remoteness from the people whom its decisions affect.

Administrative Science and Other Social Sciences

Public Administration—Art or Science

Public Administration had been recognised as an art or skill quite early in human history. It was practised as a skill amongst the Chinese, the Egyptians, the Indian and Romans in the Ancient Period and has continued to do so in larger or smaller degree ever since. There had also grown several axioms and proverbs of general applicability in the field of administration. Some astray books had also appeared on the subject. Kautilya's Arthashastra, and Abdul Fazal's Ain-e-Akbari in India. Works of Micino in China, Cicero's "De Officils" in Rome, Machievalli's Prince in Europe and other scattered pieces are books written primarily with the purpose of passion on "tips of the trade" to rulers and officials.

But with the unprecedented development of administration in government and in industry, Administration has also begun to make a claim to be a science. Of course, all the social scientists do not accept this contention. There are many thinkers who sharply refute, this claim of Public Administration. For example, Jacob Viner, Professor of Economics at Princeton University has said that "no one knows better than the occupants of the social science chairs that their discipline is so fallible and erratic that to persist in the term, scientific, is an open invitation to ridicule." Similarly, Morris R. Cohen in his contribution of 'Scientific Method' in the Encyclopedia of Social Sciences denies it the status of a science. He argues that even if human affairs obey causality rules, it may be true that because of the infinite complexity of human affairs, these affairs would not demonstrate any "laws" at all to be a finite being in finite time. Similarly, Dr. Finer says that "we cannot say quite clearly what administrative principles are or what they are not." Dr. White, an established authority on Public Administration, made a very lucid and critical study of Principles of Public Administration in a paper entitled "Meaning of the Principles of Public Administration." He arrived at the conclusion that the work of discovering and disseminating principles in Public Administration would have to be postponed to an uncertain date in the future.

These writers emphasize the empirical aspect of Public Administration which is primarily an art. Administration consists of acts or series of acts which have some practical purpose. Whether it is an official on tour or a clerk filing papers in th office or a postman delivering letters, all are carrying on administration. No doubt, it is an art or a skill which has chiefly to be acquired through practice. And like any other skill. "Administrative skill," as L. Urwick says, cannot be bought. There are no hints and tips and short cuts. It has to be paid for in the only currency which is sound in this market—hard study and harder thinking, mastery of intellectual principles reinforced by genuine reflection on actual problems, for which the individual has real responsibility." But like all other arts, to be perfected and be of greater use to its practitioner as well as to the society, it must be based on science. Painting is a purely empirical art. But it too needs the help of science." Hence there is a science of painting which lays down the rules of juxtaposition of colours, decomposition of light etc.

There is a body of thinkers who have been striving to build up a science of Public Administration. In fact, there are many who do not only claim that there already exists such a science but also declare that "if our civilisation breaks down, it will be mainly a break-down of administration", as Brooks Adams says. Cleun Necley of the Duke University says, "Administration is an activity which demands correct analysis and accurate orientation with relation to other sciences. To analyse and through analysis to understand and through understanding to make possible the final function of rational and creative action—this is the highest end which man can conceive for himself." Wallace B. Donham in his "Theory and Practice of Administration" writes. "Administration as conceived in this paper is, therefore, a social science with its own techniques, its own abstractions clustering around the concept of action through human organisations, and its own problems of theory. It is vitally concerned in integrating other sciences, physical, biological, psychological and social, at the point where action is involved." Prof. Beard, one of its greatest exponents, writers in his "Philosophy, Science and Art of Public Administration". "The word, science of administration, has been used. There are many who object to the term. Now, if by science is meant a conceptual scheme of things in which every particularity covered may be assigned a mathematical value, them administration is not a science. In this sense, only astro-physics may be called a science. If on the other hand, we may rightly use the term, science in connection with a body of exact knowledge, derived from experience and observation, and a body of rules or axioms which experience has demonstrated to be applicable in concrete practice, and to work out in practice approximately as forecast, then we may if we please, appropriately and for convenience, speak of a science of administration."

Before we enter into the discussion of whether there is a science of administration or not, it is necessary to understand the meaning of the term, science. Science may be defined as a systematised mass of knowledge, relating to a particular subject, acquired by observation, experience and study, the facts of which have been coordinated, systematised and verified. The term, therefore, signifies more a method or intellectual discipline than a particular subject. It is a discipline which "has generally been held to be one in which objectively verifiable laws or principles function in a casual sequence." The knowledge, thus acquired, must be characterised by precision and predictability.

Efforts were made since the systematic study of Public Administration began to discover the laws or principles of Public Administration and there "to rescue executive methods from the confusion and costliness of empirical experiment and set them upon foundations laid deep in stable principle." The scientific Management Movement intenesified this search for Principles. In the words of Harvey Walker they were "derived from the most successful technique used in governments or in private business." He classified them into the following heads:—(1) Organisation, (2) Budget, (3) Accounting and Auditing (4) Purchasing, (5) Personnel, and (6) Miscellaneous Services. On organisation, there are "canons of integration", e.g. the principle of departmental or unifunctional organisation, the principle of 'span of control.' The principle of delegation etc.; on personnel there is the Merit Principle, the Chain of Command, Principle of Authority and Control and so on. Thus W.F. Willoughby wrote in 1937. "There are fundamental principles of general application, analogous to those characterising any science, which must be observed if the end of administration, efficiency in operation is to be secured; and, these principles are to be determined, and their significance made known only by the rigid application of scienficic methods.

But since the forties of this century a 'Pragmatic Revolt' has taken place in human thought and this revolt has had a radical effect upon the study of Public Administration as well. The 'principles' approach of the Naturalists has been abandoned and a more pragmatic and objective approach has been made to the understanding of the administrative phenomena. The pragmatists hold that the 'principles' approach was really not scientific because the principles were normative rules which involve ethical considerations, while a scientific approach is never to value-questions (i.e. questions of ought) but to fact-questions (i.e. questions of 'is'). Thus Henry Division says, "The abstract validity of theories of government or of human rights—whether they be called moral, legal or natural—is from a strictly engineering point of view wholly impossible to determine. For the governmental engineer, the only question of fact is what appeal the various theories make in any social group—what force they exert and hence, what reactions may follow from them or may be expected to result from them." Advocating the "Need for the Development of Political Science Engineering", he said, "If political science is to furnish the basis for the engineering approach to the problems of government, it must view any community it is studying as a field of forces—psychological, biological and physical. In view of what it can discover about these forces, it must determine the measures and structures of government which can be expected to use these forces and to relate them so as to bring about development in the direction of the fundamental adopted by and appropriate to a particular social group." They, therefore, separate 'facts' from 'values' and base their study only on the analysis of 'facts' i.e. what is? and not on what ought to be? In the words of Prof. Simon the great exponent of this School—their concern with administration as a science is "in the sense of an objective understanding of the phenomena without confusion between facts and values". Clarifying his position further, he says, "This emphasis on the factual does not mean that we discount the importance of values. It simply reflects our belief that the competent practitioner reaches his desired ends—whatever they may be—through a mastery of the phenomena he is dealing with and a clear, objective understanding of their behaviour." Their main objections to the "how to" approach are:

Firstly, human problems are not so mechanical or automatic as to subject themselves to such mechanical solutions. So "Practical administrators find that formal principles of administration are of far less importance to them than an ability to size up an administrative situation—to understand the psychological processes at work—and then to apply common sense once the situation is thoroughly understood."

Secondly, Rules as to how an administrator ought to behave are of little practical use to him, because training and not precepts change a man's attitude.

Thirdly, it is maintained that the "principles" themselves involve value questions—that is, the ethical standards of the framers and hence cannot be called scientific or objective rules.

So in order to avoid these pitfalls of the earlier thinkers, the pragmatists give themselves to the objective study of the administrative phenomena, that is, with the situation as it is. And this enables them to verify their propositions empirically.

Enunciating his "Propositions of an Administrative Science" Prof. Simon defines science as concerned with the factual, and not the ethical, aspects of a situation and classifies science into practical and theoretical. The Administrative Science, he holds, is both. As a theoretical science, it is concerned with factual matters in general in establishing causal relations between the administrative phenomena without regard to immediate use e.g., "such and a state of affairs is invariably accompanied by such and such conditions." As a practical science, it is concerned with putting the propositions of theoretical science of administration into use. e.g., "In order to produce such and such a state of affairs, such and such things must be done" Although this involves an "ought" question yet it does not bring in the value' considerations. It is an 'ought' based on technical or factual considerations. To put it in Prof. Simon's own words, "The terms "good" and "bad" when they occur in a study on administration are seldom employed in a purely ethical sense. Procedures are termed "good" when they are conducive to the attainment of specified objectives, "bad" when they are not conducive to such attainment. That they are, or are not, so conducive is purely a matter of fact, and it is the factual element which makes up the real substance of an administrative science."

This "Pure science" approach has, however, been assailed by later thinkers. Prof. Waldo, for example, says," Administrative study, as any "Social Science", is concerned primarily with human beings, a type of being characterised by thinking and valuing. Thinking implies creativeness free will. Valuing implies morality, conceptions of right and wrong. It is submitted that the established techniques of science are inapplicable to thinking and valuing human beings." Administration involves questions of value as well as of facts. Therefore, the pure science methods cannot always be applied to it, in fact, not to any of the social sciences.

This, however, does not mean that administrative phenomena are not amenable to scientific investigation. "It is not denied" as Waldo himself admits, "that some administrative matters are susceptible to treatment in the mode of natural science." The subjects, which are susceptible to such treatment are budgetary, accounting, purchase and other auxiliary and allied activities. But matters of human relationships are not amenable to the techniques of physical science. But even in such matters there is need of a "scientific outlook" and "common sense" approach. Defining the 'scientific outlook', Waldo writes "There is undoubtedly a temper of mind characterised by general awareness, preciseness, and a disposition to inquire into things. It is called the scientific outlook." The "commonsense" approach is described by him "as general facility of mind, as balance of emotions and "reasonableness" of judgement, as adherence to and progress toward the Golden Mean or Wisdom." Therefore, where the pure science methods are not applicable to administrative phenomena, the scientific approach and the common sense approach should be made use of.

Relation with other Social Sciences

The earlier writers on Public Administration seemed to be more concerned with establishing Public Administration as a separate and independent academic discipline and hence emphasised its distinction and independence from other studies. And as chronologically Public Administration was a part of Political science they were more aggressive towards it. They built up a theory of the dichotomy of Politics and Administration and considered the former as characterised by passion, chance, chicanery and spoils, while the latter as characterised by the cool, calculating and rational spirit of science, and therefore, advocated that politics should not be allowed to meddle or interfere with administration.

But when Public Administration passed its age of adolescence, it regained a sense of security and began to recognize its debt to other sciences, more specifically to Political Science. Another factor which has brought about a greater inter-action between Public Administration and other Social Sciences is the penetrating and critical inquiry made by the 'Pragmatists' in every aspect of human activity. More specially, the sociologists and social psychologists find administration as a very productive field of their research.

Another factor which has brought about greater inter-relation between Public Administration and other sciences is the feeling that "the chief cause of the disasters under which humanity is at present suffering is a lack of balance between man's knowledge of the physical sciences and his grasp of the laws of social organisation necessary to control the power which that knowledge has created." Yet another factor which has helped in bringing the Administrative study close to other studies, specially of a scientific nature, was the Scientific Management Movement. It turned man's mind into the working of the laws of dynamics and statics and thus introduced scientific thinking and terminology in the study of administration.

With these general remarks we now pass on the analysis of the relations of Public Administration with specific subjects. First we would take Political Science which is chronologically as well as substantially closest to Public Administration.

Political Science

In its earlier phase, as noted above, Public Administration was drawn far apart from Political Science. Prof. Wilson, one of the earliest writers on the subject, wrote in 1887, "Although politics sets the tasks for administration, it should not be suffered to manipulate its offices. The field of administration is a field of business. It is removed from the hurry and strife of politics; it at most points stands apart even from debatable ground of constitutional study." Similarly Goodnow said. "The fact is....that there is a large part of administration which is unconnected with politics, which should be relieved very largely, if not altogether, from the control of political bodies. It is unconnected with politics because it embraces fields of semi-scientific, quasi-judicial and quasi-business or commercial activities work which has little, if any, influence on the expression of the true state will".

But since the thirties of this century, there has taken place a revaluation of the earlier relationship and more and more writers are emphasizing the close relation between the two. Today, as Leslie Lipson says, "the attempt to democrate clear-cut functions of government is impossible. Government is a continuous process. It is true that the process contains phases. Legislation is one phase, administration another. But these are merged together and at certain points become indisinguishale." Similarly, Luther Gulick says, "It is impossible to analyse the work of any public employee from the time he steps into his office in the morning until he leaves at night without discovering that his every act is a seamless web of discretion and action." Prof. Herbert Simon designated the whole process of government and administration as one of "decision making" Prof. Homer Durham accepted the concept of "Administrative Politics" and Prof. J. Donald Kingsley announced. Administration is a branch of Politics." Dwight Waldo after reviewing this "rise of heterodoxy" in his scholarly treatise "The Administration State", concluded. "The tone of recent writings strongly suggests that politics—administration, at least in the you-go-your-way and I'll go mine form is fast becoming an outworn credo".

The result of this change has been a very great widening of the scope of Public. Administration. The study of Public Administration is no longer a terse and dull study of legal concepts or of mechanical formulae but a lively discussion of human problems. Administration is no longer conceived as a set of mechanistic acts but as a dynamic process involving wide discretion at every level. Therefore, its study now includes all the processes of policy-formulation, Politics, Parties and Public Opinion. The method and technique of studying these new elements are the same as those as of Political Science—namely, the behavioural research. Thus the two subjects have been drawn so close to each other than, as John M. Gaus remarks, "A theory of Public Administration means in our time a theory of politics too."

There are other areas of political science in which public administration is very much interested. They are constitutional law, local government and international relations. The relation between constitution and administration is so close that the laymen and even some writers in this country, fail to distinguish the two. In our Constitution itself there is, at places, a fusion of principles of construction and principles of administration. Though public administration is not a part of the constitutional law of a country, yet its form and structure is largely determined by the Constitution. In the domain of local government also there is much overlapping of subject matter between political science and public administration. It is that part of the community life which is of vital importance to both the politician and the administrator. Hence there is greater need of collaboration between the researchers not only in the two sciences but also in all the social sciences.

Until fifteen years back there was practically no relation between Public Administration and International Relations. The latter was considered to be, and to a very large extent actually was a field of diplomacy and hence unworthy of the attention of administrative scientists. But with the growth of the international life into a compact community of nations, international politics presents not only problems of diplomacy but also those of administration. Since the establishment of permanent international organisation like the League of Nations, the International Labour Organisation, the U.N.O. and its various organs, the World Bank, the International Monetary Fund etc. "Public Administration has been given not only a new level, the international, but a new dimension, intercultural." Donald C. Stone with a very long experience in international organisations, says, "When we consider the problem of governments collaborating through international organisations, we tend to think only in terms of foreign policy and of issues involving conflict among countries. This is, of course, natural since these are the questions uppermost in the news. But there is another side to international collaboration. If international organisations are to be successful in dealing with world problems, the policy organs through which negotiations are conducted and the secretariats which handle the administrative work must be properly organised and administered." Proceeding further he says, "I have found no support for the contention that international administration is fundamentally different in nature from any other kind of administration. It is always necessary, of course, in transferring administrative experience from smaller to larger enterprises from one level of government to another, or from one cultural environment to another, to interprete such experience in the light of different conditions." International Relations and Public Administration meet not only in matters of organisation but also in those of management and technique. Raushofen—Wertheimer after a long experience in the League of Natior's secretariat said,

"From a technical viewpoint, international administration uses the same media for the dispatch of its business as national administration in the modern sense of the term, meaning those rational processes of organisation that have evolved since centralised government and professional civil service merged in the eighteenth century".

Lastly, there is the field of political theory whose relation with public administration has never been close or cordial. The reason is that public administration is empirical, while political theory is philosophical. One regards the other as foreign to its nature. But of lately, as Prof. Waldo says, "students of administration have been reaching out toward political theory; and have been themselves contributing in an important way to political theory." In his "Administrative State" Waldo himself has tried to prove that the American literature on Public Administration is a special contribution of U.S.A. to the field of political theory and this he gives the name of the Administrative theory of the State.

History

Public Administration in its early days was indifferent to history. This attitude of indifference arose because of its practical and empirical origins. The early writers were practical persons and were imbued with the naturalistic tendency. Jean Henry Fabre, a leading light in administrative studies during the last decade of the Nineteenth Century and first decade of the Twentieth, advised: "Study nature not books" The Scientific Management Movement had the same effect.

But of late writers on administration have begun to give themselves to the historical study of administration. As the experimental and other methods of physical science are difficult to apply in the social field, administrative scientists have turned to history in order to draw comparisons between parallel administrative situations. Dr. L.D. White has produced two remarkable books on the administrative history of U.S.A. Max Weber's Essays in Sociology', S.B. Chrimes's "An Introduction to the Administrative History of Mediaeval England in the West and Prof. Mookherji's Local Government in Ancient India and

J.N. Sarkar's Moghal Administration' in India are only a few examples of the contributions by students of Public Administration in the field of history and of the historians in that of administration. History is no longer a record of warfare or the story of dynasties but a scientific analysis of the social, political, administrative, economic and cultural life of the people in the past. While a historical outlook on the part of the administrative scientists would broaden their perspective, the administrative outlook of the historians would make the study of history more fruitful.

Harvey C. Mansfield has very scholarly analysed the 'Uses of History in administrative history. He says, "What kinds of generalisations can be derived from administrative history? Tentatively, I suggest that for our purposes at least three types, or levels of particularity, may usefully be distinguished. I shall call them, philosophical observations, analytical or problem—solving techniques, and administrative techniques". Philosophical observations, by which he meant general observations, would "help establish a mood of understanding in those who have the job to do again." The analytical and the administrative techniques are respectively "middle gauged" and "narrow-gauged conclusions which "are of the if you have to do it again, -do-it-this-way variety of lessons, on a par with the techniques of the factory, the department store, or the farmer cultivating his crops". It is hoped that with the further growth of the study of public administration social writers and thinkers will develop a historical perspective which would not only enrich the administrative literature but would also enrich the experience of administrators.

Sociology

Sociology is the study of society in its fundamentals, forms and ramifications, while administration is the mechanics of social action. Therefore the relation between Sociology and public administrative is very deep. Sociology provides administration very useful hypothesis and develops in the administrators keen and penetrating insight. It studies the various social and group processes, its origins, development, functioning and inter-relations. The sociological studies of status, class, power, occupation, family, caste, prestige and similar social forces are of special interest to the student of public administration. It is a clear influence of sociology that the present writers on public administration study all administrative problems in their environmental contest. A generation back they used to apply mechanical rules to the administrative process and thus had built up mathematical formulas like the "canons of integration".

Sociology has given public administration not only a new perspective but it has added much to the literature of administration. There is a large number of sociologists who have selected administration, private or public or both, as their field of research and have made very valuable contributions. Max Weber's essay on Bureaucracy' produced very great influence upon the study and practice of public administration. He proved that bureaucracy was a natural institution which arises under certain given conditions and works in a fixed pattern. To put it in own words. "Once it is fully established, bureaucracy is among those social structures which are the hardest to destroy. Bureaucracy is the means of carrying community 'action' over into rationally ordered 'societal action.' Therefore, as an instrument for 'societalizing' relations of power, bureaucracy has been and is a power instrument of the first order—for the one who controls the bureaucratic apparatus. Under otherwise equals conditions, a societal action, which is methodically ordered and led, is superior to every resistance of 'mass' or even of 'communal action'. And where the bureaucratisation of administration has been completely carried through, a form of power relation is established that is practically unshatterable."

The result of such studies has been that social relationships have begun to be looked in their environmental setting. Private and governmental research agencies have sprout up to study the adaptive responses of the people in given conditions. The administrator is no longer left to himself to quarrel either with his tools or his clients but is provided with a necessary sociological background of the place and people where and whom he is called upon to serve. In fact, the administrator is now himself a social scientist in action.

Social Psychology

Social psychology is the study of human behaviour in society and administration is the study of human action in society. And as action in motivated by a person's psychological behaviour, psychology and administration are very intimately related. In its early days, however, public administration was not influenced by psychology. The early writers were under the deep influence of rationalism which was the most distinguishing feature of Eighteenth and Nineteenth centuries thought. Taking human activities as perfectly rational, they proceeded to discover immutable laws of organisation and management for the guidance of practical administrators. But with the growth of psychological studies, they have found out that man is not so rational as they considered him to be. This has brought about a radical change in the study of Public Administration. By this is not, however, meant that the psychological approach has brought about any radical change in the administrative theory. The changes have been "entirely on the empirical level", as Prof. Waldo says, "there are no sweeping conclusions about the irrationality of man based even at second or third and on psychological study. What cognizance there is of psychology is chiefly of the Win-Friends-and-Influence-People school-a reflection that it is a handy tool for administrators, hence its potentialities should be exploited—and seems to have come by a process of osmesis, from the literature of business administration and scientific management."

But it is not only the Public Relations field in which psychology has influenced Public Administration. There are, in addition, many other phases of public and private administration which have been and, are being, influenced by the psychological researches. They are administrative leadership indoctinatrination of public employees, building up of morale and esprit de corps, test and measurements aid in recruitment and promotion and polling and sampling techniques of public opinion.

Ethics

Ethics has to do with the moral values of the community and questions of value had till recently been traditionally and designedly excluded from the study of Public Administration. So long as administrative writers believed in the dichotomy of politics and administration, there was no place for value questions in administration. Woodrow Wilson had definitely said, "We can learn from a murderous rogue his technique of sharpening a knife without borrowing also his intent to commit murder. So can we learn efficient techniques of administration from the autocracies of Europe and use these efficient technique the better to realize the goals of our democracy." The modern positivists, though they do not believe in the end and means dichotomy, also separate value questions from their study, as they feel that science is concerned only with questions of what is? and not with questions of what ought to be? For example, Prof. Simon says, 'Propositions so stated may be adopted to any set of values what the persons using the information may hold".

But since the Thirties of this century, there has arisen a class of thinkers of the hard-headed school who are not prepared to separate means from ends. They believe to put in Waldo's words, that 'it is most realistic and fruitful to think of means as intermediate goals and goals except the ultimate goals we state in abstract terms—as means to further goals."

The findings of the sociologists also lead to the same conclusion that forms and institutions reflect the genius and cultural complex of the community and hence administrative forms and procedures are inseparable from the cultural values. In the actual practice also we see that every form of government whether it is democratic or dictatorial, utilizes the same system of hierarchical organisation, a bureaucracy and the same method and technique and yet the administrative machinery of the two behave differently and function usually at cross-purposes.

The present writers realize this and in democratic countries, an earnest effort is being made to implant moral values both in the machinery and personnel of the state. Dr. Appleby says, "All human organisations are systematic persuits of various values. In turn, their conduct becomes a more and more important aspect of the pursuit of values. Public organisation is a part of the whole organisational complex, differentiated as a systematic pursuit of values." Continuing he says, "At the point of action the problem of morality becomes an organizational problem and hence also a problem in administration. Democracy itself is largely a means for the determination of, and arrival at, values; but the means are capable of many organisational variational, and if "the end pre-exists in the means', the specific organisational forms themselves pose important value questions. So, it is, too, with the action means of administration."

Public morality and professional morality are now taken as the integral parts of any study of Public Administration which no modern text book on the subject can afford to leave. As a specimen of writings on morality in Public Administration, we give below Appleby's view. "Moral performance begins in individual self-discipline on the part of officials, involving all that is meant by the word 'character'. But this is not enough. It also requires systematic process which supports individual group judgement enriched by contributions from persons variously equipped and concerned, and differentations in responsibilities to each other and to a whole-public responsibility. The official individually and organisationally must be concerned to go beyond simple honesty to a devoted guardianship of the continuing reality of democracy.

Economics

The study of Public Administration has much in common with that of Economics. Public Finance, Budgeting and Fiscal Administration are subject common to both. The forms and procedure of administration depend very largely upon the economic factors and considerations. Of late, there is a tendency on the part of governments to intervene more and more in the economic life of the community and thus the areas of government and economics which had been separated during the Nineteenth century are fast converging, thus the giving rise to a separate academic discipline like the Political Economy of the Nineteenth century. The greatest similarity between public administration and economics is on the points of economic institutions. And this has developed into a separate study called Economic or Business Administration.

Business Administration

Business Administration arose as a result of the Industrial Revolution. But it took definable shape only during the course of the Scientific Management Movement. Under the inspiring guidance of the Scientific Management Society, it grew into a perfect academic discipline with its own terminology, tools and technique. Public Administration which arose almost simultaneously, borrowed much from it. Most of the organisational forms and principles, personnel management techniques and office methods have been borrowed by Public Administration from Business Administration. In our own times, the system of labour-representation in management has come into Public Administration from Business Administration in the guise of Whitely or Staff committees. There is still much give and take between the two. Presently both are following the case-method of study and research.

Books for Further Study

1. Dwight Waldo: *The Study of Public Administration.* (Doubleday and Company, N.Y. 1955).
2. Dwight Waldo: *The Administration State.*
3. Simon, Smithbury and Thompson: *Public Administration* (Alfred A. Kropp. New York 1950 Chapter 1).
4. Simon: *Administrative Behaviour.* (The Macmillan Company, New York, 1954).

8

Development Administration

Edward W. Weidner was the first political scientist to propound the concept of development administration. Development administration is a new dimension of public administration. It is a dynamic concept which brings about social, economic and political changes in society. Attaching top priority to development, it strives for change, growth, progress and all-sided development in all fields of a country. It lays stress upon development of administration on the one side and the administration for development on the other.

Prof. F.W. Riggs, Joseph La Palambra, Albert Wilson etc. Played important roles in the development of the concept of development administration which is very much related to the administration of developing countries of Asia, Africa and South America popularly known as the third world. These countries had to face serious problems of illiteracy, underdeveloped economy, undeveloped political and administrative institutions, lack of scientific techniques in management, social immovability etc. Their first uphill task was to solve these problems. Therefore the traditional administration was converted into development administration.

Meaning and Definition

Concise Oxford Dictionary has defined the word 'development' as the growth into a higher, fuller and mature condition. Under public administration development means growth of a social structure towards progress. In any society changes in the direction of progress are called development. Development is a dynamic change in a society which aims to achieve higher conditions in every sphere of life. It is a functional part of government which executes policies formulated in public welfare. Following are some well known definitions of development administration.

1. *Edward Weidner:* "A rapidly developing country is a goal-oriented country, headed to the direction of modernity with special emphasis on nation building and socio-economic progress."

2. *Fainsod:* "Development administration is a carrier of innovating value. It embraces the array of new functions assumed by developing countries embarking on the path of modernisation and industrialisation. Development administration ordinarily involves establishment of machinery for planning, economic growth and mobilisation and allocating resources to extend national income."

3. *G.F. Gont:* "Development administration is that aspect of public administration in which the focus of attention is on organising and administering public agencies in such a way as to stimulate and facilitate defined programme of social and economic progress. It has the purpose of making change attractive and possible to the population generally."

4. *J.D. Montgomery:* "Development administration means carrying out planned change in economy (agriculture, industry and capital), and to a lesser extent in the social service of the state (education and health)."

Among the above definitions, the definition by Fainsod is narrow while the definitions by Weidner and Riggs present the broader view of the development administration. All writers point out the fact that it is goal-oriented and work-oriented concept.

(i) It is a process to move towards higher position.

(ii) It is a perpetual and a dynamic process.

(iii) It is a joint effort for the achievement of determined goals.

(iv) It is a work-oriented and goal-oriented administration.

(v) It is a significant instrument to solve the diverse problems of the third world.

(vi) It is not only the administration of development but also the development of administration.

(vii) It is an administrative machinery for a change and modernisation of backward society.

Characteristics of Development Administration

1. *Change-oriented:* Development administration aims to bring social and economic change. Even in the developing countries the administration has to undergo a series of social, economic and political changes. As and when the administration loses its dynamism, the changes of development become remote.

2. *Developmental Tendency:* Fainsod holds that development administration is a vehicle of developmental values. It goes with development programme. Thus, the criterion of its success is development of administration which means maximum welfare of people. Its chief aim is to develop a socially, economically and politically backward society.

3. *Related to Democratic Values:* Development administration is related to democratic values, for it implies the feelings of responsibility, aim of public welfare and respect to the human values and rights. Since it is concerned with the effort of public administration, the public activities are undertaken keeping public welfare and democratic values in view.

4. *Administrative Efficiency:* Development administration leads to administrative efficiency in whose absence

aim of maximum development cannot be achieved. If the aims of projects formulated for development administration are achieved in minimum time it is called administrative efficiency. The development administration always endeavours to increase administrative efficiency through administrative development with the result that there is no wastage of time and resources.

5. *Modernisation:* Development administration makes efforts for the modernisation in the social, economic and industrial fields. It has to prepare itself for these new and modern aims. Modernisation has to be encouraged. Its models are taken from developed countries. Development of science and technology helps in the administrative modernisation. Modernisation takes place of traditional values and the development administration has to be made stable and aim-oriented.

6. *Fulfilment of Public Demands:* Development administration makes efforts for the fulfilment of public demands. It is conscious of the civic services. It makes constant efforts to achieve fixed objects and aspirations of people. Satisfaction of public wishes affects political and administrative development of the country. Development programmes are enforced to keep in view the public welfare and convenience. The development administration should be familiar with sishes and aspriation of the people.

7. *Administration of Industrial Societies:* Development administration is concerned with the society which is industrially and economically progressive. The industrial society fixes standards for administrative behaviour and performance of functions which become models for development administration. In such societies the methods of procedure and administrative organisation take practical shape. Those countries which have been industrialised, have developed in other walks of life. Thus the industrialisation, progress

and development go together. All these are part of the development administration.

8. *Economic Development:* Development administration is primarily related to the economic development. Along with administrative development it has to make similar efforts for economic development. The different economic plans and development programmes of developing countries are executed with the cooperation of development administration. It erects and administrative organisation, which makes the economic advancement of the country possible and paves the way for economic development. When change, modernisation modernisation take place, huge sums of money are needed to enforce modernisation plans. Thus, planning is made to achieve financial autonomy.

9. *Fear of Bureaucracy:* New projects for development, launched in both developing and developed countries, impose new and additional responsibility upon the administration. The administration wields additional powers and authority to execute these plans for progress. It aggravates fear of misuse of authority by bureaucracy which becomes all powerful. The public servants take undue advantage of additional discretionary responsibility.

10. *Result-oriented:* Development administration is result-oriented for it has to enforce development programme within specific time limit and is expected to achieve the best result within this time limit. Here the emphasis is laid upon the results achieved from the efforts. Edward Weidner rightly maitnains that development administration is a work-oriented and result-oriented administrative system.

Scope of Development Administration

Development administration is a recent and vast branch of public administration. It owes its growth to the latest administrative plans and projects in developing countries. Its functions are concerned with the formulation of programmes, policies, plans and projects. In a developing country all administration is a development administration. Prof. Demock holds that practically public administration, in modern time has overlapped all our life and activities. It has become a fundamental basis of our civilisation. Public administration is an integral part of modern civilised society. The State has development administration which includes activities performed by the government concerned about social, political, economic, industrial and administrative development.

1. *POSDCORB:* These are the same as explained by Prof. Luther Gullick in his book under the chapter, The Scope of Public Administration.

2. *Legislative Functions:* In modern time both the government and legislature have excess of work and little time. Thus, the responsibility of legislation also falls upon the shoulders of the administration. The development administration is concerned with that legislation which is essential for running the development programme. The system of delegated legislation has led to the inclusion of legislation in the field of development administration.

3. *Administrative Reforms and Management Improvement:* The administrative reforms and management improvements are very important in the field of development administration. Administration and management reforms become necessary in all administrative and development organisations. The chief aim of administrative reforms is to simplify the complex activities and procedures, and to evolve those methods which may be able to achieve maximum productive results by spending least labour and money. Many Commissions and Committees are set up for this purpose from time to time to submit their reports for administrative reforms.

4. *Education and Training for Public Servants:* The development administration has to enforce new projects and programmes of specialised nature whose personnel are to be educated and trained afresh. They are sent to different specialised training institutions, where they are oriented about new administrative problems and organisational management. Various types of orientation courses, refresher courses, training weeks and workshops are organised for their training, on national and international level.

5. *International Cooperation and Coordination:* For development programmes, the projects are enforced, the internal agencies are approached for their help. The developing countries seek financial assistance of international agencies. World Bank, International Monetary Funds, World Health Organisation, UNESCO etc. International institutions provide loan to underdeveloped and developing countries. Development administration has to make proper use of the assistance within proper time limit so as to receive the next instalment in time.

6. *Use of Modern Management Techniques:* Development administration searches those modern management techniques which help in increasing efficiency. The developing countries use management techniques which have been successfully used by the developed countries. A development administration has also to face some challenges to meet which proper modern techniques and procedures are used.

7. *Use of Computer:* According to former Secretary General of the U.N.O. Jevier Perej de Queliar, a computer can help the development of developing countries. The development administration of every developing country has to make use of computer system for data processing, modernisation, all-sided development and other changes.

8. *Rural and Urban Development Programme:* Development administration enforces programmes for rural and urban development. Projects and programmes launched for rural development include irrigation, construction of roads and hospitals, provision of drinking water, telegraph and communication etc. The Government of India has set up a separate ministry for rural and urban development at the centre.

9. *Public Relations and Public Cooperation:* Public relations and public cooperation occupy an important place in development administration. Maximum public cooperation is required in development programme. In the absence of public relations, no public cooperation can be obtained. Public relations is the medium through which it has tried to learn the public reaction to development programmes launched by the government. Through the means of communication and public relation, the public is informed about what the government is doing for the people and what are its future plans. Public cooperation is essential for development administration and for public cooperation, cordial public relationship is necessary.

10. *Development of Economic, Social and Political Structure:* Development administration has to develop the economic, social and political structure of the country for reforming the traditional structure and procedure and to develop new economic, social and political structure. If the dynamic and changeable structures are left untouched, they lag behind time and tide, and fail to face due challenges. India adopted five-year plans for the economic development of the country. According to socialistic concept, reservations in jobs were made in bridge the gap between the rich and the poor. Panchayats have been vested with powers and authority for democratic decentralisation.

11. *Regional Development Councils:* Establishment of Regional Development Councils is a new dimension

in the field of democratic administration. In every country there are many fields which are left underdeveloped or undeveloped. The public of such regions demands for the establishment of regional development councils for their development. After a serious deliberation over all the problems of the region the council formulates plans and submits them to the government for approval. In India, Gorkha Hill Development Council, Chota Nagpur Hill Development Council etc. Have been established for this reason.

Development Administration in India

Soon after India achieved freedom, the public administration started taking shape of development administration. The plans were prepared and enforced. These were evaluated by development administration which has acquired an honourable status and is going ahead with fast speed. The public relations are being attached importance. Efforts are being made to achieve public cooperation through community development projects and Panchayati Raj. The Regional Development Councils are being set up to remove regional imbalance. Different types of plans for production of electricity, irrigation, river valleys, or canals, are being enforced. Through public relations public is being informed of these projects and other government welfare activities. A network of development institutions has spread all over India. Right from the apex of administration to the lowest level the public is being made to participate in the development programmes.

Development Administration at State Level

For the development administration a chain of officials has been created in every State with Development Commissioners at the apex. He directs and controls all development programmes through a Development Committee. To enforce development programmes through District Development Committee there are District Development Officers. Under him there are Block Development Officers who look after development programme through Block Committee. The District Magistrate coordinates development works. Through the Panchayat Raj Act, the heads of Gram Panchayats are vested with powers to take decisions about village development. In almost all States there are separate ministers in charge for rural and urban development.

Central Development Administration

The Union Government has also strengthened the development administration and has helped in its extension. The development of the country is being achieved through five-year plans. A National Development Council has been set up to deliberate and plan the fresh plånning for development. The Ministry for Urban Development has been set up for the development of cities. The Rural Development Ministry docs all this for the villages. The development of rural agencies has been the goal of all five-year plans. For the extension of education, health, drinking water, electrification, roads and buildings, the villages are being accorded all possible financial assistance. The goal of this programme is to raise the income of poor village people, to raise them from poverty line. National Rural Employment Programme (NREP), has been launched with this aim. Thus development administration is playing a significant role in the economic, social, political, industrial and administrative development of India. Very soon India shall occupy its place among developed countries of the world.

Problems of Development Administration

Prof. Riggs holds that the modern administration of developed countries has not been able to adapt itself to the changing needs. Apter has stated, in the book '*The Politics of Modernity*' that there is a need of excessive administration for various developmental activities. But due to the lack of proper education and training, the administrators have not been prepared in sufficient number consequently there has been a fall in the standard of administration. In such a condition the establishment of development administration has become difficult. Though casually the achievements of development administration in India, from the first decade after independence to last decade of 20th century appear to be satisfactory, still there are following problems of the development administration.

1. *Relationship with Regulatory Administration:* In India, the district administration has not been able to adapt itself according to the changing needs. The agencies of development administration could not become powerful, they depend upon the regular administration which is awfully busy with daily routine business.

2. *Political Intervention:* Increasing political intervention in development administration causes tension in the administration. On the one hand the administrative officials are looked upon with suspicion, by people, and the politicians intend to take undue advantage from the administration. On the other hand under the false ego of their powers and positions, the administrative officials, do not attach importance to the politicians, and ignore their good suggestions as intervention. In the recent years the political intervention in the administrative fields has very much increased, adversely affecting development administration.

3. *No Constitutional Recognition:* In India, as yet no constitutional recognition has been accorded to Panchayati Raj institution. In 1984. Late Rajiv Gandhi had presented a Panchayati Raj Act in the Parliament, but it could not be passed. Shri P.V. Narashima Rao has also agreed to remove this discrepancy by legislating Panchayati Raj Act. Though Institutions of Panchayati Raj and rural development work as agents of State Government .but there is no provision for decision-making at village level. As they use the delegated authority from the State Government, their decisions are neither practical nor attuned to public welfare.

4. *Dual Responsibility:* There is a dual responsibility upon the development officials. At district level the District Magistrate, and at sub-division level, the S.D.O. has to look after the functions relating to law and order, alongwith development activities. They

ignore developmental work, and are busy with law and order all the time. Hence, there is a demand that there should be independent officials for development activities, so that the development administration can successfully achieve its goals.

5. *Irregular Elections:* In India, the elections for Panchayats and District Boards are very irregular. Many plans are launched after approval but soon after, the next administration freezes funds. Consequently, half-begun plans end in disaster. Every new government reconsiders past plans and makes all possible efforts to change or to stop them.

Despite the above problems, there is no need to be disappointed at the achievements of development administration. Development and change have to face hurdles and problems. The development administration and administrative development go together. Through the administrative development efforts are made to remove the problems faced by development administration in India. Recently the number of educated people has gone up, and so the national income has increased. There has been an increase in the consciousness among people towards national and international problems. All this inspires hopes in future development.

Questions for Exercise

1. What is Development Administration? Explain its characteristics.

2. "The birth of development administration in a broad way may be attributed to the adoption of democratic polity, pressures of economic growth, adult suffrage, universal education, welfare programmes and other rural development schemes." Discuss.

3. Discuss and explain the scope of Development Administration.

4. Write a short note on Development Administration in India.

9

Comparative Public Administration

The significance of the study of comparative public administration has been recognised by almost all the civilised countries of the world. It is endeavouring to make public administration scientific and purposeful. The discipline of comparative public administration was independently accepted as a subject of study in California University in 1948 due to Prof. Dwight Waldo. In other developing countries as well, it is being accepted for study in their universities. Even in India, many universities are teaching it as a compulsory paper at Post-graduate level.

Meaning and Definitions

1. *T.N. Chaturvedi.* Comparative public administration is a comparative study of public administrative institutions of different States.

2. *R.K. Arora.* Comparative administrative group has broadened the horizon of public administration. By study of various administrative systems in their ecology, it has made the scope of public administration most scientific, and has inspired the interest of its members into the problems of development administration.

3. *A.R. Tyagi.* Comparative public administration is a discipline which uses empirical tools of comparison to study the total universe of public administration irrespective of time, place or cultural variables."

4. *Rumki Basu.* "Through comparative public administration, we learn about the administrative procedures followed in various nations and then we can endevavour to adopt those practices which can fit in our own nations and systems.

Thus, comparative public administration is a comparative study of diverse administrative systems, on whose conclusions most scientific efforts are made in public administration.

Under the comparative public administration the achievements and political systems of different countries are compared. Analysis is made to learn in any specific country, how some specific plan was launched and how many people were benefitted from it. Under comparative public administration it has become easier to study the administrative system of developing and developed countries.

Significance of Study

The comparative public administration is significant for the development administration. Both have been developed after the World War II. The development administration has to face new challenges. In the context of new development projects, the administrative development and reforms become essential. By analysing the administrative system of various countries the writers of comparative public administration try to suggest the use of administrative techniques for development administration, and for increasing the efficiency in the administrative structure. The conclusions, received from the comparison, guide the development administration.

Merits of Study of Comparative Public Administration

1. Comparative public administration has broadened the field of social research, while previously it was limited by natural cultural bonds.

2. The revolution of comparative approach has made the principle formation more scientific.

3. Comparative methodology makes our outlook broader, with the result we do not watch the world subjectively.

4. Comparative public administration is broadening the process of social analysis.

Objectives of Comparative Public Administration

1. To formulate general principles and concepts by studying specific administrative problems and systems.
2. To present far-reaching analysis of different cultures, nations and systems, and thereby extend the scope of modern public administration.
3. To find out the causes of their successes and failures by locating comparative circumstances of diverse administrative forms and systems.
4. To point out the necessity of administrative improvement in the context of comparative studies, to bring out the shortcomings into light.
5. To make experiences dynamic by making their use.
6. To contribute in the policy determination of the government.
7. To broaden the horizon of public administration and to make it practical.
8. To encourage the use of the new techniques of managerial and administrative science in the developing countries.

Factors in Evolution of Comparative Public Administration

1. *Contact with Developing Countries:* During Second World War, the writers of public administration of the U.S.A., U.K., and other European countries came into contact with the principles and procedures of the public administration of developing countries. They found many novelties and new characteristics in those systems. They were encouraged to make comparative analysis and study of these systems to learn their characteristics and fundamentals intensively.

2. *New Challenges of World War II:* The traditional public administration could not face the new challenges of World War II. Dwight Waldo has remarked, "The student of traditional public administration can acquire knowledge of a single country alone, and is unable to make the similarities or distinctions with other countries." Modern writers of public administration were not prepared to compromise with these shortcomings of traditional public administration. Therefore, new philosophy of public administration came into light.

3. *International Cooperation and Coordination:* The Second World War helped in the extraordinary development of international cooperation and coordination. Different countries had to increase their dependence upon other nations. This dependence was not confined to economic, industrial and technical fields, but also extended to the field of administration. Every country became interested in making use of administrative principles and achievements of other countries, this has created international cooperation and coordination, this has helped the development of comparative public administration. Increasing dependence among different countries contributed to the development of comparative public administration.

4. *Claim for a Science:* In the post-war era almost every social science claimed to be a science. The public administration could not present its claims due to the lack of comparative approach. In 1947, Prof. Robert A. Dahl admitted in an essay. "Unless the study of public administration was comparative, it cannot be accepted as a science". Importance was attached to the comparative study of public administration to make it meet the criterion of a science.

5. *Demarcation of Subject-Matter:* On the beginning there was no clear-cut systematic demarcation of the subject-

matter of public administration. Prof. Edward Shields holds that by systematic comparison of diverse societies their similarities and peculiarities were observed and indicated. Thus development of comparative methodology was essential for the systematic explanation of subject matter of public administration.

6. *Cold War:* After the Second World War, the world was bifurcated into American and Russian blocs. These engaged in intense cold war. Both blocs competed to turn all developing countries in their favour. The U.S.A. and USSR took recourse to diplomacy, providing all sorts of assistance in the field of economic, industrial and technical development. It could only be properly utilised when these countries used the know-how to make use of new technology. Thus the personnel of these countries were sent abroad to be trained in developed countries, and the administrative systems of these countries were employed in developing countries.

7. *Development of Comparative Public Administration as a Discipline:* From the beginning the authors of public administration considered the comparative approach so significant that they were sure of its bright future as an independent discipline.

8. *Relationship between Administration and Society:* The close relationship between administration and society played an important role in the development of comparative public administration. It became essential for the writers of public administration to study the relationship between social and administrative structure.

Scope of Comparative Public Administration

1. *Macro-level Study:* Under Macro-level study the emphasis is laid on the compression of total administrative system of a country with that of another country. All significant aspects of administrative

system of a concerning country are analysed. Both countries economic, social and cultural ecology is included. The conclusions are drawn after the comparative analysis of total administrative system.

2. *Middle Range Study:* Under middle range study of comparative public administration the comparatively greater part of the administration system of a country, the large and more significant organs of administration systems of two countries are compared. This is neither complete study of administration systems, nor of a minute part of the administration.

3. *Micro-level Study:* Nowadays micro-level study is more popular in comparative public administration. In some specific departments or specific procedures of the department are compared with those of another country. In the field of comparative public administration this system is being used for administrative research.

Approaches to the Study

1. *Structural Functional Approach:* In 1955 Prof. Dwight Waldo referred to structural-functional approach in comparative public administration for the first time. Prof. Riggs approved the idea of Prof. Waldo. In 1957, Prof. Riggs presented an agrarian industrial model on the basis of this approach. Prog. Riggs was considered to be the person to have introduced the structural functional approach in the field of comparative public administration. Talcott Parsons, Robert Merton, G. Almond, David Aptor etc. Did not support its application in public administration. The exposition of structural-functional approach in the field of public administration is that there is a structure of every administrative system. By the structure and its organs (components) various functions are performed. The comparative study and analysis of these structures, performing diverse functions is the principal aim of functional-structural approach.

The supporters of this approach hold that public administration is like a planned dynamic machine which can be studied like a scooter, motor car or a cycle and their parts. All these parts perform their functions with coordination and interdependence and are called organisational structural functions.

2. *Ecological Approach:* The credit for ecological approach in the study of comparative public administration goes to Prof. F.W. Riggs, Robert A. Dahl, J.M. Gaus, Roscoe Mastin etc. According to ecological approach, as all plants cannot grow in all climates, likewise all administrative systems cannot be useful or successful in the ecology of all countries. The public administration is also affected by the economic, social and political circumstances, and the ecology of the country. The study of public administration should be made keeping the local ecology and circumstances in view. The prismatic sala model of Prof. F.W. Riggs is based upon ecological approach.

3. *Behavioural Approach:* It is the latest approach in comparative public administration introduced by Prof. Herbert Simon, Blow Merton, Weidner, Haddy Stokes, Calton etc. It was introduced in comparative public administration, to make public administration more pragmatic and useful.

In his book, *Administration Behaviour,* Prof. Herbert Simon discarded traditional methods of study for the study of public administration. He remarked that if we wished a correct and scientific analysis of the organisation, our study should be made upon behaviour. Attaching importance to the behavioural aspect of the administration, Prof. Simon stated that everyone working in an organisation, harbours some feelings and aspirations, and his behaviour is affected by psychological conditions and inspirations or motivations. The individual and social conditions of an individual mould his behaviour. The behavioural study can successfully express the behaviour of the person working in an organisation. While the period upto 1960 is called the apex of the behaviouralism, the period of post-behavioural revolution are after 1970.

4. *Post-behavioural Approach:* The post-behavioriualism holds that though the behaviouralism has played a significant role in studying administration system it is insufficient for the full comprehension. The new challenges came for behaviorualism, the period hereinafter was called the period of post-behaviouralism. However, this revolution has not yet taken a concrete shape.

Questions for Exercise

1. Discuss the meaning and significance of Comparative Public Administration.
2. What Factors that have led to development of comparative public administration after the World War II?
3. What are the objectives of comparative public administration? Discuss causes of its evolution.
4. Explain the scope of comparative public administration. Point out various approaches to its study.

10

International Public Administration

According to Prof. C.P. Schleichar, our chief requirements are peace and prosperity, and to achieve them we aspire for international cooperation. This is an age of internationalism. The nations must cooperate with each other. They must provide all sorts of assistance to other countries, and in turn, receive assistance from some countries. Interdependence of nations must be recognised. Every country, today, is linked with other countries through ideology, treaties, pacts and assurances. Therefore, cooperation can be achieved through some sort of international organisation.

The terms world peace, international cooperation, international conference, international community, international morality etc. form a useful terminology. However, today if we talk of international administration, people are shocked. An organisation, be it local, national or international, when it take a permanent shape, it possesses an organisation—an administration; and a huge army of personnel is requried to achieve goals of administration and to perform functions.

Meaning of International Administration

The international organisation had a temporary character in the beginning. The organisations were formed; the objectives were determined; the international conferences were organised; the foreign diplomats went home after participating in the conferences. Official and administrative functions were performed by personnel of the external departments of different governments. Due to temporary character of international organisation, international administration could not take a concrete shape. Graphally, however, the nature of international organisation started stabilizing. Many worldwide organisations were developed such as League of Nations, UNO, OAS. Commonwealth of Nations, SAARC, NATO, CENTO etc. At international level many permanent organisations concerning agriculture, health, banking, communication, labour and transport etc. are working. They have their own administrative set-up and objectives. A number of personnel we recruited, and are made to work to achieve these objectives. Today international administration is a vitally important necessity in the field of international cooperation and technical assistance.

International Parliament

Prof. Dean Rusk, the American political scientist, was the first writer who addressed the U.N. General Assembly as International Parliament and pronounced it as Parliamentary Diplomacy. In his book *The Fundations of Diplomacy* Prof. L.S. Rathore has remarked. "The General Assembly shows a remarkable similarity with National Parliament. In fact, there is hardly a country in the world which is not a member of the General Assembly today. The membership of General Assembly has gone up to 163 by admission of Marshall Islands and Micronesia in Sept. 1991. These 163 members of General Assembly *represent their countries* just as M.P.s. represent their constituencies."

There is much similarity in the proceedings of both General Assembly and the Parliament. The representatives of different countries in General Assembly of U.N.O. deliberate over international problems. They participate in debates and take decisions by majority. The proceedings of General Assembly, deliberations, and use of committees, are similar to Parliamentary process of many countries. The draft proposals and debates correspond to the Parliamentary process of General Assembly. Recruitment of different officials, budgetary process, annual report of the Secretary General and many other things are like Parliamentary procedure of National Legislatures.

International Chief Executive

The ideology of international administration has been further developed since the U.N.O. started taking interest in the field of economic and social development of backward countries. Some authors have underlined the role of U.S. Secretary General as an International Chief Executive. If the world government is ever realised, in future the UN General Assembly would be the world Parliament, and the U.N. Secretary General would be the International Chief Executive. Even today if in any part of the world any emergency arises U.N. Secretary General becomes active as a guardian of international community. At the time of Gulf crisis, Mr. Javier Parez De Cuellar, the Secretary General, immediately started activity, persuasion, requests, courage and patience. Such role makes him the guardian of International Committee. As International Chief Executive, the Secretary General behaves at the time of some crisis as a head of a State does, at the time of national crisis.

Whenever there is some danger to international peace and security, the war is on, the conditions of tension arise, or there is a clash between two countries. Without waiting for the session of either General Assembly or Security Council, the Secretary General takes all possible steps for the solution of these world problems. He makes all efforts to avert war and seeks the way of amicable solution. If he fails and war breaks out, his disappointment is seen explicitly. Just after the Gulf War the Secretary General confessed, "I am constrained to admit, all diplomatic efforts failed and we could not check war." In fact these roles point out that the U.N. Secretary General, really acts like International Chief Executive.

To assist in its multifarious activities Art. 97 of the U.N. Charter provides that there should be Secretary General and personnel according to needs and requirements of the United Nations. At the recommendation of the Security Council, the Secretary General shall be appointed by the General Assembly. He shall be the Chief Executive of the United Nations. Art. 101 further provides that the Secretary General shall appoint officials and subordinate staff for the secretariat. As there is a central secretariat in every country which is the central office for all the executive departments of the country, in the same way, there is a secretariat of the United Nations which performs all international functions concerning all member countries. Some authors have described international secretariat as national or central secretariat as in all departments and ministries all information are classified in the central secretariat. As head of the ministry takes his seat in the secretariat, similarly all the departments of U.N. have their central office in the U.N. Secretariat. World information is collected there and all heads of departmental organisations have their officers there. This U.N. secretariat is world secretariat. Its working procedure is similar to central secretariat of major countries of the world. The personnel working in the central secretariat are also chosen from all countries of the world.

NATURE OF INTERNATIONAL ADMINISTRATION

From the technical point of view, International Administration uses the same media for the despatch of its business as national administration. U.N. Secretariat has been classified into various departments. The departments are sub-divided into bureaus, sections etc. The heads of the departments are Secretary, Asst. Secretaries, Directors, Chief of the Office, Chief of the Bureau etc. They are all in hierarchical order. Delegation of power comes from top to bottom. Every subordinate member personnel is responsible to his superior official.

POSDCORB

Under International Administration the performance of work is done on the basis of Luther Gullick's POSDCORB concept. Planning organising, staffing, directing, coordinating, reporting, budgeting etc. are followed in the working of International Administration. Like national administration the methods of communication, coordination, direction and supervision, are employed in international administration.

Unique Characteristics

U.N. Secretariat is a permanent executive institution. Its legislative institution is not a legislature, but a diplomatic body. International administration is always influenced by a theory of practice of U.S. Administration. The latter tries to run it on the pattern of U.S. administrative system. Prof. Lapawaski has accepted this fact in his book, *The Art of Management*. Americans have to learn to treat lightly in imposing their own administration concept on international agencies.

International Personnel Systems

All permanent international organisations possess their own personnel systems. Small temporary international organisations may not possess stable personnel system but the permanent international organisations have their own personnel who are duly recruited, their service conditions well determined, and who are properly trained according to their functions.

Articles 97-101 govern determination and provision regarding the establishment of secretariat. Secretariat General officials and personnel. The Secretary General is the Chief Administrative Officer of the Secretariat. There are 8 other Deputy General Secretaries, working as heads of different departments in the U.N. Secretariat. In 1955 the highest offices were recognised, and two Under Secretariats General were added to increase the efficiency of the Secretariat. The Secretary General appoints other officials and staff requried for the performance of functions of Secretariat. Of these three-fourth work in the U.N. Secretariat Headquarters and the rest in offices of different U.N. agencies scattered all over the world. The Headquarters of the U.N. Secretariat is at New York (U.S.A.) The personnel of the U.N. Secretariat are members of International Civil Service who work with the feeling of internationalism.

1. *Recruitment of Personnel:* Unlike that of national civil servants the recruitment of personnel for the U.N. Secretariat is a complex process. According to the provisions of the Charter, efficiency, honesty, experience and capability of personnel is to be considered in the recruitment. Secondly, representation in the civil service shall be given to the citizens of the whole world. Each geographical area shall have representation in the international civil service. Theoretically the Secretary General possess the power to make all appointments and dismissals, but in practice, he has to consult the concerning governments for all recruitments.

2. *Oath and Conditions of Service:* The U.N. Secretariat is a symbol of internationalism. It has strengthened the concept of international bureaucracy. The Secretariat staff play role of international bureaucracy. As the personnel of the world, they have to take an oath before taking charge of their duties. Article 100 of U.N. Charter provides that in the performance of their duties the U.N. Secretary General and personnel shall not accept command from any other government or official—other than the U.N. The provision of the U.N. Charter makes it clear that members and officials of secretariat are members of International administration. The conditions of their service inspire them to work in the interest of international administration. The members of international administration are paid sufficient salaries and allowances. They also get the benefit of two return T.A.'s for return (home) journey, which includes their family. They are provided with free residence and medical facilities besides promotion, pay increment etc.

International Civil Service Advisory Board

In every country an Advisory Committee or Board is set up for the personnel management and for determining the salaries, allowances and other service conditions. The Board makes recommendations about all problems concerning administration. In the U.N. Secretariat, presently an international civil service advisory board has been set up. The U.N. Secretary General is its ex-officio chairman. He nominates 10 other members of the board, who assist him in the performance of his functions. The functions of international civil service advisory board is to provide valuable advises and suggestions regarding personnel policies to different executive heads of departments of the U.N. At the suggestion of the advisory board new system of training for personnel of secretariat has also been implemented. In the beginning two-third personnel of the secretariat were from U.S.A. Canada and Western Europe. However, when countries from Asia and Africa became members of the U.N., they opposed the traditional system. According a recommendation for a change was made by the advisory board.

Grade System of Posts

The services of the personnel of International Civil Service, can be bifurcated as—career service of permanent spot, and short-term posts. The technical services, diplomatic services, missions services are short-term posts. These posts are given to the members of national civil services generally and are recruited on the recommendation of member countries. But written and oral competitive examinations are arranged for the recruitment to career services. Successful candidates are duly appointed. The permanent members of international civil service are legally entitled to promotion, increments and pension. Their service records are maintained in the U.N. Secretariat.

New Classification

According to the latest system, the personnel of the U.N. Secretariat and International Civil Cervices are classified into four categories.

1. A. The personnel of category 'A' are administrative officers, which include under secretary general, assistant secretary general, directors (D-2) and Chief Officers. (D-1).

2. B. Under category 'B' come officers (professional) which are of 5 classes as I senior officials (P-5), first officer (P-4), second officer (P-3) etc.

3. C. Category 'C' comprises personnel of clerical grade who are also of 9 types.

4. D. Under category 'D' come the personnel of regional services who work in different parts of the world, for international functions. 'D' category is further classified into 7 classes having high officials and personnel of clerical grade. There are separate pay-grades for all personnel. They pay grades run between 4500 U.S. dollars to 3500 U.S. dollars per annum. The U.N. Secretary General is an exception. The personnel of all categories work under the Secretary General who has power to superintend, inspect and control their

functions. He has the right of both, appointment and dismissal.

Critical Evaluation

The study of international administration opens new dimensions for public administration. The functions and responsibilities of U.N. Chief Executive, Secretary General are similar to the international chief executive. The U.N. General Assembly has become an International Parliament, where 163 members from various countries of the world participate and represent their countries. International Court of Justice has the status of a world court of justice, the status of a world court. The U.N. Secretariat has become international secretariat and so is the form of international civil services. The personnel of U.N. Secretariat have become the members of international civil service by taking oath for service. Thus, all the three organs of a government are set up at international level. However, the international government is missing. The concept of world government has not been realised.

The international civil services comprises the backbone of the U.N. As a body of competent, loyal and permanent civil servants. It has been able to give the necessary assistance to the Secretary General. Much of the success of the U.N. depends upon the cooperation of the Secretary General. So long as the august office is filled in by a person of imagination, courage and devotion the U.N. has been able to face many a severe crises. While the elected organs of the international organisation come and go, the secretariat with the Secretary General and the international civil services continues permanently. This is the greatest strength of the system of the international administration.

Questions for Exercise

1. What do you understand by International Administration? Discuss its nature.

2. 'U.N. Secretary General is working like a Chief Executive and U.N. General Assembly-working like an International Parliament." Examine this statement.

11

State of Public Administration in India Today

Auguste, Comte, the famous French Sociologist, was of the view that social sciences are the most backward of sciences and the natural sciences the most advanced. The reason for such an uneven and lop-sided development of sciences was that the natural sciences were not interwoven with the lives of men and could be studied dispassionately and objectively and in complete insulation, ensuring scientific study, whereas social sciences are a bewildering mix of thought and action, interest and morality, reason and impulse, passion and wisdom. Human lives with all their hopes and aspirations, strengths and infirmities, inconsistencies and contradictions constitute the warp and woof of social sciences. Political Science, an appendage to Political Economy, Philosophy and History for centuries in England, to Law on the continent of Europe and the Ethics in the ancient civilisations and oriental countries emerged out of the shadows as an independent discipline in the first quarter of this century. Public Administration, an appendage to an appendage and overshadowed completely by Political Science emerged as a semi-independent discipline much later, around the late forties or after the Second World War. The independence or self containedness of a discipline can be judged by its theoretical foundations, its social relevance, the contribution made by outstanding thinkers and by the interest taken by the common man, not necessarily in an articulate manner but even mutely. Political Scientists dismissed Public Administration as an inconsequential aberration which did not deserve an independent niche in the pantheon of Sciences. They said with considerable assurance but no less contempt that after all what the students of

Public Administration were seeking were changes of emphases on certain areas of study and certain institutions, most notably bureaucracy. It is true that Political Scientists concentrated on the political-legal institutions like the executive, the legislature, the judiciary and political parties and through calculated indifference allowed purely administrative institutions and ideas to recede into the background. No political thinker until the nineteenth century undertook a careful and systematic study of Public Administration. There are passing references to administrative structures in some of the works. Even Marx who intended to study society almost in its entirety treated it rather cavalierly.

Max Weber's Pioneering Contribution

It was Max Weber, the German Sociologist, a neo-Kantian and positivist who re-examined socio-economic phenomenon and the weight of his ideas was directed against Marxist teaching on socio-economic formations. According to Weber the essence of any socio-economic formation is determined not so much by its objective aspects as by the viewpoint of the investigator and by the cultural significance attached to any given process. Weber proceeded from the assumption that social sciences study only individual aspects of various phenomena and tried to substitute for scientific abstraction the notion of an 'ideal type'. This, Weber averred, had no basis in reality, but was only a means, a device, to systematise and understand individual facts. His theory of 'ideal types', his conception of the plurality of historical facts and the idea of rationality as the basis on which bureaucratic institutions function was a stunningly new contribution and the beginning of a world-wide study of bureaucracy and the administrative structure together with the controversies the theory spawned.

Weber was the pioneer, who through painstaking researches discovered that the burgeoning German State was governed not so much by the glaringly visible institutions like Monarchy and the Bundestag but by the sprawling new apparatus of the state, the bureaucracy. It was a new culture, administrative-political culture evolving a new work ethic as it grew. Weber's researches in Sociology were a trail-blazer and were followed by a host of writers, most notably in America Woodrow Wilson's contribution to Public Administration in its most formative period was weighty enough to be taken note of by serious students of Public Administration.

INSTITUTIONAL EFFORTS

Universities in the United Kingdom being very cautious and conservative were wary of the developments in America. Universities on the Continent also dragged their feet instead of keeping pace with some of the most prestigious universities in the Unites State. In India, as is well-known, the University of Madras was the first to have instituted a diploma course in Public Administration in 1937 followed by the University of Allahabad which started a diploma course in local-self government in 1938. Seven years later the Universities of Lucknow and Nagpur started a diploma course in Public Administration and in 1949 Nagpur University established the first full-fledged department of Public Administration, and Local-Self Government. Barring Nagpur, no other university founded a separate department of Public Administration, though diploma course were taught in the universities of Osmania, Andhra, Calcutta, Aligarh and Patna. Public Administration came to be grudgingly accepted by being introduced in the form of a paper in some of the universities at the post-graduate level. Undergraduate teaching had to wait for quite some time. At the moment Public Administration at the postgraduate level with full-fledged independent departments is being taught at thirteen universities and undergraduate teaching is being done with or without separate departments in fifteen universities.

The progress has so far been frustratingly slow but the trend for expansion is distinctly visible. Expansion has been taking place in at least two ways. The departments of Political Science are being re-christened as departments of Political Science and Public Administration or separate departments are being opened with facilities for M. Phil courses and research. In the integrated departments, Political Science continues to be the major or mother discipline and Public Administration usually takes a back seat. In the independent departments of Public Administration, however, there are no such hassles.

Growing Relevance

The greatest impediment to the development of Public Administration as an independent discipline is the ingrained reluctance on the part of all social scientists to recognise it as a self-contained discipline because of its being relatively young and not yet in possession of works of great distinction and traditions of thinking and writing. It's theoretical base is still wobbly and its debt to Political Science is so great and extensive that despite best efforts it still continues to languish under the foster care of the mother discipline. Despite these drawbacks, Public Administration had acquired an enormous relevance firstly from the State which has been undergoing rapid transformation both in regard to its nature and its responsibilities and secondly on account of the complete transfiguration politics has undergone in the last fifty years or so both in the developing and developed countries, most noticeably in the former. The modern state is no longer a merely welfare state. It has transcended practically at limits set by liberal democratic thought, the socialist doctrine and the exigencies of socio-economic development. It is total or near-total state bearing the burden of responsibilities in every conceivable area of human life and endeavour. If responsibilities have increased, so have the powers and as a consequence of the expansion of both responsibilities and powers, the state impinges upon the life of the commonest of men more than ever before. It is indeed imperative that every citizen should know how the law and administrative rules are made and implemented. How does the machinery of government operate must be made known to the people for whom it operates.

If people know how does the government function, they would be in a position to make it function within the four corners of the laws and rules and keep it from becoming highhanded and irresponsible. Ignorance of the working of government encourages willful arbitrariness on the part of the government; knowledge of its working compels responsible behaviour on the part of those who man the government at all levels. The common farmer should know all that is relevant in the revenue administration and he should not look up to the village *Patwari* like hungry sheep and be not fed. In fact every village school should teach all that is relevant administratively from the village upwards to the district. Some knowledge of Public Administration in a condensed form must be made available to all those who are affected by it. Every school-going boy should know how from village upwards to the State, administration is organised and carried on. Teaching of Public Administration, therefore, must not start in universities and colleges but at the secondary, higher secondary level by integrating a condensed course on district and State administration with social studies, Indian Constitution, history and culture. All that is taught presently is a broad outline of the Indian Constitution, leaving the most relevant part concerning the administration of India in the elementary, but most important segment untaught. But more than half the population being still illiterate, effort should be made to teach the rudiments of administration to the common man through adult literacy centres, social and culture organisations and political parties. As in the Western countries evening classes can be organised by the universities, colleges and Higher secondary schools. These measures, if adopted with sincerity and worked with determination, can go a long way to popularize Public Administration and equip common citizen with the necessary knowledge and information about the administration of the area of segment they are most concerned with.

ADMINISTRATION FOR DEVELOPMENT

The socio-economic development that is taking place has placed enormous responsibility on the bureaucracy or the civil services. So long as administration was merely a holding operation, designed to maintain law and order, collecting revenue, defending against foreign invasion and protecting against internal turmoil, the task of the civil services was simple. But to eradicate poverty and give people adequate social security and open up avenues of gainful employment the whole administrative machinery has got to be geared up, reorganised and motivated to achieve results. But developmental administration without the active participation of the people at every stage is bound to result in undemocratic practices and uncontrollable bureaucratic domination. Planned economy needs a vast bureaucratic organisation, which if not controlled and made to respond to public needs, results in a totalitarian set-up. The perils that attend developmental administration and the vast bureaucratic expansion that is inevitable can be to a great extent checked and stymied by an up-to-date knowledge of public Administration. Soviet Union and the East European countries, despite protestations to the contrary sank into dictatorship controlled by a vast and powerful bureaucracy. In a developing country, the temptation to set aside cumbrous democratic processes to achieve results is always great. In order to make sure that such practices as would inevitably result in the establishment of an undemocratic administration, teaching of Public Administration and researches into every branch and aspect of it is absolutely essential. The consciousness generated by the acquisition of knowledge of Public Administration will go a long way in remedying the defects likely to arise as a result of the expansion of the administrative machinery for developmental purposes.

Identity and Interdependence

Besides the practical or the utilitarian aspect dwelt upon so far, there is the intellectual and the academic aspect of it. As a social science, public administration, cannot but draw upon all other sciences dealing with society and also the natural sciences which vitally affect life and demeanour of a society. The more it absorbs the knowledge dug up by other social sciences, the richer it becomes. No social science or natural science can develop in isolation, but a line has to be drawn between what is fundamentally and purely an inseparable part of Public Administration and what is borrowed and absorbed from other social sciences for broadening its horizons and deepening its understanding of society. No social science can afford to ignore Economics and Political Science. Public Administration can illafford to ignore either of them because administration is squarely based on the economic activities of the people which, in turn, cannot be isolated from the political activities of the classes, parties, institutions and individuals. Those who believe that Public Administration has not been allowed to grow and expand fully on account of its excessive reliance on Political Science forget that to wean Public Administration from Political Science is to truncate both of them and make their growth impossible. But there are areas of study and specialisation which ought to be clearly marked so that overlapping may be avoided as far as possible. Business management or administration, administration in government undertakings, in the corporate sector, in the private sector, in local-self governing bodies, recruitment of personnel and training, conditions of service, organisation of government departments and their working, the bodies operating at different levels in the *panchayati raj,* administration of such bodies as Universities, Public Service Commissions and Revenue Boards all should fall within the territory clearly marked off as of Public Administration. All these areas have more or less been regarded tacitly by all concerned as the exclusive responsibility of the students of Public Administration. What is, however, needed is that these areas should not continue to be only skeletally a part of the Public Administration curricula. These areas of study should be provided with firm theoretical foundation so that the charge of unlimited but rickety empericism against Public Administration be laid to rest. All this can be achieved if right-minded Political Scientists, Sociologists, Economists and scholars and practitioners of administration strive hard to give Public Administration the much needed shot in the arm and define comprehensively its Parameters. Public Administration is more dependent on empirical research than any other social science. A modest beginning has been made though in putting together some administrative theories, but to be can did, they lack intellectual depth and philosophical perception. There is no doubt that social sciences must of necessity rely more on empirical research but there must also be a well coordinated effort to coalesce together the results of such researches and to discover a pattern, if any. No social science can be independent or self-contained unless it is based on viable theoretical foundations, a large part of which has to depend upon creative imagination, speculative thinking and constructive hunches. Public Administration's approach so far has been, to the regret of most of us, pedestrian and it has never tried to take off the ground. Parkinson's laws and management theories smartly put together might delight some and astonish others but they cannot form part of a discipline.

Need for Genuine Scholarly Pursuit

In order to give Public Administration a new orientation and to remove the reasons which have put it in an inferior position, it is necessary that the U.G.C. set up a committee consisting of senior and enlightened professors of Public Administration and distinguished practitioners to design courses for all levels of instruction and identify areas of fruitful research, which the universities and other academic bodies may, with necessary adjustment and changes, adopt. This will provide the discipline with the much-needed uniformity and purposefulness and do away with the unnecessary and disposable innovations which unfortunately are the hall-mark of the current courses in Public Administration.

The Institutes of Public Administration at the Centre and State levels have done enough useful work as far as training the fresh recruits to the All-India and State Services and conducting refresher courses and seminars are concerned. But they have created a good deal of confusion too. Studying Public Administration as a discipline is one thing and providing training in the art and science of administration is quite another. The former operates within the well-defined parameters of academic relevance and propriety, the latter is concerned only with communicating some results of the studies to those whose interest in the subject is peripheral and whose orientation is different from the dedicated students of Public Administration. Institutes were meant to be centres of serious study of Public Administration. A university has the necessary ethos and temper for the scholarly pursuit of the subject; the institutes are good enough for transferring some of the rudiments of administration to a motley crowd of the practitioners of administration. Unfortunately, courses in the universities are designed to suit the requirements of the competitive examinations, for All-India and State Services and usually scholars of Public Administration consider it an honour and a great boon to be appointed teachers at the National Academy or State Institutes for the training of officers. The Union and State governments should look up to the universities for guidance and help instead of the other way round. The increasing influence and interference of administrators is perhaps one of the reasons why Public Administration could not attain the status of an independent and self-contained social science and remained chained to men and institutions without the freedom to think and act independently.

Towards A Vibrant Science

But Public Administration has a very important role to play in the not too distant future. The days of one-party dominant system are over and coalitions in the Centre and the States will become increasingly acceptable as years roll by. Not stability, but continuity and efficiency, will be what would be expected of governments. And, when political changes will be frequent and span of life of coalitional governments short, the civil services will have a great role lined up for them. Multi-party system in a parliamentary democracy cannot escape frequent changes and the burden of administration will have to be borne by the civil services. Public Administration instead of continuing to be under the tutelage of Political Science will come into its own. Larger number of better educated and better trained civil servants would be needed and scholars of Public Administration will have much larger share of academic and social responsibility. Besides, in the coming years there is bound to be greater demand for the expert than the generalist. A political scientist, to all interests and purposes, is a generalist and a student of Public Administration is an experts and a specialist. One of the most infallible indicators of a progressive society is that it is guided and led increasingly by the expert and less and less by the generalists. Public Administration, of course, while playing such a pivotal role will have not only to enrich its intellectual and academic resources but encourage purposeful research in every and in all its ramifications. A live and vibrant science cannot rest on its oars. Perpetual and unceasing effort to discover, to comprehend, to interpret, to analyze and to weed out the out-of -date and usher in new ideas and theories is what is needed by Public Administration. Hopefully, it would perform its role well and live upto our expectations.

—A.B. Mathur

12

Perspectives on Public Administration for the 21st Century

Future of Indian Public Administration

"Ideas are the spectacles with which we look at facts," said Edward De Bono. What we see depends on what ideological spectacles we wear. To peer into the future of public administration on the 21st century is difficult, as one can't predict anything about the future. Imagine someone trying to give a talk on the perspectives on public administration for the 20th century in the year 1896! One wonders whether he would have been able to anticipate the cataclysmic changes that took place in the 20th century resulting in India becoming an independent country, the disappearance of the 600+ states and so on.

We can therefore approach the whole issue of perspectives for the 21st century from different angles. One would be to look at the inherent dynamics of public administration and draw conclusions about the likely trend of developments in the years to come. The other would be to assume that there would be a vision and a systematic effort at realising that vision which means that the dynamics of public administration will be focused in certain directions. Ultimately the perspectives depend on whether we are going to assume a mode of drift in which case certain inherent factors will come into play or whether we are going to have a vision and work towards it in which case there will be certain specific directions of development.

So far as the drift mode is concerned, we can look at external factors and those within the administration. After all, public administration is closely linked with development of society and therefore when we talk about the external factors they will relate to some of the broad trends for which we can offer analogies from geology as well as biology as has been done by Lestor Thurow.

Lestor Thurow has borrowed two concepts from geology and biology in his attempt to look into the future of capitalism in his recent book *"The Future of Capitalism"*. From geology he has borrowed the concept of plate tectonics to perceive and describe massive changes which are taking place and which have developed a force of their own. As regards to biology, he draws inspiration from the concept of the "punctuated equilibrium" in describing evolution. The disappearance of dinosaurs as a result of the catastrophe that took place 65 million years ago is an example of punctuated equilibrium. Of course, one commentator has pointed out that dinosaurs have really not been eliminated but have evolved into the birds we see today. Even if this is true, the scenario from when dinosaurs ruled the earth has undergone a sea change.

It is always good to remember one important principle of scenario planning and futurology. We have to think of the unthinkable or the showstopper. That will be the catalyst for punctuated equilibrium. Otherwise we will be like the futurologist who, looking into the 20th century in the 1890s, speculated that the roads of London would have seven feet of horse dung covering them by the year 1920. He had just extrapolated the figures of horse drawn carriages, which were quite common in the late 19th century in London. He never anticipated the automobile, the horseless carriage that was the showstopper in this case.

When it comes to internal dynamics of administration perhaps the laws of physics will apply. Newton's Law, particularly the first and third law of motion are relevant in this context. The first law is the Law of Inertia. Anybody who has dealt with large bureaucracies knows about Inertia. Unless there is a strong force to change it, the inertia is not going to change. This is where perhaps the pace of development will depend upon whether we are in the drift mode or in the focused vision mode. The third Law of Newton "every action has an equal and opposite reaction" is also relevant. This will explain the difficulties and resistance in any process of reform. While the bureaucracy and public administration will be subject to these laws, there is also another Universal Law, the second Law of Thermodynamics according to which in any system there is a tendency for entropy to increase. In other words, there is always a movement from order to disorder unless we are careful, and unless we intervene.

The Drift Mode: Plate Tectonics

We can begin our exercise by looking into three broad sets of issues. The first: What are the major forces shaping our society today, which will have an impact on public administration? These will be the plate tectonics aspect of administration. The second set of issues would be to see what would be the features that will continue in any administration irrespective of the state of the society or the perceived role of the government. These are the internal factors of administration. The third aspect will be to speculate on the showstopper signifying the punctuated equilibrium.

Let us look at the first aspect of plate tectonics. The most significant aspect of public administration is the public, the people. We have already a population of about 1 billion and in the 21st century it may be stabilise at around 15 billion. Another aspect of our demography is that with the growing improvement in health services, the population is growing. The population of old people will become increasingly significant. After all, the average life expectancy for an Indian has gone up from 32 in 1947 to 56 today. So, in the 21st century we can reasonably hope that the average life expectancy of an Indian may even go up to 65. This has to be seen in the context of the other sociological phenomenon of the breaking up of the joint family and the growth of nuclear families. We can therefore, visualise new pressures on our public administration in the social sector in the form of old age care and assistance. This aspect also has to be considered in the context of the progress made by the Asian Tigers vis-a-vis the western countries. One of the reasons given for explaining the success of the Asian tigers is that thanks to Asian values, the elders are taken care of by their families. Hence the burden of social insurance, which developed social economies have to bear, is not there in the societies of the East. This has helped the Asian countries to chalk up faster rates of growth than achieved in the West.

Another demographic fact of our population will be the significantly large population of those below 25 years of age. We can expect hopefully that the family planning and the family welfare initiatives of the government will succeed. If we are moving towards a stable population by mid-21st century, we can expect for the next say 20 years or so, a large percentage of those below 25 or 30 years in the population. This may gradually reduce as the growing of India becomes more significant.

The importance of this large young population and the pressures it will bring will be in the following areas:

(a) *Public Health:* As it will be directly linked with the effort of controlling the population and the need for any modern society to provide basic health services. One showstopper in the public health area will be AIDS. There was a recent report in TIME, which said that India was likely to become the AIDS capital of the world. If this happens, it will pose a major challenge in public administration.

(b) *Public Education:* The danger we are facing is that as we enter the 21st century we may have the notoriety of having the largest illiterate population in the world. At present, we are only 52% literate. The challenge of achieving universal literacy has already been taken up by the government. The additional challenge in the 21st century will be the challenge of technological literacy and creation of technology through effective R&D.

(c) *Law and Order:* We have already seen the continuing low intensity warfare or terrorism in the Northeast, J&K, in some parts of Andhra Pradesh in the Naxalite movement, etc. The danger of such violent local disturbances will increase if we are not able to ensure

> that economic growth does not lead to greater disparities in income and quality of life. The Human Development Report 1996 highlights five types of defective growths: jobless growth, the rootless growth, the ruthless growth, the voiceless growth and futureless growth. So far as we are concerned, we face the danger of all these types of defective growth except voiceless growth. For nearly five decades we have imbibed the democratic tradition and our people will continue to have their voice and so the danger of voiceless growth is not there. The HDI report will indicates one of the long-standing challenges to the public administration, which will continue well into the 21st century---that of continuously trying to improve the quality of life.

The second factor in the plate tectonics shaping the future of public administration is the geo political forces. The end of the Cold War signifies that in the future, geo politics is going to be dominated by economic competition on the one hand and tensions arising from nationalities and ethnic groups on the other. We are now living in a period when in our politics the regional parties are having an increasing say in the Centre. Will this trend continue and regional forces become more dominant? Or will the economic process of integration bring a new perspective by which India will become India Inc. and the economic factors play a dominant role?

The 21st century will definitely be influenced by the GATT agreement and the WTO. Up to the year 2005 also we will see coming into force of some important aspects relating to the intellectual property rights. This means that in the area of economic administration, the role of the government will change from being an active player to being a catalyst. It will have to do more of steering than rowing. At the same time, the government will also have to increasingly play the role of an objective umpire and ensure a level playing ground for competitive market forces to operate.

The third important aspect of plate tectonics is the area of technology. In fact, the world has already become a global village in the 20th century. This process will be further accentuated in the 21st century. For public administration, the advances in technology will pose two types of challenges. For example, in the area of communications and broadcasting, already we see the impact of satellite communication and how this had an impact on the aspirations, culture and thinking of the emerging generation. Perhaps we will see more and more of a global culture. Of course, there will be those who would like to preserve Indian culture and will rail against cultural colonisation. However, technology being what it is, to what extent will they be successful? For example, even in France they are finding the American influence more dominant as a result of the impact of electronic media.

The other dimension of technology is the growing application of Information Technology and computers. Simultaneously with the liberalisation process there will be greater demand for more transparency in government operations. Hopefully an act like the Freedom of Information Act may be enacted in due course of time. We will then face the issues of national security and guarding national secrets on the one hand and also ensuring privacy of the individual on the other. However, the social tensions that will be created as a result of the electronic media is a public administration issue that will probably be posed with greater acuity in the 21st century.

There will arise new technology related issues in specific areas like energy. As we move towards the next century and as fossil based fuels are consumed, energy will become an increasingly dominant issue. Energy is vital for growth. Alternative sources of energy will have to be developed. Necessity is the mother of invention. We will have to focus on technologies like solar energy and biotechnology. The green revolution saved India in the 60s. Biotechnology may be the method by which we feed our large population in the 21st century.

While these factors relating to plate tectonics of public administration will have their own dynamics, another important factor would be the political pressures of the day. But politics is ultimately the reflection of the social pressures and the demographic changes that are taking place. It is not possible to visualise the lines on which these factors are going to affect public administration. A safe assumption will be to think in terms of an oscillation theory or continuous action and reaction (Newton's third law.) Our politics generally so far has been based on the distributive approach. We started with land reform, wealth and jobs. Perhaps this has had mixed results. We can create a better future if we focus on the positive approach of creating more jobs and wealth. Again, the recent possibility of genderising Indian politics by providing 33% reservation of seats in the political institutions if rightly implemented will have a dramatic impact not only on politics but also on society as a whole. The neglect of the girl child will hopefully become a thing of the past.

Apart from the factors that are external to the public administration, changes in public administration also may come from internal factors, i.e. change agents within the public administration system who may be able to provide the leadership and make the administration perform more effectively and make it better suited for tackling the problems of the day.

One issue that will be relevant at any time in the future would be the perennial issue of corruption. Another would be the issue of efficiency and effectiveness of the government and this in turn would mean to what extent the government is able to change its systems and internalise emerging technologies. This will essentially depend on the leaders within the government, the bureaucrats (though political pressures will continue) and as the demographic analysis shows, the focus will have to be given in the immediate few years to the issue of social justice. But as the years go by, other issues perhaps relating to environment and old age will become significant. In view of the continuous growth in population, the pressure on urban cities will continue and urban management will increasingly become a key factor especially for effective administration.

As regards punctuated equilibrium in public administration one showstopper may be AIDS. Another could be an environmental disaster arising from some of the major projects under implementation about which the environmentalists are raising objection. 'Murphy's Law can operate in a vicious manner. Yet another disaster may be a large asteroid strike on the earth or some phenomenon like the one at Tungustu early this century (1908) in Russia when a vast area in Siberia was devastated. By their very nature the punctuated equilibrium will be the blind spot in our exercise.

A Vision for the Future: India as a Superpower

When we look at the perspectives for the 21st century, we can be more confident of the directions in which public administration will evolve if we had a vision of what our country would be like in the years to come. Unfortunately in our country, we do not seem to have any vision. A small country like Singapore has a vision of "Singapore as an intelligent island by the year 2000". Malaysia looks a little beyond and by 2020 wants to be a fully developed country. South Korea wants to join the G-7. We in India lack such a super ordinate goal. With our population, we should think of India emerging as an economic super power by the year 2020. Such a vision will give us ideas on how we can make public administration evolve to achieve this goal. In the absence of such a vision, we will only be drifting and be subject to the blind plàte tectonic forces as mentioned above.

The government of India started the process of economic liberalisation in 1991. It has initiated a process by which the activist role played by the government in the economic administration will sooner or later be replaced by a more catalytic role. But there are certain areas where the government, whatever the political complexion, can never abandon its responsibility and as a result it will always be significant in administration. These are the areas:

(a) We are a nation of poor people and public health is one issue, which the government will have to look after for the simple reason that if public health fails we may have disasters like the plague we had in 1994. Further, many people cannot afford private doctors. Even the medical insurance system invented in the United States is also leading to problems of funding

and this is an issue they are wrestling with. For us, running public health institutions would be a major area of challenge in public administration. We must see how we can make hospitals and the public health system effective by using the resources that are available. Imaginative use of Information Technology would be very useful in this area both in terms of collecting information about the health of the population and also in terms of providing excellent medical care. Nearly 20-30% of the costly equipment in most of our hospitals is our of order. A systematic programme of seeing that our hospitals are not sick and that our equipments have the maximum uptime will bring about substantial improvement. In this we will be facing the problem of AIDS and other diseases like TB and malaria, which probably are once again becoming challenges at present. So, public health is going to be one major area of challenge in the 21st century.

(b) The next important area is education. It has already been mentioned that India will have the largest population of illiterate people at the beginning of the 21st century. At least we must try to see that we make our country literate as quickly as possible. In this effort we must be able to use all the techniques of modern technology of distance education and also make widespread use of the NGOs that have been effective in spreading the literacy movement.

(c) Creating adequate productive employment will be another major area of concern. With the growing population and better education would arise the challenge of getting adequate productive employment. This is where the role of the government will be very critical. On the one hand, the government will be playing a catalytic role in the economic development. We need not visualise a larger number of public sector enterprises growing but at the same time, we will have

to think of innovative methods by which the employment in this country can be enhanced. We must think of new opportunities for growth. The employment opportunities provided by electronics whether it is in software or techno coolies by way of bibliographic database industry is a case in point. Another area would be to focus attention on industry based on waste because as industrial and economic development takes place, we will see that the red tape will be replaced with the green tape. A strategy where every waste product including even the municipal waste is utilised for productive purposes will be a challenge for the administration.

(d) The fourth area will be the area of law and order. The pressures of the population, the aspirations of the people leading to greater demands on the society and the increasing accentuation of the ethnic and regional identities will pose problems of tackling the perennial problems of law and order. If we look at the past 50 years after Independence, we have tackled these issues as and when they arose. Many a time one gets a feeling that the movements exhausted themselves. It is not clear whether the movements for regional separation and regional identity have a dynamics of their own but a lot of loss of life, tension and unhappiness can be reduced if we are able to handle intelligently and anticipate the growing tension. Simultaneously, we will also need to look into our entire legal system and maintenance of law and order for better results. When we look at our legal and criminal administration system, it appears as if the criminal has an advantage because our legal process is so slow. The blatant manner in which Charles Sobhraj escaped punishment from Thailand through our inefficient legal and judicial system is a glaring example. We will have to think of effective handling of law and order problems. Ofcourse, there will be the

related issue of human rights. This is an area where there will be continuous challenges for all time to come.

Education, public health, employment and law and order will definitely be the areas of concern in public administration. The government will have to think of taking initiatives to ensure productive employment of people because if there is failure on this front, there will be greater tension with political consequences like separatism, violence and so on.

We can now look at some of the specific areas where initiatives will have to be taken if we want India to be an economic superpower. The first requirement is that we have to strengthen our infrastructure and ensure for example that we have the requisite energy to power the process of growth. As the conventional source of energy will become increasingly difficult in the 21st century, we will have to focus attention on non-conventional energy sources. We should particularly try to exploit solar energy because India is well placed with perhaps the maximum number of sunny days.

The other area where we have to focus would be the area of technology. As we will be living in an era of world intellectual property rights and as Indians have shown marked capacity particularly in hi-tech areas like electronics and biotechnology, we will have to think increasingly of joint R&D with institutions and countries abroad. As Dr. Mashelkar says, we must try to see whether India can become a platform for global R&D.

We will also have to look at the whole network of our laws to see whether the pace of administration can be stepped up. If today our administration can be blamed, it is for corruption and delays. Delays can be eliminated if we can review all the various procedure we have and see how red tape can be eliminated. We must increasingly realise the value of time. This itself can eliminate to some extent petty corruption. Checking of corruption will be successful only if we are also able to evolve systems for prompt punishment and exposure of the corrupt elements. Our media is performing the role today but the administration will have to evolve its own internal system to weed out the corrupt.

One aspect of the liberalisation policy, which will become increasingly prominent relates to regional disparities. It has been said that perhaps if we draw a vertical line across the map of India, the state in the west seem to be doing better than those in the east. Liberalisation has introduced a feeling of competition among the states. Those who are in charge of less developed states will have to think of particularly innovative strategies to attract investment and growth.

In this connection a report appeared in Business Today, some time back giving a gist of the Global Competitiveness Report 1996, points out that "India ranks 45th among 49, ahead only of Russia, Brazil, Venezuela and Hungary. From 35th in 1994 to 39th in 1995 and now 45th India's declining position is a mocking commentary on its liberalisation and reform. Equating competitiveness with the likelihood of sustaining growth in per capita income over a period of such in between next 5 to 10 years, the GCR clearly implies that India's prospects are dim.

The factors that determine the management ranking in the GCR experts report India's ranking in this area as follows: In overall management ranking out of the 49 countries India is 43rd. In entrepreneurship India is no.19, risk taking and initiatives 13, willingness to delegate 38, use of Infotech 44, customer orientation 43, time to innovate 47, time to market 44, TQM 42, strategy implementation 43, absence of monopoly 32, global managerial experience 44, managerial breadth 28. strong corporate boards 46, efficient corporate boards 45, work place organisation 47, availability of managers 18 and non wage incentive 18.

To achieve the goal of India as an economic superpower by the year 2020, we will also have think of making our public administration more effective. We will have to in a way re-invent the government. One starting point in this exercise, which has been mentioned before, for re-inventing the government may be to consider the ten ideas mentioned by Ted Gaebler and David Osborne in their book *Government*.

Broadly we can look at the entire issue from two angles. The first is to take note of the massive plate tectonic forces, which shape the administration. The other is to have a focused vision to make our country an economic superpower by 2020 and start the systematic process of re-inventing the government and take specific measures to see that we improve our position as a country from the human development index point of view and the competitiveness index point of view.

The future scenario of public administration in terms of the organisation is also worth looking into. Logically, if public health, education and law and order are going to be the basic functions of the government, these should carry maximum prestige. However today for example, the economic ministries and those relating to regulatory functions seem to have greater glamour than those dealing with the social sector. Will a change in perception come about? Definitely, as the role of the government decreases in economic administration, perhaps the social sectors may become more attractive for the bureaucrats advancing in their career.

Another issue would be to what extent the governmental systems and procedures will start using modern technology. This depends essentially on the leaders within the government. For example today it is possible to use Information Technology extensively in administration but the forces of inertia seem to be more dominant. If we really want to become an economic superpower, perhaps the system of public administration ought to be modernised by simplifying procedures and speeding up the decision making process and using Information Technology extensively.

Another related issue would be the degree of centralisation and decentralisation. Information Technology helps in both. In the Indian context, this will also depend on the equilibrium of forces between the regional forces and the central forces, between the regional polity and the national polity. In the mechanisms of the Constitution, the present constitutional framework should continue unless very severe developments distort the system. This type of punctuated equilibrium, which will propel such a development cannot be foreseen at this stage.

What will be the skills required from the bureaucrat and what will be the role of the bureaucrat in the 21st century? In his book *The Shape Of Things To Come,* Peter Drucker said that in the next century, the Chief Executives would have to be more like the collectors, presidents of the universities or the superintendents of the hospitals. They will have to coordinate the work of many specialists. For this there has to be a massive change in the type of skills of the bureaucrats in the different services and the organisations to meet the emerging challenges. Innovativeness and creative thinking should be inculcated in all civil servants so that public administration does not suffer from massive inertia.

After all, the future is what we make it to be.

Civil Service: A National Perspective

The Indian Civil Service was called the steel frame and looking into the future about the shape of things to come, Peter Drucker says that the type of management needed in a society where there is going to be so much technology and specialisation, must be like the old ICS. The British had, with less than a thousand people, run the administration of a country of 300 million people. The Indian Administrative Service is the successor to the Indian Civil Service. It was the vision of Sardar Patel who saw to it that this framework needed for the administration of the country was nurtured properly. On the eve of the 21st century we need to address the question as to what are the perspectives of administration? We can look at the past and we can look to the future. A look at the past can give us concepts about the sound principles that have prevailed, how deterioration has crept in and what should now be done. While if we look to the future, we can try to anticipate the shape of things to come.

One of the doyens of the Indian Civil Service, B.K. Nehru, has made some remarkable observations. The first point he made was that we Indians have never really been democratic. If at all there was a democracy, it was only at the level of panchayats or at the level of the castes. The concept of the parliamentary democracy, which we adopted in our Constitution, is a direct result of our experience with the British where Indian leaders also became aware of the working of this system. The division between the political executive and the permanent bureaucracy was also appreciated. In the early years, thanks to visionary leaders like Jawaharlal Nehru and Sardar Patel, we were able to build the administrative service and maintain this fine distinction between the responsibility of the civil servant and the role of political leadership.

Nehru gave an interesting example of the role played by the civil servants in the early days. T.T. Krishnamachari was a very powerful Finance Minister and he wanted to see the confidential file of income tax relating to individuals. A.K. Roy, who later on became the Controller and Auditor General of the India, was the chairman of the Central Board of Revenue. When the minister asked for this file, Roy politely declined saying that he could not see the file. When the minister retorted that Roy as the chairman of the central board of revenue could see the file, why not the Finance Minister, Roy pointed out that under the rules, the files were confidential and only an income tax officer could see it and therefore the chairman, central board of revenue could see the file and not the Finance Minister. At the end, T.T. Krishnamachri fell in with this argument. Therefore, the rules were modified later on to permit access to files for ministers as well.

Another example given by Nehru related to Jawaharlal Nehru himself. Jawaharlal had a servant called Hari who was very faithful to him and worked with him for a long time. He wanted a piece of land in UP and he could not get it. When B.K. Nehru asked him why he could not talk to the Prime Minister who would support him, Hari replied: "The Prime Minister supports me but the government does not support me." Hari made a distinction between the views of the political leader and the will of the government. The point made by B.K. Nehru was to indicate how in the early years of the civil service this distinction between the role of the bureaucracy and the political leadership was maintained and even at the highest level, powerful politicians like JLN and TTK had to operate within the system. In fact BKN added as a polite afterthought "JLN could make Hari an MLA because that was within his powers but he could not get the piece of land which he wanted so badly."

Over a period of years, according to BKN, our Indianness has asserted itself in our administration. He said that Indian tradition states that the ruler is absolute. The king can do no wrong. Emperors and kings might have had Maulvis or Brahmin pundits to advise them but ultimately the decision of the ruler was final. True to this tradition, in today's context, every MLA or MP thinks he is a ruler. Therefore, if the civil servant were to quote the rules to him, he feels that his right are being violated. This is a major change that has come about in the four decades of administration after Independence. BKN gave a very telling story to bring out a change in the political perspective. It seems a young IAS officer of the UP cadre was transferred from Delhi to Arunachal Pradesh and he was taken by one of the senior civil servants of HKL Bhagat who was a very powerful politician in Delhi in those days. Bhagat asked him: "What category of officer are you?" The young man was confused and he said that he belonged to the UP cadre and gave the year of his allotment. Bhagat said: "Look, I am not interested in that. I want to know which of the category of officers you belong to. According to me there are three categories. Category A are those type of officers who when told to do a thing bring to our notice the legal position and the rules and conventions and say it cannot be done. Category B are those who point out the legal difficulties and resist but if we press for a certain time they carry out our orders. Category C are those who carry out whatever we say. If you belong to the first or second category, you have no chance. You have to go to Arunachal Pradesh. If you belong to the third category, I can see that your transfer gets cancelled." This is typical of the problem, which many civil servants face even today. We have seen some officials associated with certain political leaders and like the American Spoil System in civil service in our country also such a system has come to prevail. This is visible whenever there is a change of government.

It would be ideal if the civil servants could focus on developing their professional skills and not be identified with the political leadership. Unfortunately the craving for plum postings is such that independent professional IAS officers may be a rarity. Officers who are idealistic and try to be professional may not get plum postings and get posted in sinecured or social sectors, which are not considered prize postings. Saxena, director of the LBSNAA has been highlighting the fact that in the IAS the craving is for posts which are connected with economic ministries, posts connected with regulations like law and order. On the other hand, if you look at the future of our country, it is areas like public health, education and rural development which are important in the long run and where one can do a lot of good work for the benefit of the people. A positive attitude, a creative approach and sound common sense are the basic skills a civil servant should have if he wants to have a successful career and also make a contribution in the process.

Looking to the future, one feels that the administration in the states will become even more important. We are witnessing the increasing role of regional parties at the Centre. We are also noticing that one consequence of the economic liberalisation process is that the state governments today have a lot more scope for showing an initiative and are competing for investment and development. Therefore, the application of managerial skills in the state government administration becomes very important. Application of Information Technology should be a very high priority because it is IT that can ensure that the common man has better services. IT also can be useful in bringing in a more transparent process of governmental working as well as direct and easy access to governmental information.

Ultimately, the motto of the IAS is efficiency in work – *"yogah karma su kausalam."* Efficiency in work is considered as the yoga according to Lord Krishna. If we could bring in effectiveness and efficiency to whatever task is entrusted to us, and if we approach it imaginatively, we would be making a small contribution in the effective administration of the country. For real effectiveness not only should we master the techniques of administration and apply modern technologies like IT but we would also be rooted in certain basic values like commitment to the public good and absolute integrity—both financial and intellectual.

13

Administrative Reorganisation in India: Some Strategic Issues

Introduction

It was in 1853 that the Parliament in London passed the Act directing that recruitment to the Indian Civil Service (ICS) be made by open competitive examination. By 1913 when my father entered the ICS, there were as many as 30 Indians in the combined Bengal - Bombay - Madras establishment of nearly 800 – strong administering the subcontinent from Burma to Baluchistan. That the ICS were then the torch bearers of the British tradition in civil service is amply borne out by the historical fact that it was not until 1870, *i.e.* nearly 27 years after the 1853 Act that the Civil Service Commissioners in London gained control over graduate recruitment for higher posts in the Home Civil Service through open competitive examination. Even in 1947 when India became independent the total cadre strength of the ICS was still in three figures. Despite these impressive bonds of heritage, was the inheritance really of any long term advantages in providing independent India with a structure and a framework without which the machinery of Government would have been poorer? This has long been a debating issue.

With the hindsight of what happened in the subsequent decades in India as well as in newly-independent countries in the commonwealth like Malaysia, Singapore and others and even taking into account the interesting developments within the British Civil Service during this period—there is today a powerful school of thought that considers this linkage as handicap rather than an advantage. According to them, this linkage merely provided a rigid hidebound framework suitable for colonial administration which made subsequent restructuring and modernisation almost an impossible task. The fact that Britain itself is fighting to modernise the bureaucracy with experiments of MBO, MINIS, FMI, etc., is another aspect of the realisation that even the structure here needed change.

The sentiment expressed by India's first Prime Minister from 1947 to 1964, Pandit Jawaharlal Nehru, that "no new order can be built up in India so long as the spirit of the ICS pervades our administration and our public services is in sense still relevant today after nearly two decades of the extinction of the last ICS from Indian bureaucracy. Ironically, the ICS tradition of high talent, integrity and independence is also extinct today with mediocrity, corruption and sycophancy in the post–ICS structure. And yet, there is still some lingering similarity between the two structures—which makes comparative analysis of our failures in India with those in UK particularly instructive. Although the degree of failure varies, there are interesting lessons to be learnt from each other.

Despite the apprehension—one often hears in England that a growing civil service can be a harbinger of collectivism, even of socialist revolution, and that democratically elected governments in the UK and India still continue to make efforts to cut civil service to size—civil service in both these two countries, as indeed in many other Commonwealth countries not only survived but expanded greatly in size as an essential instrument in the establishment of a welfare state and a managed economy.

Challenge of Bureaucracy in the Third World

Since the civil service is not an end in itself but only a means to achieving the ends of a welfare state and a well managed economy, it is necessary to analyse the size of the challenge faced in the Third World countries. Two thirds of the world's Population continues to live in abject poverty. This is only one of the dimensions of challenge of development in the Third World where almost all the World's poor live. In this context, is the question of a choice between market forces and state intervention—which seemed to be raised in the wake of "perestroika"—really relevant? And yet the track record of Third World bureaucracies in the last four decades seems to confirm one's belief that it is far easier for government to intervene badly than to intervene at all. State's intervention and involvement in the management of the national Economies of these countries is also inescapable. This underlines the equally urgent need for improving performance of the government in its changing role.

On the other hand, the civil services of the Third World find themselves unable to move with the time. They are not able to cope adequately even with the problems of law and order. In the new managerial functions of goal setting and goal definition, of entrepreneurship and management, bureaucracy in the Third World continue to demonstrate an almost trained in capacity, isolation from the people, excessive concern for power and privilege, commitment of rules and procedures rater than to results, misplaced faith in the capabilities of the generalist administrator and inability to adapt. Even where democracy has been achieved as a sustainable political system, like India, democratic decentralisation is still very much a far cry. At the same time, issues of political neutrality and permanency in the civil service are being questioned. Consequently, authority in bureaucracy is yet to be adequately balanced by accountability. Despite allocation of massive resources through planning models, utilisation of these resources continue to lag behind.

How to change the role of civil services and of the government is an issue which requires immediate attention. It is necessary to identify and re-state the areas where government is still necessary in these countries. What should be the role of the other sub-systems within the governmental systems? To illustrate, what should be the interface between the government, industry and the other equally necessary parasitical organisations, whether they are the executive agencies of the massive public action programmes in rural employment, education, housing, health, etc., or the massive public enterprises and major industrial projects in economy? In most developing countries, the civil services are changed today with tackling poverty and agricultural productivity, supervising the performance of public and private enterprises expected to deliver results of industrialisation, and also with formulation and implementation of all major projects in such infrastructure sectors of the economy like ports, railways and telecommunications, where delay has been endemic. Are the civil services in these countries appropriately structured for this purpose? Is the education and training needed by the civil servants to respond to these challenges adequate and imparted in the required measure? Are behavioural and cultural needs met adequately?

India: An Overview of the Economic Challenge

It was soon realised after the country attained political independence that this was meaningless without the content of economic independence, growth and development. The first question which should therefore be asked in considering the strategic issues in India's administrative reorganisation of the last four decades is the extent to which the challenge of managing India's economy has been responded by the bureaucracy assisting the political masters who have been in the driving seat during these years. Although there is no simple answer to this extremely complex question, some general observations can be made which underscore the tremendous scope that still remains for improving the performance of the economy, which can at best be termed and "mixed" and "poor". India's per capita annual growth rate of barely one per cent during 1951-85 is lower than the average growth rate of the developing countries. In area 13 times UK's size and in population about 14 times, India's per capita annual income of an Indian estimated at $ 340 is marginally higher than the comparable $ 330 estimated for China. Distribution of income in China is stated to be much less inequitable than in India where nearly 30 per cent of the population numbering 250-300 million still continue to live below the poverty line. Thus the Indian economy does not "take off" but continues to "muddle through". The main achievement of India's economic management which has been "self-reliance" in industry and more recently in agriculture is now once again being questioned which the import of nearly 2 million tonnes of food grain necessitated in 1988 and critical shortage of foreign exchange during the current fiscal year caused by an equally serious crisis in the country's balance of payments with the total external debt of over US $ 70 billion.

The public enterprises which provided the engine of growth for a vibrant mixed economy in the 1950s and 1960s, and still provide the basic industrial infrastructure of the economy, are today facing the serious managerial challenges of modernisation and restructuring. In the central public enterprises, overall profitability ratio ranging from 12 to 13% is lower than the current cost of capital. In a heavily protected economy—and this was a price that the country paid for achieving self reliance—India's corporate sector has been left at the starting gate for the past two decades. This puzzle can only be explained by two opposite perceptions of this sector's performance, namely, that India is still one of the few recession-free economies of the world, even if it grows at a snail's pace, and that the reality of India's economy continues to be conditioned by government controls of various kinds, like raw material allocations, control of labour where it is not easy to lay off employees, the licensing regime where the enterprises could be shut down if they produced more than they were licensed.

The recent efforts of liberalisation are seen as no more than feeble attempts to inject competitive vigour in an over-controlled, over-protected and over-priced economy. Indeed, the controllers do not change their style and attitude even when controls are reduced. India's continued fiscal imbalance, characterised by budget deficit currently running at nearly 10% of FDP, annual inflation rate of 12-13%, current account deficit running at 50% of India's exports, with debt to GDP ratio around 12-15%—requires immediate attention in curbing fiscal deficit, improving balance of payments and arresting any further decline in the value of the Rupee. At the same time poverty alleviation programmes have to be managed efficiently and public enterprise reforms have to be undertaken without a day's delay. Even the social indicators in India like life expectancy is less than China's, infant mortality twice that of the Philippines and literacy rate half that of Sri Lanka. These are only some of the measures of the immediate challenges which the country's bureaucracy faces in 1991.

There are other measures of direct government "failure" in India's economic management—which can be categorised under continuing errors in resource utilisation despite reasonable successes in resource mobilisation. The slow growth rate of the country's economy u—it was barely 3% in GDP in 1991—can be explained by this phenomenon despite an impressive domestic savings ratio of over 20 per cent. In agriculture, this reflected in continued poor yield per acre in principal crops, like wheat, rice, barley, maize and pulses-where India's achievement was less than half that of China. Another aspect of this failure has been enormous delays in the implementation of public sector projects in atomic energy, coal, fertilizer, nonferrous metal, steel, petroleum, petrochemical, railways, power, paper, cement and telecommunications sector. Three hundred projects reported tatal delays exceeding 600 years! Even where projects are completed after such enormous delays, they continue to suffer from the phenomenon of under–utilised capacity which range from 40-50% of installed capacity of power, steel, cement and other sectors.

It is true that the low performance of the Indian economy has been caused by the protectionist policy framework of the 1950s and 1960s which proved difficult to dismantle or change. Thus despite efforts to liberalise, not a single instrument of control has been given up and the hassle factor has continued to operate against the interests of speedy growth even where controls, quotas and tariff barriers were lowered. Thus poor performance of the country's public enterprises has been caused not because of any inherent inefficiency in the instrument of the "public enterprises-nor because of "managerial failure" of the boards of these enterprises.

In India, managers of public enterprise are as efficient as those in the private sector. Indeed, current research shows that the principal factor has been the "governmental failure" caused by several sub-optimal investment decisions, wrong pricing and wage decisions, government's inability to provide an efficient managerial personnel policy and in various other areas of decision-making where the wrong strategic decisions taken by the bureaucracy pre-empted any possible managerial success of these enterprises. analysis also shows that even in the area of managing public action programmes for alleviating poverty, where India's achievement in the last 40 years has really been dismal, the challenge is basically for the administrators to respond with better and more innovative management capability and in restructuring the bureaucracy with a view to decentralising the decision-making effectively involving people's elected representatives fat grassroots level. Thus it will not be enough to reshape the policy package for the industrial, trade and other sectors. Past experience shows that changes in policy are not enough if initiatives are not taken at the same time to modernize the bureaucracy along truly managerial lines where administrators are judged not by their promises but by their promises but by their performance—for which they must be made accountable. This is all the more relevant in a developing country like India where government's involvement in the business of the economy will have to continue for some more years.

SIZE OF THE INDIAN BUREAUCRACY

Has the size of India's "ever proliferating bureaucracy" become unduly large? In absolute terms, the growth of India's bureaucracy has been phenomenal. If, however, we compare the bureaucracy in developed countries and compare India's size, the statistical results do not entirely confirm this. The estimated current employment of less than 20 million in India's central government, state and local government, general government and public enterprises is less than 2.5% of the population. In a recent study conducted on the size of bureaucracy in developed and developing countries, the findings confirm that public employees as a percentage of the population range from 16% in Sweden and Denmark to 13% in the UK, 8% in USA and Canada to one of the lowest figures of the developed countries of 4.5% in Japan. This ratio is, however, much lower in developing countries ranging from about 6% in Argentina to less than 2% in Guatemala. The developing countries like India, Korea, Kenya, Philippines and Tanzania were in the range of 2-3%. Interestingly enough the analysis also shows that the cost of the civil service in many of the developing countries—in India, it is around Rupees 7000 crores—also remained at levels comparatively lower than those in the developed countries.

An Overview of Organisation and Personnel Reforms in India: 1947-1991

The administrative reorganisation of modern India after the country attained independence in 1947 can logically be studied under two broad headings *(a)* Administrative Reforms and *(b)* Personnel Reforms. The latter included reforms in the structure of the Civil Services, their pay, pensions, training and management succession including the issue of political neutrality, permanency, corruption etc.

Organisational and administrative Reforms

Three distinct periods can be identified in the last four decades of organisational reforms, namely: *(i)* Reforms up to the 1970s: *(ii)* Reforms during the 1970s which followed the recommendations of the Administrative Reforms Commission set up in 1966 and *(iii)* Reforms in the 1980s.

Reforms up to the 1970s

A committee known as the Secretariat Reorganisation Committee headed by Girija Shankar Bajpai was set up soon after the country attained independence in 1947 to inquire into the question of personnel shortages, better utilisation of the available manpower and improvement of methods of work in the Central Secretariat. This was followed by a review of the working of the machinery of the Central Government undertaken towards the end of 1949 by N. Gopalaswami Ayyangar (Report on Reorganisation of the Machinery of Government, 1949). In July 1951 A.D. Gorwala, an eminent planner and ICS officer, was asked to assess how far the existing administrative machinery and methods were adequate to meet the requirements of planned development (Report on Public Administration 1951). Two subsequent reports which had a significant impact on Administrative Reforms were Paul H. Appleby's first report "Public Administration in India: Report of a Survey, 1953" followed by his second report "Re-examination of India's Administrative System which spcial reference to Administration of Government's Industrial and Commercial Enterprises, 1956".

The Appleby report of 1953 emphasised the need for the establishment of a central office charged with the responsibility of reviewing structures, management and procedures. As one of the outcomes of the report, an O&M division was set up in 1954 in the Cabinet Secretariat, Supported by O&M units in the various ministries The thrust of this division was by and large directed towards effecting improvement in paper management through manualisation and a system of inspections. Among its more important achievements was the publication of a Manual of Office Procedure for all Ministries. However, its ambit of activity remained limited.

In 1963, a mid-term appraisal of the Third Plan showed that although significant progress had been made in a number of directions, the pace of economic growth was slow. It became apparent that administrative deficiencies had something to do with the shortfall in economic achievement. Central and State Governments were called upon to raise the level of administrative efficiency and strengthen the implementation of development programmes. It was against this background that the machinery for administrative reforms came to be reviewed. The first outcome of this review was the setting-up of a Department of Administrative Reforms within the Ministry of Home Affairs in March 1964. The O&M Division was transferred to its charge from the Cabinet Secretariat. The intention was that the Department would be the Government's standing machinery for administrative reforms. It was expected to raise the level of the reform process from mere O&M operations to something more likely to yield positive results. In 1965, a new Bureau of Public Enterprises was also set up within the Government of India to provide an in-house management consultancy agency for the public enterprises and economic ministries controlling public enterprises in the federal government. This was followed by the setting-up of similar organisations in the State Governments of the Indian Union.

Reforms During the 1970s

As piecemeal efforts aimed at reforms proved inadequate to meet the new challenges thrown up by the development activities, it was felt necessary to explore the basic and significant sectors to adopt a coordinated approach to the administrative requirements. Accordingly, the Administrative Reforms Commission (ARC) was set up in January 1966. The terms of reference of ARC were perhaps the widest ever entrusted to any commission and covered the entire gamut of public administration at the centre as well as in the states. The ARC was asked to give consideration to the need for ensuring the highest standards of efficiency and the integrity in public services, for making public administration a fit instrument for carrying out the social and economic goals of development and also for making administration responsive to the people. During 1966 to 1970, the Committee submitted 20 reports containing 537 recommendations. These recommendations covered a series of suggested changes, big and small, in all important sectors of administration. Equally important, these stimulated further thinking on a variety of administrative problems which led to newer and more medical reforms.

In the decade of 1970-80 there were enormous changes in the administrative structure, systems and procedures, partly as a result of implementation of ARC's recommendations and partly due to the efforts of the central reforms agency. Some of the more important reforms effected during this period on the recommendations of the ARC were:

- a central personnel agency, the Department of Personnel, was set up;
- the role of the Department of Administrative Reforms was redefined and its structure streamlined;
- new systems of secretariat working, including the desk officer system, were introduced;
- performance budgeting was adopted by all development ministries;
- a new principle in delegating financial and administrative powers was adopted, viz., that the powers to be delegated should be the maximum possible rather than the minimum necessary; and

- the Bureau of Public Enterprises was strengthened pursuant to ARC's Report on Public Sector submitted in 1967 and several new initiatives were taken for professionalising public sector operations in the country.

Based on the recommendations of ARC, the following functions came to be assigned to the Department of Administrative Reforms:

(i) Advising the Central Government on policy matters concerning administrative reforms;

(ii) Providing management consultancy services to the organisation of the Central Government, State Governments, public sector and local bodies and promoting modern management practices in these organisations;

(iii) Promotion and development of the management services efforts in ministries/departments; and

(iv) Imparting management education and dissemination information on administrative practices and modern management techniques.

Management studies occupied an important place in the scheme of administrative reforms. A number of reform measures were introduced as a result of the studies carried out by the Department of Administrative Reforms. Specific areas of management covered in the study reports include:

- organisational structure and relationship;
- methods and procedures
- financial administration;
- information systems;
- records management;
- use of modern office machines and equipment;

- citizen satisfaction;
- employee satisfaction

These brought about considerable improvement in the working of the offices and helped to increase the level of citizen and employee satisfaction. Some of the measures introduced as a result of the studies were:

- Integration of internal and associate finance in Ministries into a single Integrated Financial Adviser;
- Departmentalisation of accounts;
- Collection of road tax through post offices;
- Payment of government dues in cash across the departmental counters;
- Evolving a revised schedule of retention periods for records common to all ministries;
- Introduction of the functional filing system which is based on a logical grouping of functions, activities and operations.

Another important reform was effected during the 1970s was the setting up of a Department of Personnel and Administrative Reforms at the State level, alongside the state level Bureau of Public Enterprises.

Reforms in the 1980s

In the 1980s, particularly since 1985, a number of reforms have been brought about in the administrative system. A full-fledged Ministry of Personnel, Public Grievances and Pensions was set up in March 1985 with three departments. Department of Personnel and Training, Department of Administrative Reforms and Public Grievances and Department of Pensions and Pensioners Welfare. A major highlight of this arrangement was that the Ministry was placed under the overall charge of the Prime Minister assisted by Minister of State.

Second, the subject of public grievances was added to Administrative Reforms. This alignment was effected under the rationale that, on the one hand, it would provide a closer and integrated view of the inadequacies of the administrative system that give rise to grievance, and on the other, how the administrative machinery could be made adaptive to changing requirements. Third, a separated department was created to handle the subject of pension and pensioners welfare.

Greater emphasis was placed on creation of a new work culture where performance and result orientation was given the highest priority. The importance of this approach was reflected notably in the then Prime Minister's address to the nation on January, 1985 when Mr. Rajiv Gandhi announced a package of measures to make administration a fit instrument for social and economic transformation. These measures included:

- decentralisation of decision-making process.
- enforcement of accountability;
- simplification of rules and procedures;
- prompt and courteous service to the citizens;
- the setting-up of effective machinery for redress of public grievances.

The second important landmark of the Reforms in the 1980s was the creation of a new Ministry of Programme Implementation (MPI) which helped to implement some of the measures emphasised in Gandhi's address in 1985 in improving the economic management of the country.

Some of the major activities/achievements in the sphere of administrative reforms and new managerial initiatives in the recent past are briefly outlined below:

(i) Coordination of Poverty Alleviation Programmes

Following the Prime Minister's broadcast to the nation on January 1985, a series of steps were initiated to bring about greater efficiency and effectiveness in the functioning of government and to make administration more responsive, accountable and result-oriented. After MPI was created in September 1985, the will towards sustained action in the above direction was reiterated in the form of the Revised Twenty Point Programme announced in August 1986, delineating the basic ingredients of the strategy to alleviate poverty and to bring forth more responsive administration, by simplification of procedures, delegation of authority, enforcement of accountability and more effective redress of public grievances. MPI and DPAR enjoined upon all the State Governments, as well Central ministries, to ensure that the administrative ingredients are integrated into all their activities including their day-to-day functioning and implementation of the specific programmes.

(ii) Enforcement of Accountability

The Jha Commission (EARC) which examined the concept of accountability in all its aspects in its report on 'Accountability' (1983) advocated the need for moving towards accountability in the positive sense, i.e. to give greater emphasis on performance and achievement of results rather than mere adherence to rules and procedures. In this respect, the recommendations closely followed those of the Fazal Committee (1980-82) on Public Enterprises. Jha Commission and Fazal Committee felt that if accountability in its positive sense were to be introduced in Government and the Public sector, certain organisational and individual requisites would also need to be brought in, viz., defining goals and objectives of the organisation, evolving a scheme of delegation of powers within the organisation, providing for a mechanism to appraise the performance in terms of achievement with an inbuilt system for reward and punishment, streamlining the process of interdepartmental consultations, evolving an appropriate system for monitoring of performance with deviation correction mechanism, etc.

Following the government's decision to implement the various recommendations of these two committees, certain concrete steps were taken by the MPI and DPAR to institutionalise accountability in Government through the introduction of Annual action plans by individual Ministries/Departments; a system of on-line monitoring of performance of infrastructure sectors of the economy as well as of all major industrial projects in the country; further delegation of powers; and streamlining of the procedures for inter-ministerial consultation.

(a) Annual Action Plan

To bring about accountable management in Government, the concept of Management by Objective (MBO) was introduced by the Ministry of Programme Implementation (MPI) under the orders of the Prime Minister, Rajiv Gandhi, in late 1985. This was in the form of an Annual Action Plan in Government Departments. The Annual Action Plan is intended to reflect the manner and time-frame of action in respect of the activities and functions to be performed during the course of the year by each individual Ministry of Department. A succinct document listing both the tasks to be performed and the timeframe for each of the tasks is prepared.

Once a programme is formulated by a Ministry/Department, it is formally adopted so that the programme gets recognised as something positively to be done rater than merely taking the form of a set of pious intentions. Again, once a programme of action gets recognised, specific tasks are allocated to individuals and units and in this manner it becomes possible to fix responsibilities specifically, both of organisations and individuals. The action points for each activity are indicated in the Action Plan, along with critical milestones to be achieved in a particular month. The Action Plan would also mention the key activities/functions and the responsibility centres at the level of Joint Secretary by name.

All the ministries/departments are currently preparing Annual Action Plans under the guidance of the MPI and the Cabinet Secretariat in the form of a calendar of activities identifying tasks and objectives which are broken down into targets, and also individual officers having primary or supervisory responsibility for the tasks, with dates for the completion of the tasks.

Monitoring of the achievement of targets is done every month at level of the Secretary/Minister of the individual Ministries and

Ministry of Programme Implementation. The progress of achievement of the items indicated as key activities is reviewed by the Prime Minister's office on a quarterly basis. The sysain of AAPs by individual Ministries/Departments has also since been underpinned by the new system of MOUs (Memorandum of Understanding) which are the Annual Action Plans drawn up by Public Enterprises and agreed upon between the PEs and the administration Ministries/ Department. The management system for introducing MOUs and their monitoring is now being taken care of by the MPI.

(b) On-line Monitoring of Infrastructure Sector Performance as well as of the Major Projects.

MPI, under the direction of Prime Minister Gandhi, also introduced on-line monitoring of the managerial performance of all enterprises in the public, private and co-operative sectors of the nine infrastructure groups, namely, Railways, Ports, Power, Telecommunications, Steel, Petroleum, Coal, Fertiliser and Cement in the length and breadth of the country. In addition, all industrial projects in the public sector valued at Rs. 20 crore or more—were brought under MPI's on-line monitoring net which introduced an effective system of problem-solving at the enterprise level, or ministry level for all those projects which were delayed by years. MPI, which emerged as an effective "management services area" of the central government, also brought within its fold the Department of Public Enterprises (earlier BPE) by 1990, which took up the work of implementing Government's decisions on three important committees which looked into marginal issues of Government and public Enterprises in the Eighties, namely, Fazal Cutta (1980-82) Jha Commission (1983-84) and Sen Gupta Committee (1984).

(c) Delegation of Powers

Attempts have been made to match responsibility for performance of tasks with authority. The dictum followed is that delegation should be the maximum possible rater than the minimum necessary. The result has been greater delegation of powers.

- by the Ministry of Finance, and other model ministries to administrative ministries;

- by administrative ministries to other lower formations; and
- inter-departmental delegation of powers.

This work continues and pressure is being kept on Ministries by DPAR to delegate more powers where necessary. A few illustrative examples are given below:

- Power of the administrative ministries to sanction expenditure on schemes/projects have been enhanced. Two-stage clearance of public sector investment proposals by the Public Investment Board is a case where administration ministries were given enhanced powers.
- The ministry of Environment and Forests has built up organisation structures so as to delegate to the operating levels financial powers for specific time-bound projects such as the Ganga Project.
- Powers of regional licensing authorities under the Chief Controller of Imports and Exports have been enhanced to grant supplementary licenses and advance licenses.
- Powers of the Company Law Board under specified sections of the Companies Act have been delegated to Regional Members of the Board.
- Powers of the Heads of Circles and subordinate offices under the Department of Posts have been increased in respect of purchases, settlements of claims, etc.

(d) Inter-ministerial Consultation

Inter-ministerial consultation often took a long time being completed, resulting in considerable delay in decision-making. In order to avoid such delays and to achieve speedy and effective decision-making, it was decided that speedy and improved procedure be evolved in cases requiring inter-ministerial consultation:

- Where consultation with or concurrence of other departments has been prescribed for taking decisions or for submission of a case to the Cabinet or its committees, a limit is set, i.e. the sponsoring ministry may ask the ministries being consulted to forward their views withing a stipulated and reasonable time period, failing which it will be presumed that other ministries have no comments, unless they have indicated otherwise.
- As far as possible, technical, specialist or appraising agencies were required to lay down broad guidelines for implementation by other Ministries so as to avoid being involved in giving a case-by-case clearance.
- It would be the responsibility of the administrative secretary to ensure timely decision after consulting the departments and organisations concerned wherever necessary either individually or jointly.

(iii) Relaxation of Industrial and Trade Controls

There has been progressive relaxation of controls of both industrial and trade policy and procedures since 1975. Important examples of these are the gradual transfer of many items earlier requiring an import licence to open general licences, and the de-licensing of 24 broad groups of industries and 82 bulk drugs and related formulation of non-MRTP/non-FERA companies. The various forms of liberalisation included, (a) De-licensing of industries up to an investment limit of Rs. 50 crores, (b) De-licensing of specific groups of industries for MRTP/FERA and non-MRTP/non-FERA companies, (c) Broad banding, (d) The minimum Economic Scales of capacity (MES), (e) re-endorsement of capacity based on past production, (f) Liberalisation of technical development fund scheme, (g) Procedural simplification for grant of approvals including extending the initial validity period of the letters of intent up to 3 years, etc. A set of new Policy Measures formulated in June 1970 is also awaiting final approval of the government.

(iv) Instances of Procedural and Systematic Improvements Introduced by Department of Administrative Reforms and Public Grievances

Till the end of December 1989, the Department completed about 469 studies. Some of the steps taken by DARPG as a result of the studies/reviews and actions initiated by the various ministries/ departments to bring about reforms in administration and procedural simplification, decentralisation/delegation and decontrol deregulation are:

1. Office Modernisation

A scheme for modernisation of government offices which has been formulated to improve the work environment through: functional layouts; creation of open offices to facilitate better supervision; redress of public grievances and better service to the public; more efficient management of data through reduction in paperwork by using modern aids, and cost-effective and space-effective records management. The scheme provides for setting up a model office. Accordingly, a section or a unit withing the office would be taken up for development into a model unit. This unit in turn, would be a model for others to emulate. A separated budget was provided under this scheme for the purchase of modern aides, e.g. photo-copiers, electronic typewriters, shredders, etc.

2. Work Improvement Teams

Another innovative measure designed to achieve higher productivity in public organisations was introduced of Work Improvement Teams (WITs). Adapted from the Japanese experience of Quality Control Circle, the WIT is essentially a small group of employees in the same work area or doing similar type of work who voluntarily meet regularly for about an hour every week to identify, analyse and resolve work-related problems. Through participation of the grassroots level, the scheme seeks to generate higher employee morale, improved productivity and reduction in cost.

The scheme formulated by DARPG envisages a few sequential steps for implementation of CIT programmes in

Government organistations. First, a small group of members of a unit will identify an operational problem. Then, they will submit it to a Steering Committee for consideration. The Committee to be in each Ministry/Public Enterprise, will consist of a few selected employees to be headed by the Secretary/Chief Executive to provide overall leadership for implementation of the programme. Each team will be given a distinct identity in the organisation and its work and contribution will be periodically monitored by the Steering Committee. The scheme also provide for appropriate training for the team leaders in various training institutions.

The scheme has been introduced in select organisations having large interface with the public, viz, Railways, Telecommunications, Delhi Development Authority, Health, Labour, Banking, Insurance and some Public Enterprises.

(v) Redress of Public Grievances

Redress of public grievances also occupied a prominent place in the agenda of government's administrative reforms. The objective of the efforts has been not only to provide speedy and effective redresses of grievances, but also to smooth the relationship between citizens and the Government. The strategy has four aspects—First to set up or strengthen the grievance machinery in various organisations and to evaluate its effectiveness; second, to concentrate more on identification of systematic deficiencies that give rise to complaints rater than on individual complaints; third, to enlist the cooperation and support of voluntary agencies to supplement the governmental effort in the sphere of public grievances; fourth, to utilize the media for transmission of information on various innovative measures taken by the government and for creating awareness among the people about their rights and privileges and the services, including grievance redress and arrangements available to them.

(a) Standing Committee of Voluntary Agencies

To supplement the governmental effort in the sphere of public grievances, voluntary agencies are being involved like the Standing Committees of Voluntary Agencies (SCOVA) in the

Ministry of Health and Family Welfare, Department of Women and Child Development, Department of Yourth Affairs and Sports, Department of Electronics and Department of Pensions and Pensioner's Welfare.

(b) Shikayat Adalat

With a view to bringing, face to face, the aggrieved with the department concerned for on-the-spot redress of public grievances, the concept of Shikayat Adalat (Grievances Court) has been introduced as an innovative scheme. The scheme has been tried out in the Department of Telecommunications and the Delhi Development Authority and has evoked good response.

LONG-TERM IMPACT OF THE ORGANISATIONAL REFORMS: AN EVALUATION

The paradoxical absence of any long-term impact of the administrative reforms from 1947 onwards outlined in the previous paragraphs can only be explained by our preoccupation with forms, facades, intentions and rituals rater than with providing any real long-term solutions to the burning issues which can truly restructure and modernize an archaic, out-of-date bureaucracy. While powers were delegated for improved management of the government, the Appointments Committee of the Cabinet continues to retain its power to approve all appointments at the relatively junior level of deputy secretaries and their equivalent. Similarly. the purpose of encouraging speedy inter-ministerial decisions through problem-solving initiatives at these fora is often defeated by the temptation of administrative ministries not to take decisions even when such decisions clearly lie within their jurisdiction. Whenever decisions involve replacing any old system for the new, intertia continues to operate strongly against such change. This has been the fate of committees and commissions and task forces appointed from time to time—many of whose reports are either not read or not considered for years.

To illustrate, the recommendations of an important committee set up by Prime Minister's Order in 1986 under the chairmanship of Mr. Ratan Tata to investigate the causes of delay in major projects and to bring about the required systematic improvements which can avoid future delays with cost over-runs running into billions of rupees have been awaiting consideration of the Government since October 1987. The various attempts made to institutionalize ministerial accountability through the system of Annual Action plans in the nature of articulation corportate objectives of different departments/ministries (who are encouraged by the MPI to identify their "mission" as well as "key result areas"), and launched with great enthusiasm, were only diluted into routine as the years passed. Thus, as against Annual Action Plans prepared by 61 departments during 1985/86 under managerial leadership and guidance of the MPI which submitted these AAP's to the then Prime Minister, the number as well as the quality of the AAPs fell sharply in subsequent years. The review meetings of monthly progress reports on the AAPs initiated by the MPI also their significance as their numbers fell from 10 meetings held during 1987/89.

Today, the Departmental AAP is as much a mere ritual as the Department Performance Budgets introduced in the 1970s. Not only is no importance attached to these Performance Budgets, but they often project non-performance and even lower performance and higher losses of the Department's Public Enterprises. These are no longer managerial documents but routine paperwork prepared without any real purpose. Thus, the Civil Service in India, like their counterparts elsewhere in the developing countries, have mastered the art of evading any accountability for their decisions and actions. All these attempts, including the latest initiative of AAPs introducing MBO in the government to provide an effective bottom-line to evaluate performance, have turned out to be abortive.

The experiment with Public Enterprise MOU, which is a sub-system of the governmental system of AAP's extended to public enterprises, also seemed to meet the same fate of being degenerated into a mere procedural imposition from the government and not seised as a management opportunity either to empower PE boards with responsibilities discharged earlier by the Administrative Ministry or even to install a modern effective system of 'Performance Evaluation for their Performance improvement.'

Unless administrative reforms encourage micro-level improvement of performance and their micro-level self-evaluation with a view to providing a managerial feed-back loop for bringing about further improvement in performance, any elaborate machinery for external evaluation can only degenerate into evaluation for evaluation's sake. In fact, performance itself often becomes a casualty. It also helps to "pass the buck" upwards and reduce accountability from those who should perform to those who supervise. The organisational reforms in India have thus tended to exist mainly in form rater than in real substance—leaving little impact on the efficiency of the system. We cannot have effective administration without a close fit between policy objectives, organisational design, operational procedure and personnel motivation. What has been lacking in India's administrative reforms in the past four decades is a congruences between strategy, structure and substance.

Finally, the effectiveness of any organisational reform would ultimately depend on whether 'planning' and 'implementation' can be under-pinned appropriately through monitoring with control. MPI's success in the initial years in setting up the monitoring machinery—one of the most effective in any developing country with its undoubted impact on improved performance of projects and infrastructure sectors of the economy, as well as in the poverty alleviation measures—eluded their grasp in later years in the absence of any effective control system whereby accountability for non-performance could be institutionalised.

Personnel Reforms in India: 1947-1991

The personnel reforms in India can be analysed under the following headings: (i) Civil Service recruitment and selection and the vertical hierarchy of government; (ii) Pay and remuneration including pensions; (iii) Training, successions and appraisal; and (iv) Issue such as political neutrality, permanency and corruption.

Civil Service Structure and Hierarchy

In terms of structure, hierarchy and selection, the transition from pre-1947 to post 1947 meant discontinuation of a unified interchangeable top cadre structure like the ICS which was replaced by a set of Group A civil services divided horizontally into administrative, foreign policy, finance and accounts, revenue, railways, post and telegraphs, ordnance factories, forest, engineering etc., on a broadly similar pay structure with some marginal variations in their promotion prospects, depending on whether their cadre reviews had been taken up from time to time. While many of these Grade A services were inherited from the pre-independence era, they were really then the 'non-covenanted' cadres supervised by the members of the unified superior service, the 'covenanted cadre' of the ICS. The purpose of the foreign ruler to have a plethora of non-covenanted cadres under-pinning the ICS was really to divide the ranks in order to provide conflict between them. By merely adding a few more new cadres to this list like the IAS, IFS, IPS etc.,—the structure of the Civil Service in India in the post- 1947 era continued to suffer from this conflict where members of different services were encouraged to protect there boundaries of strong vested interest of power, privilege and promotion in reserved appointments within their cadre, often with low salaries and poor fringe benefits. Instead, if the services were unified and competition built into the structure for promotion on merit, the overall effectiveness of the services would undoubtedly have improved.

What was even more unfortunate was that the elaborate vertical hierarchy only made the impact of horizontal hierarchy of multiplicity of services even more disastrous. Between the Permanent Secretary and the section officer in Federal Ministry at New Delhi there are today ten levels in the hierarchy—causing enormous delay in decision-making as well as avoidable dilutions of responsibility centres. On top of this, the system of written competitive examination now being conducted in 14 regional languages causes its own difficulties in merit rating-although the objectivity of the Civil Service Commission both at the federal and state level continues to be an important hallmark of impartial selection.

While the Civil Service structure remained more or less unchanged over the decades, Governments' decision to organise two new "high talent fast track" cadres in 1957, by the setting up of the

Industrial Management Pool and the Central Administrative Pool, broke refreshingly new ground. This followed the recommendation of the second Appleby Report as well as reports of several parliamentary committees which foresaw and emphasised the need for professional managerial cadres within the public services—distinct from the various administrative cadres already in existence. An abortive attempt was also made in 1986/87 to organise a Senior Management Pool within the central government as select group of high talent fast track managers—civil servants to fill top management posts in the central secretariat and the public sector.

Salary, Pensions and Other Fringe Benefits

Four central commissions in the last 40 years have succeeded in progressively revisiting and substantially improving the salary structure in the civil services in India. Thus the basic pay of a Permanent Secretary at New Delhi which was reduced overnight from Rs. 40,000 per month applicable to ICS officers on 14.8.1947 to Rs. 3,000 per month to non-ICS officers on 15.8.1947 increased to Rs. 8,000 per month from 1.1.1985 on the recommendations of the Fourth Pay Commission. In addition an index-linked dearness allowance scheme has also been introduced for all levels of civil servants up to the level of Permanent Secretary, who currently draws nearly Rs. 2,000 in dearness allowance. Similarly, the entry pay into Group A civil service which was reduced to Rs. 350 per month in 1947 from Rs. 450 per month in the ICS has now been revised to Rs. 2200 per month with an index-linked dearness allowance. The other major reforms which were introduced on the basis of the Fourth Central Pay Commission were:

- Introduction of elongated scales of pay with efficiency bars, to eliminate the problem of stagnation;
- Rationalisation of pay scales from the minimum Rs. 750 per month to maximum Rs. 8,000 per month and the consequent reduction in the number of scales from 153 to 36;
- Other fringe benefits including provision of government accommodation as well as use of

exclusive/sharing chauffeur driven cars for the senior officers at the level of Joint Secretary and above.

The setting-up of a separate Department of Pensions and Pensioners' Welfare in 1985 translated the Government's intention of introducing pension as an instrument to instil confidence in civil servants that they and their families would not be in penury when the breadwinner retires from service or dies. It has also been recognised that the pensions structure is as important as the pay structure in attracting talent into the government services.

Training, Succession and Appraisal

One of thc major items in the agenda for civil service reforms is training. The objective of training is not only to sharpen the professional skills of the participants, but also to bring about attitudinal changes. A comprehensive training strategy was evolved in the middle of the 1980s which sought to make training compulsory and to cover all the civil servants at all levels.

A major step in this direction was the introduction of compulsory training programmes for senior officers. An annual one-week mandatory refresher course, with a vertical mix of participants, has been started for all officers belonging to Group A Services. In addition, a three-stage training programme of 4 weeks' duration has been developed to ensure regular training depending upon the work requirements at specific intervals. These programmes were structured to meet the needs of officers at various levels viz., 6-9 years' service (Programme Implementation), 10-16 years (management Concepts and Decision-making Techniques), 17-20 years (Policy Planning and Analysis)

Greater emphasis is also given to training in decentralised administration as civil servants are increasingly being entrusted with the task of planning and implementation of programmes in agriculture, industrial and other related fields. Training in project formulation, implementation, monitoring and evaluation is imparted to them wherever appropriate.

Broadly categorised as Plan and non-Plan training programmes, to cater for different categories of officers in the

Central Ministries/Departments, State Governments, Public Enterprises and the nationalised banks the table shows the reduction in the number of training programmes conducted, but a sharp rise in the number of officers trained during the period 1985-86 to 1988-89.

Year	*Non Plan No. of Programme Officers trained*	*Plan No. of Programme Officers Trained*
1985-86	44 151	1157 3179
1986-87	33 133	1008 3439
1987-89	38 159	998 4193
1988-89	28 229	745 5080

Source: Department of Personnel, GOI, New Delhi.

The cadere authorities were asked to formulate training plans for officials of organised Group A Services in consultation with the Training Division of the Department of Personnel and Training and implement them so as to give every officer a refresher course relevant to his stage of career by the end of 1990. For non group officials, the ministries/departments have been requested to organise the programme themselves on account of the large numbers involved.

A new thrust was also given to management education for civil servants by launching an intensive 15–month National Management Programme specially designed for a mix of young officers from government as well as managers of public and private sector organisations. The programme is held with the academic cooperation of all the four Indian Institutes of management at Calcutta, Bangalore and Lucknow and Xavier Labour Relations Institute, Jamsedpur.

Training in computerisation and information technology also started in earnest in 1985 and has been implemented over the last

5/6 years. The National Information Centre and the Ministry of Programme Implementation, in collaboration with the Indian Institute of Project Management New Delhi, have run several courses in the last few years for civil servants and senior public enterprise managers.

Because succession in the civil services depends on the appraisal of performance as well as training, the system of reportion on the performance of civil servants has been streamlined to make the performance appraisal a tool for human resources development. The Annual Confidential Report has been revised and designed to provide an objective appraisal in the form of a joint exercise between thc officers reported upon the reporting officer who both evaluate performance against pre-set performance targets, where these are quantifiable.

Permanency, Political Neutrality and Corruption

One of the main attractions of a civil service career apart from the challenge it provides to young man or a woman in various facets of administration and management of this vast sub-continent, is security of service guaranteed under the Constitution. Unlike the permanent civil servant in a government department, managers of public enterprises do not enjoy security of tenure as they are invariably hired on contracts where a termination clause of 3 months' notice on either side is incorporated. The permanency of civil services is also considered to be one of the main preconditions for ensuring political neutrality of civil servants in a democratic government. In the interest of reaping the benefits of competition through opening of the cadres, as well as ensuring loyalty and commitment of individual civil servants particularly at the top level of the government, both these concepts of permanency and political neutrality are being questioned. The issue of corruption is linked to this as it is extremely difficult to dislodge a civil servant on the groups of corruption unless the charges are framed and established after going through elaborate procedures which involve years of litigation. On the other hand it is an open secret that there is an unwritten scale of 'dowry' payment for officers of different Group A services.

A three-pronged strategy, i.e. prevention, surveillance and direction, and deterrent punishment has been adopted by the Department of Personnel to fight the malaise of corruption. An Action plan an anti-corruption measure has also been formulated along with a calendar or vigilance action. The Action plan includes; identification of corruption-prone areas: simplification of rules and procedures; strengthening of the departmental vigilance machinery; the expeditious finalisation of vigilance cases; regular review of the cases under FR. 56 (J) of the government employees who attain the age of 50/55 years or who will be completing 30 years of service, with a view to weeding out the corrupt and inefficient elements; and a close watch on the officers of doubtful integrity.

The existing anti-corruption laws and procedures and mechanisms for detecting the corrupt practices and punishing the corrupt among public servants have been strengthened with the enactment of the Prevention of Corruption Bill, 1988. The Act brings together the various provisions relating to the prevention of corruption to make the law more stringent. Some of the salient features of the Act are: widening the scope of the definition of the term "Public Servant"; empowering the Central Government to appoint special Judges and investing these judges with civil powers and functions exercisable by a District Judge for attachment of property; incorporating the offences under Section 161 to 165-A of Indian Penal Code and day-to-day trial of cases.

As stated earlier, government can under Rs 56(J), terminate the services of permanent civil servant on attaining the age of 50/55 and this is the only restriction that has been placed at present on the permanency of government service in India. The government has been considering for some time whether the provision of this rule should be extended to include similar termination of civil servants' tenure when they attain the age of 40/45. In fact when the Senior Management Pool Scheme was drafted in 1986/87. One of the provisions of this scheme was to weed out civil servants found unfit through a second mid-career selection procedure on the basis of 10/15 years performance of the officers-proposed to be conducted by the civil service commission as and when the civil servants attain the age of 40. The proposal was to introduce a limited written competitive examination and sort the civil servants into three categories: (a) top category, found fit for the SMP, i.e. the post of Joint Secretary and above in central government including public enterprises; (b) middle category, found fit to remain in the Group A services to which the officer belonged and (c) to be weeded out through application of FR 56(J) at the age of 40 instead of 50/55 so as to facilitate their rehabilitation in another career at a relatively younger age.

Unfortunately, no final decision on the SMP proposal could be taken before the government changed in 1989 and Rajiv Gandhi relinquished charge. The two subsequent governments did not revive the proposal. It ought to be mentioned that the civil service associations did not take too kindly to the SMP idea. They saw in it a threat not only to their long-term security and promotion on seniority inertia, but also introduction of the threat of competition at mid-career.

Long Term Impact of these Personnel Reforms: An Evaluation

The impact of personnel reforms in India's civil services was as diffused and unsatisfactory as the impact of organisational reforms discussed in previous paragraphs. Not only has the civil services structure—horizontally fragmented into a multiplicity of services providing little scope for healthy competition, pre-empted by their closed career pattern—become out-of-date, but the vertical structure of the hierarchy is unsuitable for either speedy decision-making or empowerment down the line to encourage bright young talent to take decisions and be accountable for them.

The only innovation of organising two fast track bodies for highly talented personnel of the Central Administrative Pool consisting of Secretaries, Additional Secretaries, Joint Secretaries and Deputy Secretaries in the Federal Government and the Industrial Management Pool (consisting of Chairman, CEO's and potential top management talent for the public enterprises) was not followed through after 1957, owing to the bargaining power of the various Group A Services who rightly viewed these pools as threats to their promotion prospects. But unless these Group A Services are unified and opened up—providing competition between them—the feasibility of organising 'pools' for high talent fast track cadres which involve "selection within selection" from the existing cadres may prove to be difficult. The proposal for the Senior management Pool mooted in the late 1980's under the leadership of Gandhi as Prime Minister could also not be implemented owing to the absence of these preconditions. And yet no civil service can be modernised unless it is opened up, unified and replenished with new talent at all levels which can provide competition to those inside the cadre.

Without restructuring of the civil service, the training and succession plans could not attract highly talented personnel. It is no secret that despite the quantitative efforts of imparting training to civil servants in India and other Third World countries, the qualitative content and impact of this training remained negligible. The impact of training efforts was also diffused in the absence of any rigorous system of surveying training needs. Training needs surveys can be conducted far more rationally in a system where personnel and position classification exercises have been taken up and updated on a regular basis—which is still a far cry from the Indian system. Indeed, without unification of services, personnel and position classification is often made unusually complicated. Unless the civil services are organised on specialised functional lines, where the best available administrators, professional managers, scientists, and engineers are pooled together within the system and trained on the job as well as through specially structured programmes with a managerial succession plan up to the topmost levels, training efforts will remain in suspended animation and not linked to the total structure and strategy of civil service reform. Today, the civil services of the Third World countries where government continues to provide the delivery system in public administration, public enterprise administration and even in business administration—separate professional groups for all three distinct professions should be built within the civil services for which education and training efforts are to be undertaken. In addition, management of public action programmes, management of scientific and engineering departments like space, atomic energy, power etc., would require specialised civil servants of the required education and training background.

In evaluating the long term impact of personnel reforms in post-independent India, it is necessary to mention the neglect of democratic decentralisation efforts in the last four decades. The administrative structure of the Indian federation today consists of (i) the central government at New Delhi (ii) 32 state government including union territories (iii) 430 districts (iv) 5092 blocks, consisting of (v) 500,000 villages, Prior to 1947, 'District' was the focal point of colonial administration with all emphasis on law and order and governance of the country. It is ironical that even after 40 years of independence, the district continues to be the focal point of administration in democratic India where we have yet to take the bureaucracy down to the masses and serve them effectively. Even the archaic designations of District Collector and Deputy Commissioner introduced by the Raj in the latter part of the 19th century have been retained although it is not clear today what these officers do.

Several committees have submitted reports and the steps to be taken on democratic decentralisation—notable among them being Balwantrai Mehta Committee 1959, G.V.K. Rao Committee in the 1970s and the Advisory Council on Programme Implementation in the late 1980s. Not only has the District Planning Procedure not been streamlined nor even effectively introduced, except in some states like Karnataka (where the new institution of District Chief Secretaries is interesting and needs a special mention), Maharashtra, Gujarat, Andhra Pradesh, West Bengal and Kerela, Panchayati Raj Institutions fell in to a state of suspended animation in most parts of the country. And yet, the Block Development Officer is entrusted on an average with executing poverty alleviation programmes amounting to nearly Rs. 2 million per month per block. This underscores the need for strengthening administration at this level. It is time we break the blocks into smaller formations like the Mandals as was done in the state of Andhra Pradesh consisting of 30 villages or so with beneficial impact on the implementation of the various social sector programmes. There is today wide recognition of the fact that to derive full benefit from the enormous amount of money being spent on poverty alleviation, where every third Rupee in the country's National Plan was allocated, as well as to improve management of Public Action Programmes in health, education, housing, drinking, waster etc., these programmes must be packaged appropriately, and implemented by a strong, democratically elected, grassroots bureaucracy.

Developments in UK

As a close witch of the civil service reforms in the UK in the last four decades since the umbilical cord of the ICS to the Home Civil Service in Britain snapped, I am left with a clear impression that the attack in UK on what is regarded as civil service mismanagement and waste combined with the attack on any obstacle to modernisation and openness of the civil service structure has been much more determined. Thus although government's reaction as well as eventual acceptance of the recommendation of the Fultion Report of 1968 appeared to be slow, the speed of reforms caught up during late 1970s and in the 1980s despite several changes of government during the last three decades. In 1964, after a long period of Conservative rule, the civil service applied itself to implementing the policies of the incoming Labour government as it did in 1979 for the radical policies of the next incoming conservative government under the leadership of Margaret Thatcher. It is significant to note that the Thatcher era was described as a 'Reign of Terror' in Whitehall by a senior civil servant.

Thatcher, who was an outsider in Whitehall—the first Prime Minister since Sir Alec Douglas Home in 1964 not previously to have been a civil servant—was characteristically not attracted by the co-called traditional qualities of "detachment, versatility, caution the ability to see things in the round" prised among British civil servants. In addition to seeing the civil service as an adversary to help the government of the day to break away from the conventional wisdoms of the post-war Britain, Mrs. Thatcher also disliked the 'privileges' which the civil services enjoyed. But her main criticism of the role of the civil service—which is shared today by almost all the developed and developing countries with a powerful civil service structure operating in them—is that they give too much time to policy making and not enough to management, especially the pursuit of efficiency and reduction of waste. It is a tribute to her leadership that the last in the country civil service history will go down as a period of great progress and modernisation in Britain, where their bureaucrats were redefined as "accountable managers", public sector operations sub-divisional into "business" and public seen as a "customer".

If we analyse the reforms in the Thatcher year in Britain, we find that the total effect was to implement the Fulton recommendations of "developing responsibility" to usher in both "accountable managements" as well as "efficient management" and to gradually do away with the "cult of the amateur". The methodology adopted by the government under Mrs. Thatcher's leadership to carry out the reform, included:

(i) Setting up of "scrutinise" of the governmental system undertaken by an in-house consultancy unit called the Efficiency Unit, set up in the Prime Minister's Office, headed and manned by renowned and professional managers from the private sector like Lord Rayner, Chief Executive of Marks and Spencer, Sir Robin IBBs, Director of ICI and later Deputy Chairman of Lloyds Bank and Sir Angus Fraser, former Chairman of the Board of Customs and Excise.

(ii) On the basis of the scrutinises, several structural changes were brought about in the civil service:

- to make the civil service open and able to face competition from those outside the service;
- to introduce a new breed of civil servant—the Chief Executive, who can respond to the challenge of restlessness;
- in addition, several institutional changes were also introduced simultaneously like;
- strengthening system of cash limits;
- introducing the Financial management initiative, supported by an infrastructure of cost and management accounting, developed to the point where the measurement of results made MBO an operative culture in government;

- breaking up large departments into relatively small 'agencies' who can take quick decisions and be accountable to them;
- privatising public enterprises and replacing dysfunctional control of government departments before privatisation, by functional regulation of enterprise after privatisation, through smaller regulatory bodies.

The most impressive aspect of the reform in the British civil services in the last decade is their ability to break the last remaining shackles of a close career structure which suffered from the self-delusion that immunity to competition from outside can keep the talents within the service secure, sharpened and up-to-date. As the present British Cabinet Secretary Butaler himself described, the change to the open structure in Britain was to make it "open to recruitment of all manner of people at all stages of their career, open to those show leave it and wish to return, open to the exercise of initiative and responsibility, open to competition with outside providers of similar services, open to public scrutiny and Parliamentary accountability, open to the ideas, initiative and enthusiasm to be found in its own ranks at all levels and throughout the country." The unification of the civil service in Britain were in-built for several years. To this unified structure, opening up of the top seven grades of the civil service, which has already been achieved in Britain, brought in a breath of fresh air. This was helped by interchange of staff between civil service and industry and commerce. Although the Formal exchange scheme was set up in 1968, a new initiative launched in 1977 increased the number of secondments which trebled between 1977 and 1985 as shown in the table below:

Interchange of Staff

Year	*Secondment Civil Service*	*Secondment to Civil Service*	*Total*
1997	63	60	123
1984	186	116	302
1985	229	157	386

Source: Management and Personnel Office, 1985 Report.

Redesignation of the permanent Secretary as a Project Manager, reorganisation of the departments as agencies like the Civil service college, Meteorological office, Passport Department and 30 other government departments—and the success achieved so far through the Next Steps Initiative to quantify the measurement of performance of the civil servants, are some of the other aspects of the modernisation process in the British Civil Service, of which the developing countries in the Commonwealth should take serious note. The current ideas of the political leaders in Britain to devote their renewed attention once again to the safeguards in the civil service against corruption, the impartiality within political parties, appointment and promotion on merit rather than by patronage—also show the vigour of the reforms in the last decade.

It is significant that the recent all—party House of Commons Select Committees on treasury and civil service matters found no evidence of "politicisation" in the service. On the other hand, there should be no room for complacency in taking these reforms forward. Although considerable efforts have been made in the UK to improve management as well as measurement of performance in government, these analyses still cannot show whether the aim should be to increase efficiency by raising output for given inputs or minimize imputs for given outputs. This issue can be critical for any modernisation process in government as any government can taxes, and destroys ant quality of public service just as easily as they can increase the output by lavishing resources on them. The final answer, however, will depend on the ability of any government to achieve either aim efficiently.

Developments in USA

The function-activity-indicator matrix of the Federal Productivity Measurement System introduced in the 890s in the USA was a similar attempt to measure the output of government with a view to measuring and improving efficiency. The structure is based in the grouping of agency measures into 28 functions which have common characteristics across reporting agencies. The current system provides evidence of reasonable productivity in US government and a vast improvement on previous management initiatives like PPES. It also shows what might be done in countries interested in developing measures of government output and productivity. Although this is also subject to a number of technical weaknesses—it does not include measures of quality and its use has been limited—some of these deficiencies could be largely overcome if productivity improvements and management were to command sufficient sustained priority.

The thrust of reforms in the UK and USA has been to institutionalise accountability of civil servants – who unlike their anonymous predecessors, cannot live by promises alone but have to show results and in doing so demonstrate their efficiency. There is today much greater scope for quantification of output, performance and efficiency in government. This is the message that developing countries in the Commonwealth should receive from administrative reorganisations attempted in the advanced countries. The use of new information technology and computers will also demand greater efficiency and decentralisation in decision–making. It is no use having information available in micro-seconds and then taking weeks or months to decide or to get authority from a higher level to act upon it. No civil service can hang on to the outdated cult of amateurism. What the civil services need today is more of the new breed of technocrats and multi-disciplinary managers like engineer managers, scientist managers, economic managers, etc.

What we need to know of the Strategic issues in Administrative Reorganisation in Developing Countries

1. Good Government is as much about well-designed, well-considered 'policies' as of the equally efficient 'delivery' of services which flow from these policies. The Indian belief that Fabian socialism, introduction of central planning in a mixed economy and pursuit of self-sufficiency would take the country forward in its growth and industrialisation is today jinxed the country faces the problem of alleviating the poverty of 300 million; grapples with large gaps between 'planning' and 'implementation' exposed by project delays; continues to suffer low yields from agriculture and low utilisation of allocated resources in industry—and now has to deal with

the problem of huge external debt with falling value of the rupee. Yet, there is a realisation with an efficient management, within Civil services a factor that has been singularly mining in India's economic growth in the last 40 years—these policies could have been implemented with the difficulty which the country faces today. The reform of the civil service and a need for a further boost in administrative reorganisation must take centre stage.

2. In measuring the efficiency of 'delivery' of public services, we have to look for a whole new set of efficiency criteria of government—against which efficiency levels of government in developing countries can be assessed as they are being done in the developed countries. There are many approaches to tackling this issue, the most common one is to assess the growth and efficiency of public spending. Experience shows, however, that this approach alone does not always lead to useful conclusions without being supplemented by other approaches.

3. A more historic approach in measuring 'efficiency' of governments in developing countries would be to review their transition and growth through different historical phases. Three such phases can be delineated as we analyse the administrative reorganisation of India—namely the phase of Governance up to 1947, which was then gradually replaced by the phase of Administration of an independent democratic federal republic, and now the struggle to usher in management.

4. During the phase of Governance, the civil services were trained to administer law and order in a predominantly 'Police State'. The concepts of the anonymity of the civil services, their permanency and political neutrality were well understood and faithfully observed. The challenge of transition from Governance to Administration is basically to move the focus towards administration of a "Western State". Development of central planning in a mixed economy, the achievement of self-reliance in industry and agriculture, the efficient management of public enterprises and public action

programmes, efforts towards greater decentralisation of the bureaucracy from the centre down to village level were all included in the agenda for ushering in Administration and then Management—replacing as quickly as possible the inheritance of Governance from the colonial past.

We somehow lost our way in this forest, not only because the challenge and promise of development itself growth in geometric progression compared with the growth of bureaucracy in arithmetic progression—but also because of a 'self-delusion' from which successive generations of bureaucracies in India suffered, namely that public administration is the same as public management. Apart from the different educational and training needs of the two professionals, the transition from Administration to Management involves a systemic leap. We are apt to forget that no country is underdeveloped. Those which seem to be are the ones which are really under Administration and Management is best described in a bureaucracy of a developing country like India by the continuing scenario—where government seeks 'results' but ends up by following 'procedure'.

5. The ultimate test of a government's ability to change its administrative structure to a managerial structure is whether it can match the quality of implementation of its programmes to the pre-determined levels of planned targets and objectives without mismanagement or waste leakage. The necessary preconditions for this transition—evident from the developments in the UK and USA—are threefold.

First, it requires a basic structural change in the civil services from the pattern of fragmented, closed-career, anonymous, generalist, permanent and neutral structure to one where the civil servant bears a name-tag, has professional managerial competence and possesses dedication and commitment to national causes irrespective of the political party of the government he serves. Second, in a large country like India, democratic government without democratic decentralisation cannot be an efficient delivery system. No system of democratic decentralisation will be acceptable without involving the elected representatives of the people at village, mandal, block and district level by the bureaucracy in the management of the government's programmes including poverty alleviation and other social sector programmes like education, health and housing. Third, the output and performance of the government in a managerial mode must be susceptible to both quantifications as well as measurement. Before attempts are made to quantify and measure performance, responsibility must be appropriately devolved from the government to its lower formations whether they are public enterprises, local government or other agencies. Such devolution can help to remove the areas of 'government failure' which pre-empt any possibility of long term 'managerial success' by these public enterprises, local governments and other decentralised executive agencies.

6. The unification and opening up of the civil services in the developing countries must follow the impressive track record in Britain in introducing mobility between government and industry, both public as well as in the private sector. Whenever efforts have been made in such a direction in India, particularly when the mobility is from industry to government, the result has been encouraging, although the extent to which such effort could be made were limited by the closed career, reserved appointment-based vested interests of the fragmented civil services in the country. The cult of the amateur can be replaced effectively by the new breed of multi-disciplinary managers in the civil services only if these structural changes precede such reforms in the administrative reorganisation.

7. Like the Next Steps Initiative in Britain, where detailed identification and scrutiny of departments is undertaken before they are reorganised as executive agencies of government's policy to achieve measurable results with reduced public expenditure, the time has come to examine, assess and identify the results and cost effectiveness of the different forms of devolution in the governmental structure in India. Whether the departmental forms of devolution (like

the Railways into several zonal railways) is more effective than the devolution of the department's function into public enterprises as in steel, mines, petroleum, coal and other sectors is an issue which needs to be reviewed. The evidence of more efficient and autonomous departmental devolution in railways, telecommunications, atomic energy, and space compared with less efficient devolution in other sectors where government's business is carried out by public enterprises, with strategic decision-making powers retained by government, reconfirms the urgent need for reconsidering the form of such devolution. In this context, the alternative of privatisation of the public enterprises should also be viewed against pragmatic consideration. Privatisation of the kind followed in Britain is obviously unwarranted in a developing country like India where the size of the capital markets is limited. But what is possible and should merit consideration is the scope of pre-privatisation restructuring and turn-around of public enterprises as was done in British Steel—as well as post-privatisation replacement of dysfunctional control by functional regulation as was done in gas, telecommunications and other sectors. For the efficient development of the private sector the time has come to dismantle protective policy barriers and make the private sector face competition of quality, service and technological modernisation.

8. A multiplicity of levels in the hierarchy of decision-making can be as harmful as the horizontal fragmentation of civil services. In a country like India this has been further aggravated by generally low remuneration of the civil services with a multiplicity of pay scales and allowances. The deficiency in these two areas in India, has been made good by successive Pay Commission Reports although efforts should continue for further rationalisation and improvement. No strategy to restructure an administrative system to a managerial mode can, however, be successful without reducing both vertical hierarch and horizontal fragmentation in the civil service. Indeed, unification and opening up of the services as well as rationalisation of the hierarchy are important preconditions which can be overlooked only at the

cost of keeping the public service structure inefficient. In the short term, efforts like the setting up of a Senior Management Pool for the government (attempted in 1986-1987 by Prime Minister Gandhi) should merit consideration. Revival of a well structured managerial Civil Service for the public sector, like the Industrial Management Pool set up in the late 50s, is also urgent. A much greater role of the scientists and engineers in both these pools should be recognised. The redesignation of government functionaries like District Collector or Secretary to Government, which we inherited from the Raj, should also merit consideration. The fact that the permanent secretary in the British government is today redesignated as Project Manager has its own message for such action to be taken in the developing countries to fight inertia wherever it has been more powerful than change in administrative reorganisation. The quest for efficiency and effectiveness must be a quest for a slimmer, fitter, and a more functional public service structure which should be a means to an end and not an end in itself.

9. Political neutrality of civil servants must be viewed in the context of increasing politicisation in the civil service in the developing countries. The fact that all three Indian Prime Ministers resorted to changing the Cabined Secretary three times during the year 1989/90 (in none of these three cases the chosen incumbent was the most senior Permanent Secretary) speaks volumes against any system which is opposed to patronage in senior public service appointments where neutrality, commitment and loyalty to the nation should be given the highest priority. While it was possible for Prime Minister Indira Gandhi to bring in technocrats and intellectuals as Permanent Secretaries in the economic ministries as well as in her own secretariat in the topmost post of the Principal Secretary to the Prime Minister, her successors were not able to capitalize on this healthy tradition. In a sense, the reforms in India have gone in the reverse direction, similarly, the openness in government and in the civil service structure makes the anonymity of civil servants in the interest of so-called ministerial responsibility an out-

of-date constitutional fiction. The Wasteland affairs, the Ponting case and the Wright case have all broken new ground in British Civil service tradition which cannot be ignored by developing countries. As far as security of tenure is concerned, re-thinking is also needed in the interest of introducing mobility and openness in the civil services.

10. Finally, the behavioural and cultural pre-conditions of the new order are perhaps going to be the most critical where education, training and management development have to play their part.

Concluding Thought

Machiavelli said in a famous remark "there is nothing more difficult to take in hand, more perilous to conduct, more uncertain in its success than to take the lead in the introduction of a new order of things". We know how difficult he found in his own life to translate this intention into action, besides spending years in prison and trying to deal with a whole lot extremely difficult Italian princeling. But no new order will serve the order to the day unless it can effectively balance authority with accountability and institutionalise this balance through an appropriate managerial system. Many of my colleagues in India often ask the cynical question whether, in democratic set-up like ours, given compulsion of political leadership with constituencies of political and economic interest and patronage, it is at all possible to usher in a managerial system-oriented government. It is my belief and affirmative if the 'pre-conditions' can be taken care of adequately. As stated earlier, the behavioural and cultural preconditions are going to be the most critical in managing change to replace status by function, hierarchy by participation and regulation by development.

The changing role of Government in National competitiveness is also another aspect worth examining. Is the role of Government in Malaysia, Hong Kong and Singapore qualitatively different from that in other Commonwealth countries like Kenya, Tanzania, Pakistan? To what extent is the hypothesis of a government role in enhancing national advantage the reverse of what is often supposed? Many see the government as a helper and supporter of industry. Yet many of the ways in which the government tries to help can actually hurt enterprises in the long run, e.g. subsidies, domestic mergers, providing guaranteed government's proper role that of a pusher, a challenger and at the broadcast level one of signalling and if so, how is this role being played by governments in Commonwealth countries in Asia and Africa?

—P.K. Basu

14

New Public Management: Challenges and Issues in an International Perspective

Introduction

While there are many common themes among the twenty-five member countries of the OCED (Organisation for Economic Cooperation and Development), there are also differences of substance, speed and emphasis in public management reform. (These are more fully analysed in Public Management Services' forthcoming publication, *Governance in Transition.*) OECD experiences range from the so-called "radicalism" of UK and New Zealand through the more "measured" approaches of Australia and the Nordic countries, to the smaller (so far) changes in most administrative law countries (Italy, Spain). There are some countries where public sector reform is not a major issue as yet—Germany at the national government level (although things are now beginning to happen) and perhaps Japan (although there appears to be a rapidly emerging consensus that fundamental reform including deregulation is required in the Japanese public sector to maintain Japanese economic growth). The USA illustrates significant reforms, in state and local governments, but with change in the federal government just beginning, reflecting both the National Performance Review and the Contract with America.

Public sector management reform is, of course, not new. In the last 30 years many countries have pursued "micro" reforms described variously as programme budgeting, management by objectives and accountable management, to name but a few. And many individual organisations at both, national and local government level, have developed their own initiatives focusing on efficiency, effectiveness and customer service. (In some cases this raises questions about the value added by "central" initiatives.) But generally what appears to be different about current reforms is their greater scope, involving in many cases significant changes to the boundaries and structure of the public sector, a greater sense of urgency and a more comprehensive or strategic, approach to reform, recognising the interdependence of different aspects of reform. New Public Management (NPM) is not now generally regarded as another passing "fad".

The origins of these changes are mixed. In all cases, increasing globalisation forces or encourages a bit of "me-tooism" in the reforms. In some cases the changes may be ideologically driven, invoking the superiority of the private sector as in the case of Thatcherism (UK) or Rogernomics (New Zealand), although to be fair a strong intellectual paradigm based on public choice and agency theory has been developed in the New Zealand case. In others, the changes represent a more direct response to government's budgetary difficulties, themselves brought on by economic contraction. While their objectives and origins may differ between countries, the strategies and directions generally converge. There are perceived new limits to the ability of the state to solve economic or social problems. The sheer weight of the public sector in the economy has grown significantly and there is a general acceptance of the view that public sector performance has a significant impact on total economic performance. There is a consensus that public sector performance can be and needs to be improved.

While origins and objectives many differ between countries, the strategies and directions generally converge. The reforms are being promoted by governments of different political persuasions. While in some countries they may be aimed at reducing the role and size of the public sector (in these cases reforms to existing organisations are seen as a prelude to privatisation), in other countries the reforms are perceived as defending and enhancing the public sector and its organisations and maintaining the legitimacy of the state. A well-performing public sector organisations may equally be a candidate for retention or survival as for sale. And only the public sector may be considered the appropriate provider of many services.

While there may be continuing role for the state, it may be to "steer" rather than to "row" or to facilitate rather than to do. At the same time, there is a greater willingness to think in terms of results of public interventions, rather than of rigid structures and processes governing such interventions. Perhaps, as has been said, the political right has become more dogmatic and the political left, less so.

Giving managers the tools and incentives to improve performance is seen as a way of enabling managers to do more with less, to minimise the impact on services of budget reductions. Public sector organisations face a more demanding public which excepts better services, a say in what it gets and how it is delivered, and which is increasingly reluctant to pay higher taxes. At the same time, demographic and other changes are adding to demands for services.

Evaluating New Public Management

In evaluating NPM, much depends on whose viewpoint is adopted. There are three potentially conflicting interests and points of view, namely:

- consumers of government services;
- taxpayers; and
- public sector employees.

At the stage public sector reforms have probably had greater impact on public sector employees who in many cases have had to adjust a major changes in organisational structures and new work methods. They have been required to work smarter, to accept continuing change and to accept competition. But in many cases, their job content and individual autonomy have also been enhanced. Quite a number have lost their jobs. Overall, the working environment has been radically changed. This issue is discussed later.

The impact on consumers also appears to have been significant in many countries. The adoption of a client focus is a simple but powerful concept which is likely to have a major and enduring influence, as discussed later. But, at the same time, consumers' perceptions will be influenced by any reductions in services. For example, train services may run on time but there may be fewer of them.

The impact on taxpayers in terms of their getting better value for money is also probably significant, but more difficult to prove and always less obvious in its impact.

In fact, we lack objective aggregate information on just what has happened to the performance of the public sector. For example, our national statisticians do not measure public sector productivity. But there is plenty of anecdotal evidence of performance improvement and partial performance indicators and a number of interesting public opinion surveys, the overall circumstantial evidence of performance improvement is compelling.

I should make my own position clear. I believe there is a positive role for well-performing and responsive public institutions. I am a general supporter of the new public management and generally optimistic about where it is taking us. I am not a believer in the "good old days" of public management propounded by some anti-managerialists. More often than not, the "good old days" were characterised by inward-looking and unresponsive public sector organisations. But the new public management needs to be done "right". Exaggerated claims about its achievements are common. And mistakes have been made. But that is no reason for turning back.

It is useful to distinguish between changes which are concerned with changing the role, boundaries and structure of governments (the macro changes) and those more concerned with the internal management "paradigm" of the public sector (the macro changes). These are sometimes called the "what" and the "how" of public management reform. This is not a total satisfactory distinction but reflects areas of lesser and greater convergence of approach.

The "Macro" Changes

It is clear that the structure and boundaries of the state are changing in all countries. Governments of a range of political persuasions are showing themselves willing to privatise (or partly so) previously state-owned airlines and banks. But there is less unanimity about privatisating public utilities such as telecoms, gas and electricity (France). In the case of the macro public service there is even less commonality of approach. A number of governments have shown an interest in vouchers but these have yet to become significant. Other market-type mechanisms such as increased use of external charging and charging for services within government are more common. There is a general willingness to contract out housekeeping activities (printing, information technology, gardening, cleaning, internal audit, etc.), and to develop new relationships with both the non-profit sector and the private sector in new forms of service delivery. While the rhetoric may be more subdued in some countries, the reality may be stronger. For example, recent labour governments in Australia, both state and federal, have pursued significant privatisation and contracting-out, but have not promoted these changes as policy plans.

Is privatisation and contracting-out reducing the size of the public sector? Unfortunately, there are no adequate comparable and recent statistics to demonstrate changes in the size of the public sector. But it appears that in the last five years, only New Zealand and the UK have seen, a significant change (a reduction of over five per cent) in the public sector share of Gross Domestic Product (GDP). The size of the public sector appears to be "sticky" in terms of downward adjustment.

Are these changes a major once-and-for-all correction of the size and role of the public sector? Or are they more a correctional adjustment viewed from a longer-term perspective? I am not sure. But clearly, we need to distinguish the question of ownership from that of control or management. Modes of operation may be changing, the number of public servants may be diminishing, but the role and influence of the state is not as much effected.

There appear to be some benefits in privatisation and contracting-out (lower real pieces and improved customer service) although of course the real issue is whether these could have been achieved without privatisation. And in few countries is privatisation politically popular. Assessing the benefits of contracting-out is more complex, at least more than its proponents claim, but PUMA's work suggests that overall there are efficiency and services quality gains.

Another structural aspect of the changes particularly associated with the UK and New Zealand is the establishment of autonomous service delivery agencies separate from ministerial departments. Depending on one's point of view, agencies involve either undesirable fragmentation or enhanced or clarified accountability. Nordic countries, particularly Sweden, have long had autonomous agencies. But in their case the agency may retain a major involvement in policy advice and evaluation as well as in service delivery. What appears to be lacking in the UK approach is comprehensive policy and programme evaluation—either in ministries or in agencies. A greater focus on management which was previously lacking is commendable, but one also needs more and better policy, analysis and evaluation, not less of it.

The "Micro" Changes

Changes in public sector management at the micro level have a more general level of acceptance and common pattern of implementation in OECD countries. They reflect a concern to improve the performance of the pubic sector or to do more with less through:

- more effective programmes, e.g., through better-targeting;
- more efficient operations; economising on staff and capital resources; and
- improved quality of services and service delivery.

Public sector organisations are seen as needing to be customer-focused, flexible and outward-looking as opposed to the highly centralised, rule bound, inward-looking organisations of the past.

To some, this new public sector management paradigm simply means invoking private sector management-techniques, a view given credence by the rhetoric of Thatcherism in the UK, Rogernomics in New Zealand and the US National Performance Review. I do not see it this way. The tools of corporate planning, performance measurement and devolution to provide clearer accountability are general "common sense" management tools. They have been in use in many public sector organisations before government, wide reforms were commenced. And the accountability from mechanisms and ethical rules under which the public sector operates continue to be different from the private sector. Although. there has been some convergence, public sector management remains much harder.

There is no need in this paper for a detailed or a tedious exposition of the themes "let the managers manage and" "make the managers manage" in new public management. But the basic components of the new paradigm are worth restating:

- a closer focus on results in terms of efficiency and effectiveness, and service quality;
- the replacement of highly centralised hierarchical organisational structures with decentralised management environments where decisions on resource allocation and service delivery are taken closer to the point of delivery, and which provide scope for feedback from clients and other interest groups;
- flexibility to explore alternatives to direct public provision which might provide more cost-effective policy outcomes.
- New personnel management policies to provide greater flexibility in the deployment of staff (e.g., through multi-skilling);
- The use of mechanisms to improve performance such as performance contracting and the creation of

competitive and a market environment within and between public sector organisations.

- Incentives to improve performance (or at least removing disincentives) through enabling organisations to retain a portion of savings from improved performance;
- The strengthening of strategic capacities at the centre to "steer" government to respond to external changes and diverse interests quickly, flexibly and at least cost; and
- Greater accountability and transparency through requirements to report on results.

. These are what I see as the components of a comprehensive approach to the new public management. Not all elements are present in all countries. Several of these aspects of the new paradigm are worth separate discussion, namely:

- a client or customer focus;
- devolution; and
- performance contracting.

A major theme associated with improving performance is the development of a customer or a client focus or service quality initiatives in the public sector. The UK Citizens Charter is probably the best-known example. These initiatives aim to improve performance in service delivery (timeliness, accuracy, etc.) as well as to provide service which meet people's needs. Thus, they involve consolation with clients about what they want and aspects of services they particularly value. Much more information on available services may be provided. Commitments to provide a certain type, volume and quality of service may be made and performance measured against their commitments. They provide greater client choice and complaint and redress mechanisms. Service may be tailored to individual needs rather than standardised. Empowerment of staff to respond appropriately to client requirements is also stressed. In a number of countries, these reforms have a strong element of debureaucratisation or administrative simplification: public servants are perceived as existing to help citizens, not to make their lives difficult. The long-term implications of this simple but powerful concept may be significant in terms of the type of decisions which may in the future be made by clients as opposed to elected officials or public servants. Developing a customer service has involved a major change in mind-set in many public sector organisations and all the difficulties in staff motivation and organisation this entails.

While there is little doubt that performance has improved in many governments as result of client focus, client perceptions are, interestingly, more mixed. A commonly-quoted standard of improvement is the time taken and documentation required to obtain a passport—an example as common in client focus literate as is rubbish collection in discussions of contracting-out. One problem is that while the quality of individual services may be improved, their overall level may diminish.

Also, the focus of most service quality initiatives is on quality of service delivery rather than on service outcomes. While waiting times for medical operations may be reduced, what about the quality of medical staff and the medical success—or survival rate? Service quality is only one aspect of overall performance. A focus only on short-term service delivery questions may divert us from more important issues of public services.

A client focus also has a management dimension within public service organisations. Support units (accounts, personnel units, etc.) exist to provide a service to operational parts of the organisation. They do not exist as ends in themselves. Their performance may be considerably improved if they can develop a client focus. The possibility of contracting-out may encourage them to do this.

Devaluation has been a major theme of public sector reform. It has a number of related elements:

- devolution of responsibilities to other levels of government.

- Devolution from the centre to operating departments, including the setting up of autonomous agencies; and
- Devolution within organisations.

In the latter two cases, a significant feature has been the removal of unnecessarily prescriptive rules and regulations.

In a number of countries, the devolution from national to lower levels of government has been substantial (Denmark, Finland, France, Sweden, but not UK). This devolution is a significant and probably enduring change. In some cases, this devolution of both responsibilities and finances has not been accompanied by clear accountability relationships between the levels of government. Arguably, if both responsibilities and financing are developed, democratic accountability/means that each level of government can keep to its own/turf without the need for such accountability arrangements.

As mentioned previously, the creation of autonomous agencies or units (Canada, Denmark, France, Sweden, UK) is another development with long-term implications for accountability and performance. As mentioned earlier, the separation of policy from administration is part of this in only a few countries (New Zealand and UK); in other such agencies may have significant policy monitoring development and advice role (Sweden). Accountability for only outputs rather than also for outcomes may be clearer, but is worryingly narrow.

There is also the question of the adequacy of policy development and steering from the centre. The greater the disaggregation, the more difficult is steering, a concern already expressed by New Zealand ministers. Clearly, there should be some sensible limit to disaggregation. Autonomous agencies, central ministries, agencies and portfolio ministries, all need to transform themselves for this new regime. There is some evidence that not enough of this transformation is taking place to ensure sustainable and significant change.

In many countries, there has also been a substantial freeing up of centrally-imposed rules on budgetary and staffing matters

(Australia, New Zealand). The level of autonomy in staffing manners raises yet unresolved issues about the future of a unified (but mobile and flexible) public service (New Zealand and UK). But while many governments have been prepared to free up appointments, job classification and promotion processes, there has been much less devolution in industrial relations and pay-fixing processes. Even in the former scenario, tight budget controls and requirements that managers live with the budgetary consequences of their negotiations have limited any "excesses".

As with any devolution, there are concerns about, for example, merit and equity policies not being observed, that some public servants may over classify positions and pay themselves too much, and so on. But it needs to be remembered that devolution of operational decisions does not mean freedom to do as one wishes. On the contrary, decisions are devolved within a policy framework and managers must be held accountable for these decisions within this framework. Reporting on and audit of decisions made are part of this accountability.

Devaluation is based on the view that decisions made closer to their actual point of impact, and therefore, with greater knowledge of likely results, are likely to be better decisions. There is little evidence that centralised decision-making is any better than devolved decision-making in avoiding inappropriate decisions. Certainly there is no evidence of budget blowouts from financial devolution. The reverse is the case-financial devolution has been a means to enable managers to achieve tight aggregate expenditure controls.

Nevertheless, "letting the managers manage" has been difficult to achieve in number of countries. An interest in compliance rather than performance, a view that managerial autonomy may give too much power to public servants at the expense of elected officials and fears of increased risk of "impropriety" have limited its progress. But even in the USA, politicians have recognised the inefficiencies created by excessive rules and regulations, as reflected in the freeing-up personnel and procurement regulations.

This is an appropriate point at which to discuss the issues of ethics and corruption which appears to be a concern in the UK and New Zealand, but less so in other countries which have extensively pursued NPM such as Australia and the Nordic countries. The issue of excessive pay for executives in the private sector is less important than the perception that NPM encourages the introduction of private sector values into public management. For a start this view is unfair to the private sector where many companies run frugal and ethical senior management regimes. The problem is that in many cases no rules or guidelines have been prescribed under the guise of "let the managers manage" or the need to use "private sector" practices. But this should be easily dealt with by clear signals and guidelines concerning executive remuneration and other "perks". Codes of conduct and ethics are essential. The public sector is not the private sector.

My own view is that devaluation or freeing-up the rules and giving managers greater flexibility and autonomy has been the key factor in improving public sector performance. Performance contracting and even performance pay may have made a contribution but the simple act of freeing up the system has been incomparably important.

One important aspect of accountability is information. In many industrial countries, there has never been so much information publicly available on the operations of government organisations. In countries with Freedom-of-Information legislation, this situation is even more pronounced. But sheer quantity is not the point: relevance is an area where more work needs to be done. Audit institutions can play an important role in assuring the reliability and even relevance or validity of performance information while not detracting from the responsibility of management to develop good, performance information as part to self-evaluation.

The concept of *performance contracting* is to a large extent the other side of the autonomy coin. It involves both an increased emphasis on performance and the development of new accountability instruments. Contracts may be between ministers and organisations, which specify levels of autonomy, required results and sanctions and rewards. They may include employment contracts for chief executives. While not normally a legal agreement, a performance contract involves mutual undertakings. As such, it may modify old, hierarchical relationships and will involve sanctions and rewards and other incentives of both a personal and institutional nature which are new in a public sector environment. It puts pressure on the performance measurement systems with all the limitations and the attendant possibilities, of game playing. Indeed, this appear to be a problem in the UK where the use of a relatively small number of board performance indicators (frequently politically determined) reflects the private sector's "rough and ready" use of performance indicators, with insufficient regard to unintended or dysfunctional consequences. Of course, in the private sector it matters less; there is always market survival as the ultimate test. We need to remember that performance measurement in the public sector is about getting a "better feel" for overall performance efficiency, effectiveness, and service quality, not about a single bottom line.

The "People" Dimension

Clearly, the new public management is not just a set of technical measures; it has a "people" dimension. In organisational terms, it implies flatter structures, some greater priority on operational units and broader or less specialised job specifications. It has seen greater emphasis on general management or supervisory skills as opposed to technical ones, as represented by the now-common concept of Senior Executive Services (SES). In theory, public servants are more empowered and more broadly skilled; there are fewer of them, but they are better paid.

But are they appropriately motivated to regard performance and a client focus as part of their professional ethic and values? While this is not the place for a detailed discussion of this issue, signals and incentives to staff are clearly important and appear to be neglected in some country's approaches to the new public management. Performance pay which has been tried in a number of countries with mixed results, is only one aspect of this. Evidence suggests that consultation and management leadership are key in converting new public management theory into reality.

Conclusion

Taken together, customer focus, autonomy and performance contracting appear to be promoting a new spirit of innovation in public service managers. There is considerable evidence, particularly in state and local governments, of a major and enduring change where such strategies are coherently implemented. The interaction between citizens, public servants and elected officials has been changed beneficially and probably permanently. In local government, there appear to be widely-accepted models of good governance and public sector management. But there is, as yet, less to report at the national government level. Of course, it is not easy to do it well. Experiences of OECD member countries suggest that success depends on sustained efforts, patience and clear and consistent signals. It is here that the role of leadership (not necessarily political), in public sector management reforms is so important.

But the changes are not yet fully in place. Some governments have scarcely begun and there are many obstacles to be overcome for those who are currently on the path. These include a failure to show demonstrable benefits, and inadequate strategic management of the change process.

The demise of the old "command and control" system of public management is not to be too much lamented. The real challenge is to get the new public management right. Care, thought, consultation and attention to the "people" dimension is what this challenge requires.

—David Shand

Bibliography

Books

Abdul Aziz and David D. Arnold, ed. Decentralised governance in Asian Countries. New Delhi: Sage, 1996.

Addy, John. Parliamentary election and reform (1807-32). London: Longmans, 1961.

Administrative Reforms Commission. Report on Centre-state Relationships. New Delhi: Manager, Publication Branch, 1969.

Administrative Staff College. Accountability of government departments. London: ASC, 1955.

Ahluwalia, Isher Judge, Rakesh Mohan and Omkar Goswami: Policy Reform in India. New Delhi: Oxford and IBH, 1996.

Alatas, Syed Hussein. Corruption: Its Nature, Causes and Functions. Aldershot: Avebury, 1990.

All India Management Association. Corporate governance and business Ethics. New Delhi: Excel Books, 1997.

Anand, D.A. Electoral Reforms: Curbing Role of Money Power. New Delhi: Indian Institute of Public Administration, 1995.

Andhyarujina, T.R. Judicial Activism and Constitutional Democracy in India. Bombay: N.M. Tripathi, 1992.

Aoki, Masahiko and Hyung-Ki Kim, eds. Corporate Governance in Transitional Economies: Insider Control and the Role of Banks. Washington, D.C.: World Bank, 1995.

Arora, Ramesh K. People's Participation in Development Process. Jaipur: HCM RIPA, 1979.

Asian and Pacific Development Administration Center, Kuala Lumpur. Administrative Reforms for Decentralised Development, Kuala Lumpur: APDAC, 1980.

Avasthi, Amreshwar and Shri Ram Maheshwari. Public Administration. Agra: Lakshmi Narain Agrawal, 1990.

Banerjee, Ajit M. and K.A. Chandrasekaran. Renewing Governance: Issues and Options. New Delhi: McGraw-Hill, 1996.

Banerji, S.K. Forty Years after Independence: The Change in India. New Delhi: Enkay, 1994.

Bansal, J.P. Supreme Court: Judicial Restraint Versus Judicial Activism. Jaipur: Unique, 1985.

Barker, James Jr., Bernard Tenenbaum and Fiona Woolf. Governance and Regulation of Power Pools and System Operators: An International Comparison. Washington, D.C.: The World Bank, 1997.

Barnabas, A.P. The Experience of Citizens in Getting Water Connections (A Survey Report on Knowledge, Communication and Corruption). New Delhi: Indian Institute of Public Administration, 1965.

Barthwal, C.P. Public Administration in India: Retrospect and Prospects. New Delhi: Ashish, 1993.

Barve, S.G. Good Government: The Administrative Malaise and Connected Issues. New Delhi: Indian Institute of Public Administration, 1964.

Basu, Debashis and Sucheta Dalal. The Scam: Who Won who Lost who Got Away. New Delhi: UBS, 1993.

Baxi, Upendra. Annual Capital Foundation Lecture 1996: On Judicial Activism, Legal Education and Research in a Globalising India. New Delhi: Capital Foundation Society, 1996.

Baxter, Craig, et.al. Government and Politics in South Asia. Lahore: Vanguard, 1988.

Betes, Robert H. and Anne O. Krueger, eds. Political and Economic Interactions in Economic Policy Reform. Oxford: Blackwell, 1993.

Bhambhri, C.P. Bureaucracy and Politics in India Delhi: Vikas, 1971.

Bhambhri, C.P. Public Administration in India. Delhi: Vikas, 1973.

Bhandari, Kusumlata. India: Electoral Reforms. Delhi: Election Archieves, 1988.

Bhargava, G.S. India's Watergate: Study of Political Corruption in India. Delhi: Arnold Heinemann Publishers, 1974.

Bhargava, G.S. Indira's India Gate: Latest Study of Political Corruption in India. Delhi: Arnold-Heinemann, 1977.

Bhatia, K.L. Judicial Review and Judicial Activism: A Comparative Study of India and Germany from an Indian Perspective. New Delhi: Deep and Deep, 1997.

Bhattacharya, Mohit. Restructuring Public Administration: Essays in Rehabilitation. New Delhi: Jawahar, 1997.

Bhushan, Prashant. Bofors: The Selling of a Nation. New Delhi: Vision, 1990.

Birkenshaw. When Citizen's Complain: Reforming Justice and Administration. Buckingham: Open University Press, 1993.

Bogdanor, Vernon. Coalition Government in Western Europe. London: Heinemann, 1983.

Bolles, Blair. Corruption in Washington, or Men of Good Intenticns. London: Gollancz, 1960.

Brautigam, Deborah. Governance and Economy: A Review. Washington, D.C.: The World Bank, 1991.

Bueno Mesquita, Bruce. Strategy, Risk and Personality in Coalition Politics: The Case of India. Cambridge: Cambridge University Press, 1975.

Buscaglia, Edgardo and Maria Dakolias. Judicial Reform in Latin American Courts: The Experience in Argentina and Ecuador. Washington, D.C.: The World Bank, 1996.

Butcher, Tony. Delivering Welfare: The Governance of the Social Services in the 1990s. Buckingham: Open Univ. Press, 1995.

Butler, David. Coalitions in British Politics. London: Macmilan, 1978.

Caiden, Gerald E. The Commonwealth Bureaucracy. London: Melbourne Univ. Press, 1967.

Caiden, Gerald E., ed. Strategies for Administrative Reform. Lexington Mass.: D.C. Health, 1982.

Campbell, Alan K. and Roy W. Bhal, eds. State and Local Government: the Political Economy of Reform. New York: Free Press, 1976.

Carter, Jimmy. A Government as Good as its People. New York: Simon and Schuster, 1977.

Chapman, Richard A. and J.R. Grenway. The Dynamics of Administrative Reform. London: Croom Helm, 1980.

Chatterjee, Partha, ed. State and Politics in India. Delhi: Oxford Univ. Press, 1997.

Chatterjee, Sibranjan. Restructuring Centre-state Relations: The Sarkaria Commission and Bengal. New Delhi: Minerva, 1997.

Chaturvedi, T.N., ed. Auditing Public Utilities. Delhi: Ashish, 1989.

Chaturvedi, T.N., ed. Perspectives of Administrative Reforms for Integrated Rural Development: India. New Delhi: Indian Institute of Public Administration, 1980.

Chaturvedi, T.N. ed. Quest for Commitment in Public Services. New Delhi: Department of Personnel and Administrative Reforms, 1975.

Chaturvedi, T.N., ed. Secrecy in Government. New Delhi: Indian Institute of Public Administration, 1980.

Chaturvedi, T.N., ed. Training in Public Administration: The Changing Perspective. New Delhi: Indian Institute of Public Administration, 1989.

Chaturvedi, T.N. and S. Venugopal Rao, eds. Police Administration. New Delhi: Indian Institute of Public Administration, 1982.

Chaturvedi, T.N. and Shanta Kohli Chandra., eds. Social Administration Development and Change: Essays in Honour of Professor V. Jagannadham. New Delhi: Indian Institute of Public Administration, 1980.

Chaturvedi, T.N. ed. Ethics in Public Life. New Delhi: Indian Institute of Public Administration, 1996.

Chaturvedi, T.N., ed. Contemporary Administrative Culture of India. New Delhi: Indian Institute of Public Administration, 1996.

Chaturvedi, T.N., ed. Administrative Accountability. New Delhi: Indian Institute of Public Administration, 1984.

Chitkara, M.G. Corruption 'N' Cure. Delhi: APH Pub., 1997.

Chopra, S.K., ed. Towards Good Governance, Delhi: Konark, 1997.

Claessens, Stijn. Corporate Governance and Equity Prices: Evidence from the Czech and Slovak Republics. Washington, D.C.: The World Bank, 1995.

Claessens, Stijn, Simeon Djankov and Gerhard Pohl Ownership and Corporate Governance; Evidence from the Czech Republic. Washington, D.C.: The World Bank, 1997.

Clarke, Michael. Corruption: Causes, Consequences and Control, London: Frances Pinter (Publishers), 1983.

Clarke, Michael and John Stewart, eds. Renewing Public Management: an Agenda for Local Governance. London: Pitman, 1996.

Claude, Jean et. al eds. Public Administration in the Global Village. Westport: Praeger, 1994.

Commonwealth Secretariat. The Changing Role of Government Administrative Structures and Reforms. London: Commonwealth Secretariat.

Commonwealth Secretariat. Current Good Practices and New Development in Public Service Management: A Profile of the Public Service of Trinidad and Tobago. London: Commonwealth Secretariat, 1995.

Commonwealth Secretariat. Current Good Practices and New Developments in Public Service Management: A Profile of the Public Service of Zimbabwe. London: Commonwealth Secretariat, 1997.

Consumer Coordination Council. An Insight into Citizen's Charter. New Delhi: CCC, December 1997.

Coolidge, Jacqueline and Susan Rose-Ackerman. High-level Rent-seeking and Corruption in African Regimes: Theory and Cases. Washington. D.C.: The World.

Cox, Archibald. The role of the Supreme court in American government. Oxford Clarendon Press, 1976.

Crane, Edgar G. Legislative review of government programmes: tools for accountability. New York: Praeger, 1977.

Curtis, Donald. Beyond government: organisation for common benefit. Hong Kong: Macmillan, 1991.

Dakolias, Maria. The judicial sector in Latin America and the Caribbean: elements of reform. Washington, D.C.: The World Bank, 1996.

Damodaran, K.M. Accountability in administration case for employees charter. New Delhi: Indian Institute of Public Administration, 1998.

Das Gupta, Monica, Lincoln C. Chen and T.N. Krishnan, eds. Health, poverty and development in India. Delhi: Oxford Univ. Press, 1996.

Das, Kartik Kumar. Poverty alleviation programmes in India: a micro study. Meerut: Anu Books, 1995.

Das, S.K. Civil services reform and structural adjustment. Oxford: Oxford University Press, 1998.

Datt, Gaurav and Martin Ravallion. Macroeconomic crises and poverty monitoring: a case study for India. Washington, D.C.: The World Bank, 1996.

De Swaan, Abram. Coalition theories and cabinet formations. Amsterdam: Elsevier Scientific Pub., 1973.

Dean, Mitchell. The constitution of poverty: toward a genealogy of liberal governance London: Routledge, 1991.

DeLeon, Peter. Thinking about political corruption, Armonk: M.E. Sharpe, 1993.

Desai, Meghnad and Paul Redfern, eds. Global governance: ethics and economics of the world order. London: Pinter, 1995.

Dia, Mamadou. A governance approach to civil service reform in Sub-Saharan Africa Washington, D.C.: The World Bank, 1993.

Docloux, Louis. From blackmail to treason: political crime and corruption in France, 1920-40. London: Andre Deutsch, 1958.

Dodd. Lawrence C. Coalitions in parliamentary government. New Jersey: Princeton University Press, 1976.

Dubey, Ajay, ed. Democratic governance: management practices in Indian cooperatives. Delhi: Kalinga, 1996.

Dubhashi, P.R. Administrative reforms in perspective. Trivandrum: Department of Publication, Univ. of Kerala, 1985.

Dwivedi, O.P. and Shri Ram Maheshwari. The public service in Canada and India. New Delhi: Jawahar, 1995.

Dwivedi, Onkar P., R.B. Jain and Dhirendra K. Vajpeyi, eds. Governing India: issues concerning public policy, institutions and administration. Delhi: B.R. Publishing, 1998.

Dwivedy, Surendranath and G.S. Bhargava. Political corruption in India. Delhi: Popular, 1967.

Echeverri-Gent, John. The State and the poor: public policy and political development in India and the United States. Oxford: Univ. of California Press. 1993.

Emery, Fred. Watergate: the corruption and fall of Richard Nixon. London: Pimlico, 1995.

Erappa, S. Dynamics of rural poverty in India. New Delhi: Discovery Pub., 1996.

Eswaran, Mukesh and Ashok Kotwal. Why poverty persists in India: a framework for understanding the Indian economy. New Delhi: Oxford Univ. Press, 1994.

Falk, Richard. On humane governance: toward a new global politics: the world order models project report of the global civilisation initiative. Cambridge: Polity Press, 1995.

Faundez, Julio, ed. Good government and law: legal and institutional reform in developing countries. London: Macmillan, 1997.

Frischtak, Leila L. Governance capacity and economic reform in Developing Countries. Washington, D.C.: The World Bank, 1994.

Furnivall, J.S. The Governance of modern Burma. New York: Institute of Public Relations, 1958.

Gadkari, S.S. Electoral reforms in India. New Delhi: Wheeler Pub., 1996.

Gary, Cheryl W. and Rebecca J. Hanson. Corporate Governance in Central and Eastern Europe. Washington, D.C.: The World Bank, 1993.

Geist, B. State audit: developments in public accountability. London: Macmillan, 1981.

Ghosh, Archana and S. Sami Ahmad. Plague in Surat: crisis in urban governance. New Delhi: Concept, 1996.

Gill, S.S. The pathology of corruption. New Delhi: Harper Collins, 1998.

Girling, John. Corruption, capitalism and democracy. London: Routledge, 1997.

Goodman, Walter. All honourable men: corruption and compromise in American life. London: Longmans, 1964.

Gopalaswami, R.A. Indian polity: a plea for reform. Bombay: Nachiketa, 1970.

Gruber, Jidith E. Controlling bureaucracies: dilemmas in democratic governance. Berkeley: University of California Press, 1987.

Guhan, S. and Samuel Paul, eds. Corruption in India: agenda for action. New Delhi: Vision Books, 1997.

Gupta, Deepak, Corporate social accountability: disclosures and practices. New Delhi: Mittal Pub., 1995.

Gupta, M.C. and R.K. Tiwari, eds. Restructuring government. New Delhi: Indian Institute of Public Administration, 1998.

Haggard, Stephan and Steven B. Webb, eds. Voting for reform: democracy, political liberalisation, and economic adjustment. Washington, D.C.: The World Bank, 1994.

Hamer, D.A. The politics of electoral pressure; a study in the history of Victorian reform agitations. Hassocks: Harvester Press, 1977.

Hanumantha Rao, C.H. and Hans Linnemann, eds. Economic reforms and poverty alleviation in India. New Delhi: Sage, 1996.

Heidenheimer, Arnold J. Political corruption: readings in comparative analysis. New York: Holt, 1970.

Held, David. Democracy and the global order: from the modern state to cosmopolitan governance. Cambridge: Polity Press, 1995.

Hempel, Lamont C. Environmental governance: the global challenge. Washington, D.C.: Island Press, 1996.

Heywood, Paul, ed. Political corruption. Oxford: Blackwell, 1997.

Hinckley, Barbara. Coalitions and politics. New York: Harcourt Brace, 1981.

Hirst, Paul. Associative democracy: new forms of economic and social governance. Cambridge: Polity Press, 1994.

Hirst, Paul and Grahame Thompson. Globalisation in question: the international economy and the possibilities of governance. Cambridge: Polity Press, 1996.

Hooja, Rakesh. District planning practice and theory with special reference to the 'how to aspects'. Jaipur: HCM State Institute of Public Administration, 1998.

Hooton, Cornell. Executive governance: presidential administrations and policy change in the federal bureaucracy. Armonk: M.E. Sharpe, 1997.

India. Administrative Reforms Commission. Report of the Study Team on machinery of the Government of India and its procedures of work. New Delhi: Administrative Reforms Commission, 1968 (Chairman: S.G. Barve).

India. Administrative Reforms Commission Study Team. Reports. New Delhi: The Commission, India. Cabinet Secretariat. Department of Personnel and Administrative Reforms. New perspectives for public administration in India. New Delhi: Training Division, 1975.

India. Committee on Electoral Reforms. Report of the Committee on Electoral Reforms. New Delhi: Legislative Department, Ministry of Law and Justice, 1990.

India. Committee on Prevention of Corruption. Report, Delhi: Controller of Publications, 1964 (Chairman K. Santhanam).

India. Committee on Reorganisation of the Machinery of Government. Report. New Delhi: Cabinet Secretariat, 1949 (Chairman: Gopalaswami N. Ayyangar).

India. Committee to Enquire into the Securities Transactions of the Banks and Financial Institutions. Interim report. Bombay: Reserve Bank of India, 1992-93.

India. Committee to Review and Rationalise Centrally Sponsored Schemes for Poverty Alleviation and Employment Generation. Report, New Delhi: Planning Commission, 1997 (Chairman: S.R. Hashim).

India. Committee to Take Stock of All Information about the Activities of Crime Syndicates/Mafia Organisations. Report. New Delhi: Ministry of Home Affairs, 1995 (Chairman: N.N. Vohra).

India. Department of Administrative Reforms. Report on the management of the Indian Administrative Service. New Delhi: The Department, 1968.

India. Department of Administrative Reforms and Public Grievances. Action plan for effective and responsive government. New Delhi: The Department, 1997.

India. Department of Personnel and Administrative Reforms. Colloquium series for higher levels in government. New Delhi: The Department, 1975.

India. Economic Administration Reforms Commission. Report on accountability. New Delhi: Department of Administrative Reforms and Public Grievances, 1986 (Chairman: L.K. Jha).

India. Expert Group on the Commercialisation of Infrastructure Projects. Infrastructure report: policy imperatives for growth and welfare. New Delhi: National Council of Applied Economic Research, 1996 (Chairman: Rakesh Mohan).

India. Lok Sabha Secretariat. Accountability in administration: report of the Sub-committee constituted by the conference of Chairman of Public Accounts Committee. New Delhi: The Secretariat, 1987.

India. Ministry of Finance. Central Pay Commission. Various reports. New Delhi: The Ministry, 1947-97.

India. Ministry of Home Affairs. Administrative changes for citizen satisfaction. New Delhi: The Ministry, 1977.

India. Ministry of Personnel, Public Grievances and Pension. An agenda for effective and responsive administration. New Delhi: The Ministry, 1966.

India. Ministry of Urban Development. Report of the task force on urban poverty alleviation in the eighth five year plan. New Delhi: The author, 1991.

India. Ministry of Urban Development. Report of the task force on urban poverty alleviation in the Eighth Five Year Plan. New Delhi: The Ministry, 1991.

Indian Institute of Public Administration. Bureaucracy in India: image and reality. New Delhi: The Institute, 1974.

Indian Institute of Public Administration, Maharashtra Regional Branch. Administrative problems of the next fifteen years. New Delhi: The Branch, 1988.

Indian Institute of Public Administration, New Delhi. Coalition government experience and prospects. New Delhi: IIPA, 1996.

Indian Institute of Public Administration, New Delhi. Conference on administrative reforms: Proceedings. New Delhi: IIPA, 1967.

Indian Institute of Public Administration, New Delhi. Electoral reforms. New Delhi: IIPA, 1994.

Indian Institute of Public Administration, New Delhi. Personnel administration: Implementing the reforms – report of the conference. New Delhi: IIPA, 1970.

Indian Institute of Public Administration, Rajasthan Branch. Administrative reforms in Rajasthan. Jaipur: IIPA, Rajasthan branch, 1981.

Indian Institute of Public Administration, New Delhi. Bureaucracy in India: Image and reality. New Delhi: Indian Institute of Public Administration, 1974.

International Labour Office. Joint Committee on the Public Service. Third Session. Geneva. 1983. The effects of structural changes and technological progress on employment in the public service. Geneva: ILO, 1983.

Irani, C.R., ed. Laloo in the dock: CBI's chargesheet in the fodder scam case. Calcutta: Statesman, 1997.

Ishwara Bhat, P. Administrative liability of the government and public servant. Delhi: Deep and Deep, 1983.

Jabbra, Joseph G. and O.P. Dwivedi, eds. Public service accountability: a comparative perspective. West Hartford: Kumarian Press, 1988.

Jayaraman, N., ed. Coalition government experience and prospects. Maharashtra: Indian Institute of Public Administration, 1997.

Jeejeebhoy, J.R.B. Bribery and corruption in Bombay. Bombay: The Author, 1952.

Jha, L.K. The role of bureaucracy in developing democracy. New Delhi: Training Division, Department of Personnel and Administrative Reforms, 1983.

Karunakaran, K.P., ed. Coalition government in India. Simla: Indian Institute of Advanced Study, 1975.

Kashyap, Subhash C. Coalition government and politics in India. New Delhi: Uppal, 1997.

Kashyap, Subhash C., ed. Crime and corruption to good governance. New Delhi: Uppal, 1997.

Kashyap, Subhash C., ed. Judicial activism and Lokpal. New Delhi: Uppal, 1997.

Kaushik, Asha Democratic concerns: the Indian experience. Jaipur: Alekh, 1994.

Kaushik, S.L. and Pardeep Sahni, eds. Public administration in India: emerging trends Allahabad: Kitab Mahal, 1983.

Khan, M. Adil. Economic development, poverty alleviation and governance: the Asian experience. Aldershot: Avebury, 1996.

Khan, Mohammad Mohabbat. Administrative reforms in Bangladesh. New Delhi: South Asian, 1998.

Khilnani, Sunil. The idea of India. London: Hamilton, 1997.

Khurana, N.K. Role of vigilance on Railways its effectiveness: a critical study of Northern Railway vigilance. New Delhi: Indian Institute of Public Administration, 1994.

Kickert, Walter J.M. Public management and administrative reform in Western Europe. Cheltenham: Edward Elgar, 1997.

Klitgaard, Robert. Controlling corruption. Berkeley: Univ. of California Press, 1988.

Koehler, Jerry W. and Joseph M. Pankowski. Quality government: designing, developing and implementing TQM. Florida: St. Lucie Press, 1996.

Kohli, Atul. Democracy and discontent India's growing crisis of Government Cambridge: Cambridge University Press, 1991.

Kohli, Suresh. Corruption in India. Delhi: Chetana Pub., 1975.

Kooiman, Jan, ed. Modern governance: new government-society interactions. London: Sage Pub., 1993.

Kothari, Rajni. State against democracy: in search of human governance. New Delhi: Ajanta, 1989.

Kothari, Shanti and Ramashray Roy. Relations between politicians and administrators at the district level: a study for the Administrative Reforms Commission. Government of India. Delhi: Indian Institute of Public Administration, 1981.

Kothari, Shanti. Relations between politicians and administrators at the district level: a study for the Administrative Reforms Commission, Government of India. New Delhi: Indian Institute of Public Administration, 1969.

Kotter, John P. and Paul R. Lawrence. Mayors in action: five approaches to urban governance. New York: John Wiley, 1974.

Kousar J. Azam, ed. Federalism and good governance: issues across cultures. New Delhi: South Asian, 1998.

Krueger, Anne O. Political economy of policy reform in developing countries. Cambridge: MIT Press, 1993.

Kshire. V. and V.G. Mandedkar, eds. Public administration in India. Jaipur: Rawat Publication, 1995.

Lahiri; Suprakas. Effectiveness of the Central Vigilance Commission. New Delhi: Indian Institute of Public Administration, 1994.

Lee, Hahn-Been and Abelardo G. Samonte, eds. Administrative reforms in Asia Manila: EROPA, 1970.

Leslie, Palmer. The control of bureaucratic corruption: case study in Asia. Delhi: Allied, 1985.

Levi, Michael and David Melken, eds. The corruption of politics and the politics of corruption. Oxford: Blackwell, 1996.

Lewis, John P. India's political economy: governance and reform. Delhi: Oxford Univ. Press, 1995.

Luebbert, Gregory M. Comparative democracy: policy making and governing coalitions in Europe and Israel. New York: Columbia Univ. Press, 1986.

Mackay, R.W.G. Coupon of free? Being a study in electoral reform and representative government. London. Secker & Warburg. 1943.

Maheshwari, Shri Ram. Administrative reform in India. New Delhi: Jawahar, 1993.

Maheshwari, Shri Ram, Administrative Reforms Commission. Agra: Lakshmi Narain Agarwal, 1972.

Maheshwari, Shri Ram. Administrative reforms in India. Delhi: Macmillan, 1981.

Maheshwari, Shri Ram. Indian administration. New Delhi: Orient Longman, 1974.

Maheshwari, Shri Ram. Indian administrative system. New Delhi: Jawahar, 1994.

Maheshwari, Shri Ram. Indian parliamentary system. Agra: Lakshmi Narain Agarwal, 1981.

Maheshwari, Shri Ram. Open government in India. New Delhi: Macmillan, 1981.

Maheshwari, Shri Ram. Problems and issues in administrative federalism. New Delhi: Allied, 1992.

Maheshwari, Shri Ram. Public administration in India: management of change Bangalore: Bangalore University. 1980.

Maheshwari, Shri Ram. Study of public administration in India. Agra: Lakshmi Narain Agarwal Educational Publishers, N.D.

Maheshwari, Shri Ram. The civil service in Great Britain. Delhi: Concept, 1976.

Maheshwari, Shri Ram. The higher civil service in Japan. Ahmedabad. Allied. 1987.

Maila. V.N. Efficiency in government. New Delhi: Indian Institute of Public Administration, 1995.

Malaysia. The civil service of Malaysia: towards excellence through ISO 9000. Kuala Lumpur: Government of Malaysia, 1996.

Mamadou Dia. A governance approach to civil service reform in Sub Saharan Africa. Washington, D.C.: The World Bank, 1993.

Mansukhani, H.C. Corruption and public servants. New Delhi: Vikas, 1979.

Mathur, A.P. Commentaries on the Prevention of Corruption Act, 1947, and the Criminal Law (Amendment) Act, 1952. Lucknow: Eastern Bk., 1963.

Mathur, Kuldeep. Development policy and administration. New Delhi: Sage, 1996.

Mathur, Kuldeep and J.W. Bjorkman. Top policy makers in India: cabinet ministers and their civil service advisors. New Delhi: Concept, 1994.

Mathur, P.C. and Hooja, Rakesh. Projects, planning and development: Jaipur: Rawat, 1996.

Mathur, P.N. The civil service of India (1731-1894): a study of the history, evolution and demand for reform in the service and the civil service question. Jodhpur: Prabahash Prakashan, N.D.

May, Peter J. et. al. Environmental management and governance; intergovernmental approaches to hazards and sustainability. London: Routledge, 1996.

Mehta, Jashwant B. Quest for a better democratic alternative. Bombay: Forum for Better Democratic Alternative, 1995.

Mishra, N.L. Responsive administration with specific reference to district administration. Jaipur: Amar Jyoti, 1989.

Mishra, Sweta. Changing pattern of district administrator. New Delhi: Mittal, 1996.

Mishra, Sweta. Democratic decentralisation in India: study in retrospect and prospect. New Delhi: Mittal, 1994.

Misra, B.B. The Bureaucracy in India: a historical analysis of development up to 1947. Delhi: Oxford Univ. Press, 1977.

Mitchell, Olivia. Public pension governance and performance: lessons for Developing Countries. Washington, D.C.: The World Bank, 1993.

Monteiro, John B. Corruption: control of maladministration. Bombay: Manaktalas, 1966.

Morrissey, Oliver and Frances Stewart, eds. Economic and political reform in Developing countries. New York: St. Martin's Press, 1995.

Motiwal, O.P., ed. Changing aspects of public administration in India. Allahabad: Chugh, 1976.

Murray, Charles. In pursuit of happiness and good government. New York: Simon and Schuster, 1988.

Nunberg, Barbara amd John Nellis. Civil service reform and the World Bank. Washington, D.C.: the World Bank, 1995.

Oliver, Dawn amd Gavin Drewry. Public Service reforms: issues of accountability and public law. New York: Pinter, 1996.

Osborne, David and Ted Gaebler. Reinventing government: how the entrepreneurial spirit is transforming the public sector. Reading: Addison-Wesley, 1992.

Oza, B.M. Bofors: the ambassador's evidence. Delhi: Konark, 1997.

Ozgediz, Selcuk. Governance and management of the CGIAR centers. Washington, D.C.: The World Bank, 1991.

Page, W., ed. The future of politics: governance, movements and world order. London: Frances Pinter, 1983.

Pai Panandiker, V.A. and Ajay K. Mehra. The Indian cabinet: a study in governance. New Delhi: Konark, 1996.

Palanithurai, G. ed. Empowering people: issues and solutions. New Delhi: Kanishka, 1996.

Palmier, Leslie. The coontrol of bureaucratic corruption: case study in Asia. Delhi: Allied, 1985.

Pannier, Domnique, ed. Corporate governance of public enterprises in transitional economies. Washington, D.C.: The World Bank, 1996.

Papola, T.S. Anti-poverty and special employment programmes in India: their role and effectiveness under the structural adjustment programme. Washington, D.C.: World Bank, 1993.

Paranjape, H.K. The Reorganised Planning Commission: A study in the implementation of administrative reforms. New Delhi: Indian Institute of Public Administration, 1970.

Paranjpe, Nalini. Administrative reforms in India. New Delhi: Uppal, 1997.

Parekh, M.P., ed. Administrative issues. Ahmedabad: Sardar Patel Institute of Public Administration, 1989.

Paul, Guhan Samuel, ed. Corruption in India: agenda for action. New Delhi: Vision, 1997.

Paul, Samuel. Accountability in public services: exit, voice and capture. Washington, D.C.: The World Bank, 1991.

Paul Samuel. Strengthening public service accountability: a conceptual framework Washington, D.C.: IBRD, 1991.

Pavarale, Vinod Interpreting corruption: elite perspective in India. New Delhi: Sage, 1996.

Picciotto, Robert. Putting institutional economics to work: from participation to governance. Washington, D.C.: The World Bank, 1995.

Prasad, A.D. Corruption and administration. Patna: Basant Pub., 1971.

Ramachandran, K.S. Scanning the scam: how and why of the securities scandal. New Delhi: NEO. 1993.

Ramachandran, Padma. Public administration in India. New Delhi: National Book 1996.

Ramakrishna, P.V.A treatise on anti-corruption laws in India: with exhaustive commentaries on the prevention of corruption act, 1988. Hyderabad: S. Gogia, 1995.

Rao G.R.S., ed. Accountability of public institutions: emerging issues in the Indian context. Hyderabad: Rajaji International Institute of Public Affairs and Administration, 1991.

Rao, M. Sankara. Public administration and management with special reference to India. New Delhi: Deep and Deep, 1991.

Ravi Prakash. Constitution, fundamental rights and judicial activism in India. Jaipur: Mangal Deep Pub., 1997.

Repetto, Robert. Second India revisited: population, poverty, and environmental stress over two decades. Washington, D.C.: World Resources Institute, 1994.

Rhodes, Gerald. Inspectorates in British government: law enforcement and standards of efficiency. London: Allen & Unwin. 1981.

Rhodes, Raw. Understanding governance: policy networks. Open University Press, 1997.

Rieselback, L.N., ed. Legislative reform: the policy impact. Lexington: Lexington Books; 1978.

Root, Hilton L. Small countries, big lessons: governance and the rise of East Asia Hong Kong: Oxford Univ. Press, 1996.

Rose, Richard, ed. Challenge to governance: studies in overloaded politics. Beverly Hills: Sage, 1980.

Rose-Ackerman, Susan. Corruption: a study in political economy. New York: Academic Press, 1978.

Roulier, Richard P. Bank governance contracts: establishing goals and accountability in bank restructuring. Washington, D.C.: The World Bank, 1995.

Rowat, Malcolm, Waleed H. Malik and Maria Dakolias, eds. Judicial reform in Latin America and the Caribbean. Washington, D.C.: The World Bank, 1995.

Sahai, Shashi B. Politics of corruption: the goddess that failed. New Delhi: Gyan Pub. House, 1995.

Sapru, R.K. Civil service administration in India. Delhi: Deep & Deep, 1985.

Sathe, V. National government: agenda for a new India Delhi: UBS, 1991.

Saxena, Pradeep K. Modern governance. Jaipur: RBSA Publishers, 1995.

Scott, James C. Comparative political corruption. N.J.: Prentice-Hall, 1972.

Searle, G.R. Corruption in British politics. 1895-1930. Oxford: Clarendon Press, 1987.

Self, Peter. Political theories of modern government, its role and reform. London: George Allen and Unwin, 1985.

Sen Gupta, Bhabani. India: problems of governance, Delhi: Konark, 1996.

Shah, Tushaar. Making farmers' co-operatives work: design, governance and management. New'Delhi: Sage, 1995.

Shakdher, S.L. Electoral reforms for India. Delhi: Voters' Council and Citizens for Democracy, 1980.

Sharma, Arvind K. Mizoram: a study of some aspects of the state's governance. New Delhi: Indian Institute of Public Administration, 1997.

Sharma, B.R. Constitutional law and judicial activism. Delhi: Ashish, 1990.

Sharma, Raju. Foundations of the principle of transparency in government. New Delhi: Indian Institute of Public Administration, 1998.

Sherman, Lawrence W. Scandal and reform: controlling police corruption. Berkeley, Calif.: University of California Press. 1978.

Shome, Parthasarathi, ed. Fiscal policy, public policy and governance. New Delhi: Centax, 1996.

Shore, Cris and Susan Wright, eds. Anthropology of policy; critical perspectives on governance and power. London: Routledge, 1997.

Shourie, H.D. Citizens' charters to promote accountability. Times of India, 10 April, 1998.

Simpson, Antony E. The literature of police corruption. New York: John Jay Press, 1977.

Singh, L.P. Electoral reform: problems and suggested solutions. New Delhi: Uppal, 1986.

Singh, Naunihal. A system of governance: parliamentary or presidential. New Delhi: Anmol, 1998.

Singh, S.S. and Mishra, S. Legislative framework of Panchayati Raj in India. New Delhi: Intellectual, 1993.

Sinha, Ajit Kumar, ed. New economic policy of India: restructuring and liberalising the economy for 21st Century. New Delhi: Deep and Deep, 1994.

Sinha, V.M. The superior civil services in India: a study in administrative development: 1947-57. Jaipur: The Institute for Research and advanced Studies, 1985.

Sivaraman, B. Bitter sweet: governance of India in transition. New Delhi: Ashish, 1991.

Smith-Sreen, Poonam. Accountability in development organisation: experiences of women's organisations in India. New Delhi: Sage, 1995.

Stacey, Frank, British government 1966 to 1975: years of reform. London: Oxford University Press. 1975.

Strategic Management Group. Report on governance and government: emerging scenarios in the 21st Century. New Delhi: Strategic Management Group, 1995.

Subramaniam, Chitra. BOFORS: the story behind the news. New Delhi: Viking, 1993.

Thakur, Upendra. Corruption in ancient India. Delhi: Abhinav, 1979.

Thomas, Graham P. Government and the economy today. New York: Manchester University Press, 1992.

Torstendahl, Roli. Bureaucratisation in north-western Europe, 1880-1985: domination and governance. London: Routledge, 1991.

Tummala, K.K. The ambiguity of ideology and administrative reform. Delhi: Allied Pub., 1979.

Tummala, Krishna K. Public administration in India Delhi: Allied, 1996.

Turner, Mark and David Hulme. Governance, administration and development: making the state work. London: Macmillan Press, 1997.

UK Commonwealth Office. Raising the Standards Britain's citizen's charter and public service reform. London: Citizen's Charter Unit, 1992.

UK Efficiency Unit. Consultancy, inspection and review services in government departments: report to the Prime Minister by Kate Jenkins, Brion Morris, Charlotte Caplan, Less Metcalfe. London: HMSO, 1984.

UK Efficiency Unit. Improving management in government: the next steps: Report to the Prime Minister, by Kote Jenkins, Karen Kaines and Andrew Jockson. London: HMSO, 1988.

UK Efficiency Unit. Making things happen: a report on the implementation of government efficiency scrutinies, by Kate Jenkins, Graham Oates and Andrew Stott. London: HMSO, 1985.

Udai, N. Parliamentary control of public administration in India. Allahabad: Chugh, 1981.

United Nations. Handbook on the improvement of administrative management in public administration. New York: United Nations, 1979.

United Nations Development Programme. Bureau for Policy and Programme Support. Management Development and Governance Division. Public sector management, governance, and sustainable human development. New York: United Nations Development Programme. Division of Public Affairs, 1995.

Venkatachalam, D. Bureaucracy: an evaluation and a scheme of accountability. New Delhi: APH Publishing, 1998.

Verghese, B.G. India's Northeast resurgent: ethnicity, insurgency, governance, development. Delhi: Konark, 1996.

Visvanathan, Shiv and Harsh Sethi, ed. Foul play: chronicles of corruption 1947-97. New Delhi: a seminar. New Delhi: Business India Publication, 1998.

Wadhwani, M. and R.K. Tiwari, eds. Indian administration the changing scenario: presidential addresses at the IIPA 1954-1994. New Delhi: Indian Institute of Public Administration, 1995.

Wannop, Urlan. The regional imperative: regional planning and governance in Britain, Europe and the United States. London: Jessica Kingsley, 1995.

Ward, Peter M., ed. Corruption, development and inequility: soft touch or hard graft. London: Routledge, 1989.

Welch, Susan and John G. Peters, ed. Legislative reform and public policy. N.Y.: Praeger, 1977.

Williamson, Oliver E. The mechanisms of governance. New York: Oxford Univ. Press, 1996.

Williamson, John, ed. The political economy of policy reform.

Washington, D.C.: Institute for International Economics, 1994.

Wilson, Harold. The governance of Britain. London: Weidenfeld and Nicolson, 1976.

Woodiwiss, Michael. Crime, crusades and corruption: prohibitions in the United States, 1900-1987. London: Pinter, 1988.

Xiaonian Xu and Yan Wang. Ownership structure, corporate governance, and corporate performance: the case of Chinese stock companies. Washington, D.C.: World Bank, 1997.

Yates, Douglas Bureaucratic democracy: the search for democracy and efficiency in American Government Cambridge, Mass.: Harvard Univ. Press, 1982.

Young, Oran R. Global governance: drawing insights from the environmental experience. Cambridge: MIT Press, 1997.

Articles

Adrian, Leftwich. Governance, the state and the politics of development. *Development and Change*. 25; 1994. pp. 363-86.

Agarwal, U.C. Case for a national level ombudsman. *Indian Journal of Public Administration* 34(2) April-June 1988. pp. 249-65.

Agarwal. U.C. Administrative reforms: no panacea for good governance. *Politics India 3 (2)* August 1998. pp. 4-7.

Agarwal. U.C. Galloping corruption: need for effective vigilance. *Indian Journal of Public Administration.* 43(3) July-September 1997. pp. 434-40.

Appu, P.S. Decline of Indian bureaucracy. *Mainstream.* 24(43) 28 June 1986. pp. 27-30.

Arora, Satish K. Political policy and the future of bureaucracy. *Indian Journal of Public Administration.* 17(3) July-September 1971. pp. 354-5.

Asmerom, H.K., K. Borgman and R. Hoppe. Good governance, decentralisation and democratisation in post-colonial states.: a comparative study of Ghana, Indonesia and Surinam. *Indian Journal of Public Administration.* 41(4) October-December 1995. pp. 735-81.

Atory, Hussain Ahmad. Administrative reforms in Malaysia.: strategies for promoting efficiency and productivity in the public service, 1981-91. *Indian Journal of Public Administration.* 41(1) January-March 1995. pp. 78-91.

Awasthi. R.K. Evolution and development of urban society and municipal governance in India. *Man in India.* 64(3) September 1984. pp. 263-79.

Bag, R.K. Judicial activism vis-a-vis public administration. *Administrator.* 42 (2) April-June 1997. pp. 167-77.

Bakshi, P.M. Judicial activism: some reflections. *Administrator.* 42(2) April-June 1997. pp. 5-8.

Balakrishnan, Suresh and K. Gopakumar. Initiatives of responsive administration. *Management in Government.* 29(2) July-September 1997. pp. 65-91.

Baldassare, Mark. Regional variations in support for regional governance. *Urban Affairs Quarterly.* 30(2) December 1994. pp. 275-84.

Bandyopadhyay, D. Administration, decentralisation and good governance. *Economic and Political Weekly.* 31(48) 30 November 1996. pp. 3109-114.

Barnes, Peter. Lessons of reform in the Ontario civil service. *Public Administration and Development*. 17(1) February 1997. pp. 27-32.

Basu, Ashok Ranjan. Improving public service delivery systems for tribal population in India.: An empirical investigation. *Prashasnika*. 14(1) January-March 1985. pp. 1-15.

Batra, J.C. Electoral reforms—role of the Election Commission. *Journal of Constitutional and Parliamentary Studies*. 28(3-4) July-December 1994. pp. 381-84.

Bava, Noorjahan. Changing role of bureaucracy in India. *Indian Journal of Public Administration*. 31(2) April-June 1985. pp. 275-94.

Been, Lee Hahn. Two critical combinations for successful administrative reform. *Prashasan*. 15(2) March 1984. pp. 131-138.

Benninger, Christopher C. Urban governance in Asia.: conference report. *Cities* 12(3) June 1995. p. 213.

Bhambhri, C.P. Legitimacy and accountability of state systems.: new challenges *Indian Journal of Public Administration*. 41(3) July-September 1995. pp. 320-30.

Bhambhri, C.P. The administrative elite and political modernisation in India. *Indian Journal of Public Administration*. 17(1) January-March 1971. pp. 47-64.

Bhat, N.B. Legal and judicial reforms for improved police effectiveness. *CBI Bulletin* 24(2) February 1990. pp. 3-6.

Bhattacharjee, G.R. Judicial activism: its message for administrators. *Administrator*. 42(2) April-June 1997. pp. 31-42.

Bhattacharya, Mohit, Rolling back the state.: public administration in the age of market supremacy. *Indian Journal of Public Administration*. 42(3) July-September 1996. pp. 245-57.

Bhattacharyya, R. Judicial activism: the motive force of public administration. *Administrator*. 42(2) April-June 1997. pp. 69-79.

Blunt, Peter, Cultural relativism, 'good' governance and sustainable human development. *Public Administration and Development*. 15(1) February 1995. pp. 1-9.

Bollens, Scott A. Fragments of regionalism: the limits of Southern California governance. *Journal of Urban Affairs*. 19(1) 1997. pp. 105-22.

Bolongaita, Emil P., Jr. Total Quality Governance (TQM): the citizen as customer. *Regional Development Dialogue*. 18(2) Autumn 1997. pp. 155-66.

Bouke, Tim Irish Public Service reform: a review of current development. *Parliamentary Affairs*. 49(3) July 1995. pp. 485-94.

Burns John P. Administrative reform in China: issues and prospects. *International Journal of Public Administration*. 16(9) September 1993. pp. 1345-369.

Caiden, Gerald E. Institutionalising administrative reform. *Management in Government*. 23(4) January-March 1992. pp. 283-304.

Caiden, Gerald E. The Vitality of administrative reform. *International Review of Administrative Sciences*. 54(3) September 1988. pp. 331-58.

Caiden, Gerald E. and Naomi J. Caiden. More on official misconduct. *Indian Journal of Public Administration*. 41(3) July-September 1995. pp. 370-82.

Callender, Guy and July Johnston. The Australian way of government and public sector commercial reform: from a lucky to a clever country? *Public Administration and Development*. 17(1) February 1997. pp. 55-70.

Chakravarthy, N.S. Management and administration in India: impact of vigilance machinery. *Indian Journal of Public Administration*. 36(4) October-December 1990. pp. 845-68.

Chakravartty, Nikhil. Judicial activism, right or wrong. *Mainstream*. 35(16) 29 March 1997. pp. 3-4.

Chan, Hon S. Agency problem and bureaucratic governance in the People's Republic of China. *International Journal of Public Administration*. 17(9) August 1994. pp. 1631-662.

Chan, Hon S. Scientizing public administration or public administration in search for quality governance. *International Journal of Public Administration*. 19(2) February 1996. pp. 261-89.

Chandrasekaran, K.A. What makes the best late 20th century public official. *Indian Journal of Public Administration*. 43(2) April-June 1997. pp. 153-72.

Chatterji, Susanta. For public administration: is judicial activism really deterrent to legislative anarchy and executive tyranny. *Administrator*. 42(2) April-June 1997. pp. 9-24.

Chaturvedi, M.K. Commitment in civil service. *Indian Journal of Public Administration*. 17(1) January-March 1971. pp. 40-46.

Chaturvedi, T.N. Parliamentary control over public expenditure: role of the office of the Comptroller and Auditor General. *Journal of Parliamentary Information*. 36(3) September 1990. pp. 290-9.

Chiang. Min-Chin. The concept of efficiency in public administration. *Chinese Public Administration Review*. 1(1) December 1991. pp. 23-51.

Ching-Hyun Ro. Social change and administrative reforms towards the year 2000. *International Review of Administrative Science*. 50(3) 1984. pp. 252-2.

Choudhry, M.A. and Hameed Akhtar Niazi Reforms in people management in Pakistan. *Asian Review of Public Administration*. 8(1) January-June 1996. pp. 65-87.

Chowdhury, M.M. Social background and bureaucratic performance. *Indian Journal of Public Administration*. 29(4) October-December 1983. pp. 865-64.

Chung-Hyun Ro. Reforms to improve performance: Korea's experience. *Asian Review of Public Administration*. 7 (2) July-September 1995. pp. 22-27.

Chung-Hyun Ro. The keynote address on social change and administrative reform in Asia towards the year 2000, *Prashasan*. 15(2) March 1984. pp. 16-22.

Cohn, Daniel. Creating crises and avoiding blame: the politics of public service reform and the new public management in Great Britain and the United States. *Administration and Society*. 29(5) November 1997. pp. 584-616.

Collins, Paul D. and Mullen, Joseph. Training administrators for improved service delivery to small farmers: experiences from Somalia. *International Journal of Public Administration*. 15(8) Summer 1992. pp. 1538-78.

Considine, Mark. Administrative reform 'down-under' recent public sector change in Australia and New Zealand. *International Review of Administrative Sciences*. 56(1) March 1990. pp. 171-84.

Dandavate, Madhu. Global governance. *Mainstream*. 34(40) 7 September 1996. pp. 7-10.

Datta, Abhijit. Institutional aspects of urban governance in India. *Indian Journal of Public Administration*. 40(4) October-December 1994. pp. 616-32.

Datta, Abhijit. Search for autonomy and accountability in civic administration. *Nagarlok*. 22(3) July-September 1990. pp. 23-9.

Datta, Prabhat Kumar. Public administration—old issue and new challenges. *Indian Journal of Political Science*. 48(1) January-March 1987. pp. 42-59.

Dauda, Bola. Global context of the Nigerian public service reform since 1945. *Chinese Public Administration Review*. 5(3) June 1996.

Davies Morton R. Governmental and administrative responsiveness in Britain: Channels of communication and information between politicians and administrators. *Indian Journal of Public Administration*. 33(2) April-June 1987. pp. 199-209.

Davis, Charles R. Gulick's efficiency: the administrative management view. *International Journal of Public Administration*. 13 (4) 1990.

Dey, Bata K. Career management in government. *Indian Journal of Public Administration*. 43(3) July-September 1997. pp. 579-95.

Dey, Bata K. What ails administration: A minimum programme in reforms *Management in Government*. 20(2) July-September 1988. pp. 143-51.

Dharmadhikari, Vinay. Elections and governance: A systems-engineered design. *Politics India*. 2(4) October 1997. pp. 25-29.

Digaetano, Alan. Urban governance in the Gilded Age: An examination of political-culture, social-control and fiscal-ideology theories. *Urban Affairs Quarterly*. 30(2) December 1994. pp. 187-209.

Dixit, Manoj. Responsive administration in India. *Journal of the Institute of Public Administration*. 6 (1-4) April 1990-March 1991. pp. 43-58.

Downs, Charles. Regionalisation, administrative reform and democratisation: Nicaragua 1979-1984. *Public Administration and Development*. 7(4) October-December 1987. pp. 363-81.

Dubhashi, P.R. Administrative reforms: Lessons from experiences abroad. *Indian Journal of Public Administration*. 29(2) April-June 1983. pp. 276-83.

Dubhashi, P.R. Administrative reforms: The current context. *Administrative Change.* 12(2) January-June 1985. pp. 174-81.

Dubhashi, P.R. Indian public administration. *Indian and Foreign Review.* 21(16) 15 June 1984. pp. 20-21.

Dubhashi, P.R. Restructuring and reform of Indian political, administrative and economic system. *Indian Journal of Public Administration.* 43(3) July-September 1997. pp. 362-68.

Dubhashi. P.R. Trends in public administration: South Asia. *Prashasan.* 17(2) March 1986. pp. 27-34.

Dubois, Marc. The governance of the Third World: A Foucauldian perspective on power relations in development. *Alternatives.* 16(1) Winter 1991. pp. 1-30.

Dunsire, Andrew. Tipping the balance: Autopoiesis and governance. *Administration and Society.* 28(3) November 1996. pp. 299-334.

Dwivedi, O.P. Administrative theology.: Dharma of public officials. *Indian Journal of Public Administration.* 36(3) July-September 1990. pp. 406-19.

Dwivedi, O.P. Ethics and values of public responsibility and accountability. *International Review of Administrative Sciences.* 51(10) 1985. pp. 61-6.

Elliott, James. Advisory commissions and administrative reform The Western model in Japan. *Philippine Journal of Public Administration.* 28 (1&2) January-April 1984. pp. 111-20.

Engineer, Asghar Ali. Globalisation, democracy and threat to diversity. *Mainstream.* 35(47) 1 November 1997. pp. 9-14.

Eswara Reddi, Agarala. Coalition government: effective and workable. *Politics India* 1(10) April 1997. pp. 26-27.

Eswara Reddi, Agarala. Towards responsive and responsible administration: revamping civil services. *Politics India.* 2 (2) August 1997. pp. 22-23.

Faber, Mike, Governance and the foreign direct investor. *IDS Bulletin.* 24(1) January 1993. pp. 51-57.

Fadia, B.L. Reforming the Election Commission. *Indian Journal of Political Science.* 53(1) January-March 1992. pp. 78-88.

Fajonyomi, S. Banji. Taming the mandarin: some reflections on the looming administrative reforms in Japan. *Indian Journal of Public Administration*. 43(4) October-December 1997. pp. 891-903.

Fischer, Frank. Ethical discourse in public administration. *Administration and Society*. 15(1) May 1983. pp. 5-42.

Fox, Jonathan. Governance and rural development in Mexico.: state intervention and public accountability. *Journal of Development Studies*. 32(1) October 1995. pp. 1-30.

Gagne, R.L. Accountability and public administration. *Canadian Public Administration*. 39(2) Summer 1996. pp. 213-25.

Garcia-Zamor C.H. and I. Mayo-Smith. Administrative reform in Haiti.: Problems, progress and prospects. *Public Administration and Development*. 3(1) January-March 1983. pp. 39-48.

Gargan, John J. Reinventing government and reformulating public administration. *International Journal of Public Administration*. 20(1) January 1997. pp. 221-47.

Gathon H.J. and Pestieau P. The implications of European Union for the performance of public enterprises. *Administration (Ireland)*. 41(2) Summer 1993. pp. 149-65.

Geng Xiao. Reforming the governance structure of China's state-owned enterprises. *Public Administration and Development*. 18(3) August 1998. pp. 273-80.

Georgiou, George A. The responsiveness of the Greece administration system to European prospects. *International Review of Administrative Sciences*. 60(1) March 1994. pp. 131-44.

Ghosh, Arun. Governance, institution-building and economic development. *Economic and Political Weekly*. 31 (24) 15 June 1996. pp. 1432-433.

Godbole, Madhav. Bureaucracy at a cross roads. *Indian Journal of Public Administration*. 43(3) July-September 1997. pp. 560-66.

Guha Roy, Jaytilak. Using liberalisation for efficient and effective administration of justice. *Indian Journal of Public Administration*. 40(3) July-September 1994. pp. 351-56.

Guhan, S. World Bank on governance: a critique. *Economic and Political Weekly*. 33(4) 24 January 1998. pp. 185-90.

Gupta, V.P. Politicised bureaucracy in India and the recommendations of Sarkaria Commission. *Indian Journal of Political Science*. 51(1) January-March 1990. pp. 75-83.

Halachmi, Arie. Civil service and accountability: Reflections on the U.S. experience. *Management in Government*. 18(3) October-December 1986. pp. 303-14.

Hamid, Ahmed Sarji Bin Abdul. Accountability in the public service. *Asian Review of Public Administration*. 3(2) July-December 1991. pp. 106-09.

Hays, Steven W. and Richard C. Kearney. Riding the crest of a wave: the national performance review and public management reform. *International Journal of Public Administration*. 20(1) January 1997. pp. 11-40.

Hazan, Reuven Y. Executive legislative relations in an era of accelerated reform: reshaping government in Israel. *Legislative Studies Quarterly*. 22(3) August 1997. pp. 329-50.

Holmes, John W. The office of the Auditor General and public service reform: an insiders perspective. *Canadian Public Administration*. 39(4) Winter 1996. pp. 524-34.

Howell, Robert, Philip McDermott and Vicki Forgie. Local government governance and management in New Zealand. *Public Sector*. 19(1) March 1996. pp. 17-21.

Hummel, Ralph P. Towards a new administrative doctrine: governance and management for the 1990's. *American Review of Public Administration*. 19(3) September 1989. pp. 175-96.

Ives, Denis. People management reform in the Australian public service. *Asian Review of Public Administration*. 8(1) January-June 1996. pp. 28-39.

Jain, L.C. Electoral reforms: money power and state funding. *Mainstream*. 34 (18) 6 April 1996. pp. 13-14.

Jain. R.B. The state of the study of comparative public administration in India. *Indian Journal of Public Administration*. 37(1) January-March 1991. pp. 17-33.

Jain, Satish Chandra. Re-structuring of police administration in India for the 21st century. *Administrator*. 36(4) October-December 1991. pp. 19-36.

Jayakumar, N.K. Limits of judicial activism vis-a-vis administrative discretion.: A preliminary inquiry. *Journal of the Indian Law Institute* . 26(1&2) January-June 1984. pp. 55-69.

Jayal, Niraja Gopal. The governance agenda: making democratic development dispensable. *Economic and Political Weekly*. 32(8) 22-28 February 1997. pp. 407-12.

Jiang Xianrong. An overview of the reform of China's administrative system and organisations and its prospects. *International Review of Administrative Sciences* 63(2) June 1997. pp. 251-56.

Jogendra Prasad. Office machines and management efficiency. *Administrative Management*. January-March 1983. pp. 1-5.

Joshi, Gopal. Administrative reforms in Nepal past efforts and future agenda. *Prashasan*. 23(2) march 1992. pp. 1-14.

Jreisat, Jakil E. Administrative reform in developing countries.: A comparative perspective *Administration and Development*. 8(1) January-March 1988. pp. 85-97.

Kamala Prasad. India's leadership and governance. *Mainstream*. 34(42) 21 September 1996. pp. 7-13.

Kambhu, Thongsri. Thai administrative structure and reform: Problem with decentralisation. *Philippine Journal of Public Administration*. 28(1&2) January-April 1984. pp. 65-96.

Karan, Anup K. District planning: administrative reforms. *Journal of Social and Economic Studies, New Series*. (2) 1989. pp. 327-37.

Kashyap, Subhash C. Urgent need for electoral reforms. *Monthly Public Opinion Surveys*. 37(10) July 1992. pp. 21.

Kashyap, Subhash C. The Lokpal Bhill. *Politics India*. 1(11) May 1997. pp. 8-10.

Keraudren, Philippe. Administrative reform, ethics and openness: the balance between effectiveness and administrative identity. *International Review of Administrative Sciences*. 61(1) March 1995.

Kernaghan, Kenneth. Evolving patterns of administrative responsiveness to the public. *Management in Government*. 18(3) October-December 1986. pp. 291-302.

Khanna, H.R. Judicial activism: courts as trustees of the constitution. *Politics India*. 1(10) April 1997. p-7-8.

Khanna, R.S. Making administration more efficient. *Manisha*. e(4) October-December 1990. pp. 7-11.

Knox, Colin. The European model of service delivery: a partnership approach in Northern Ireland. *Public Administration and Development*. 18(2) May 1998. pp. 151-68.

Kothari, Rajni. On human governance. *Alternatives*. 11(3) July 1987.

Kothari, Rajni. Public Administration and democratic upsurge. *Indian Journal of Public administration*. 43(3) July-September 1997. pp. 289-92.

Krishna Iyer, V.R. Judicial activism and administrative autonomy. *Administrator*. 42(2) April-June 1997. pp. 1-4.

Lam Tao-Chiu and Hon S. Chan. Reforming China's cadre management system: two views of a civil service. *Asian Survey*. 36(8) August 1996. pp. 772-86.

Landry, Rejean. Administrative reform and political control in Canada. *International Political Science Review*. 14(1) October 1993. pp. 335-49.

Larmour, Peter. Models of governance and public administration. *International Review of Administrative Sciences*. 63(3) September 1997. pp. 383-94.

Lewis, Norman. The citizen's charter and next steps.: a way of governing? *Political Quarterly*. 64(3) July-September 1993. pp. 316-26.

Lindquist, Evert A. Recent administrative reform in Canada as decentralisation: who is spreading what around to whom and why. *Canadian Public Administration*. 37(3) Fall 1994. pp. 416-30.

Littlewood, Stephen and Aidan While. A new agenda for governance? agenda 21 and the prospects for holistic local decision-making. *Local Government Studies*. 23(4) Winter 1997. pp. 111-23.

Liu Yichang. Reform and open to the outside world to meet the challenges on public administration in the 1990's. *Prashasan*. 21(3) July 1990. pp. 43-55.

Madan, Shirin. Introducing administrative reform through the application of computer based information systems: a case study in India. *Public Administration and Development*. 13(1) February 1993. pp. 37-48.

Madhava Menon, N.R. Can judicial activism contribute to a responsive and responsible administration? *Administrator*. 42(2) April-June 1997. pp. 25-30.

Maheshwari, Shriram. Ethics for civil service in India. *Indian Journal of Public Administration*. 41(3) July-September 1995 pp. 492-505.

Maheshwari, Sriram. Public policy making in India. *Indian Journal of Political Science*. 48(3) July-September 1987. pp. 336-53.

Malhotra, D.D. Local government institutions in India: recent developments and dimensions of reforms. *Administrative Change*. 23(1&2) July 1995-June 1996. pp. 70-95.

Malhotra, G.C. Democratic governance of Delhi. *Journal of Constitutional and Parliamentary Studies*. 2(1-4) January-December 1990. pp. 106-28.

Marini, Frank and Kyung Deuk Kwon. Some ethical implications of representative bureaucracy. *Indian Journal of Public Administration*. 41(3) July-September 1995. pp. 486-91.

Marwah. Ved. Need for police reforms. *Politics India*. 3(1) July 1998. pp. 25-27.

Maslen, A.T.J. The politics of administrative reform.: The special review of Lambeth Borough Council. *Local Government Studies*. 9(3) May-June 1983. pp. 45-65.

Mathur, P.C. Integrative capabilities of the Indian administrative system. *Gandhi Marg*. 4(12) March 1983. pp. 996-1000.

Mehrotra, V.K. India's governance an agenda for change. *Politics India*. 11(7) January 1998. pp. 46-48.

Milkis, Sidney M. The new deal, administrative reform, and the transcendence of Pakistan politics. *Administration and Society*. 18(4) February 1987. pp. 433-72.

Minocha, O.P. Good governance: concept and operational issues. *Management in Government*. 29(3) October-December 197. pp. 1-9.

Mishra, S.N. Basic minimum services and people's participation. *Kurukshetra*. 45(1-2) October-November 1996. pp. 29-33.

Misra, C. Tshering. Administrative reform. *Nirnay*. 1(1) June 1984. pp. 39-43.

Mitra, Ashoke. Reorganisation of judicial administration in India. *Indian Journal of Public Administration*. 40(4) October-December 1994. pp. 633-42.

Mohammad Mohabbat Khan. Politics of administrative reform and reorganisation in Bangladesh. *Public Administration and Development*. 7(4) October-December 1987. pp. 351-62.

Mohammad Mohabbat Khan. Urban local governance in Bangladesh: an overview. *Nagarlok*. 38(3) July-September 1996. pp. 22-40.

Mohanan, B. Sustainable development, good governance and gram swaraj. *ISDA Journal*. 7(2-3) April-September 1997. pp. 121-28.

Mohanty, Amarendra and Narayan Hazary. Evolution of prison administration and reform in India.: The Orissa scene. *Indian Journal of Public Administration*. 31(4) October-December 1985. pp. 1331-42.

Mohanty, Manoranjan. The city and the citizen: people's participation and structure of urban governance in India and China. *Nagarlok*. 30(2) April-June 1998. pp. 26-38.

Mohanty, Prasanna K. Municipal decentralisation and governance: autonomy, accountability and participation. *Indian Journal of Public Administration*. 41(1) January-March 1995. pp. 11-30.

Moore, Mick. Declining to learn from the East: the World Bank on governance and development. *IDS Bulletin*. 24(1) 1993. p. 39.

Mooshahary, Ranjit S. Towards more efficient all India services. *Administrator*. 28(3&4) Autumn-Winter 1983. pp. 339-44.

Mountfied, Robin. Organisational reform within government: accountability and policy management. *Public Administration and Development*. 17(1) February 1997. pp. 71-76.

Mukarji, Nirmal. Democratic decentralisation and system of governance. *Mainstream*. 27(33) 13 May 1989. pp. 5-8,10.

Mukarji, Nirmal. Changeful society and changeless governance. *Economic and Political Weekly*. 24(28) 15 July 1989. pp. 1577-81.

Mukarji, Nirmal. Restructuring district administration. *Mainstream* 24(3) 21 September 1985. pp. 11-13.

Mukherjee, Neela. Delivering basic minimum services through people's participation. *Kurukshetra*. 45(1-2) October-November 1996. pp. 38-41.

Mukhopadhyay, Asok. Politics and bureaucracy in urban governance.: the Indian experience. *Indian Journal of Public Administration*. 42(1) January-March 1996. pp. 32-47.

Mukhopadhyay, Asok. Ethics in governance.: the Indian perspective. *Indian Journal of public Administration.* 41(3) July-September 1995. pp. 395-401.

Mukhopadhyay, Asok. Public administration in India.: immediate reform agenda. *Indian Journal of Public Administration.* 40(3) July-September 1994. pp. 467-78.

Mukwena, Royson M. Zambian civil service structure, training programmes and transnational inducement of administrative reforms. *Indian Journal of Public Administration.* 38(2) April-June 1992. pp. 187-95.

Muslehuddin Ahmed. Administrative reform/reorganisation in Bangladesh (1971-1995): politics, change and consequences. *Administrative Change.* 24(1) July-December 1996. pp. 59-73.

Nafees Ahmad. Constitution and judicial activism. *Politics India.* 1(10) April 1997. p. 25.

Nageswara Rao, V. Judicial activism and administrative authorities in India in retrospect and prospect. *Administrator.* 42(2) April-June 1997. pp. 145-52.

Naidu, W.G. Responsive administration.: Attitudes and styles of Deputy Collectors. *Manisha.* 1(2) July-September 1989. pp. 13-14.

Nakamura, Akira. Public accountability and responsible governance: the case of Japanese public administration. *Asian Review of Public Administration.* 3(2) July-December 1991. pp. 47-53.

Nakano, Koichi. The politics of administrative reform in Japan, 1993-1998: toward more accountable government. *Asian Survey.* 38(3) March 1998. pp. 291-309.

Narain, Yogendra. Government functioning in the centre.: An agenda for freedom. *Indian Journal of Public Administration.* 36(4) October-December 1990. pp. 840-4.

Nehru, B.K. Changing the modes of governance. *Politics India.* 11(7) January 1998. pp. 3-7.

Nehru, B.K. The public services. *Man and Development.* 8(1) March 1986. pp. 47-62.

O'Toole Laurence J., Jr. American public administration and the idea of reform. *Administration and Society.* 16(2) August 1984. pp. 141-66.

Ohashi Tomohiro. Japan: administrative reform. *Productivity*. 34(4) January-March 1994. pp. 590-98.

Pachauri, S.K. Administration of justice in Indian administration: role of Committees and Commissions. *Indian Journal of Public Administration*. 40(3) July-September 1994. pp. 357-63.

Pachauri, S.K. Concept of efficiency in administration: from Curzon onward. *Indian Journal of Public Administration*. 43(4) October-December 1997. pp. 910-20.

Palmer, Geoffrey. Reforming parliamentary select committccs: A personal view. *Public Sector*. 5(3&4) May 1983. pp. 14-18.

Pareek, Udai. Decentralisation for effective governance. *Administrative Change*. 16(2) January-June 1989. pp. 105-14.

Pateria, A.K. Development role of bureaucracy in post-independence India. *Indian Journal of Social Research*. 25(1) April 1984. pp. 49-57.

Patil, V.T. and K.P. Singh. Bureaucracy in a developing society like India: its adequacies and limitations. *Journal of Karnataka University (Social Sciences)*. 22 1986. pp. 98-107.

Paymaster, B.B. This business of administrative reforms. *Public Administrator* (Special issues) 1986-87. pp. 100-10.

Pedersen, Jorgen Dige. State, bureaucracy and change in India. *Journal of Development Studies*. 28(4) July 1992. pp. 616-39.

Perry, James L and Shui-Yan-Tang. Applying research on administrative reform to Hong Kong's 1977 transition. *Asian Journal of Public Administration*. 9(2) December 1987. pp. 113-36.

Perumal, C.A. Indian bureaucratic system and responsive administration. *Indian Journal of Political Science*. 49(4) October-December 1988. pp. 580-90.

Peters, B. Guy. Government reorganisation: a theoretical analysis. *International Political Science Review*. 13(2) April 1992. pp. 199-217.

Picherack, J. Richard. Service delivery and client satisfaction in the public sector. *Canadian Public Administration*. 30(2) Summer 1987. pp. 243-54.

Pinto, Marina R. Civil service neutrality in India – the career of a concept. *Indian Journal of Public Administration*. 43(3) July-September 1997. pp. 596-610.

Pirotta, Godfrey. Politics and public service reform in small states: Malta, *Public Administration and Development*. 17(1) February 1997. pp. 197-207.

Polidando, Charles and David Hulme. No magic wands: accountability and governance in developing countries. *Regional Development Dialogue*. 18(2) Autumn 1997. pp. 1-18.

Ponnoly, Joseph. Dealing with maladministration –the need for ombudsman in India. *CBI Bulletin*. 4(12) December 1996. pp. 22-27.

Potter, David C. Mobility patterns in state government departments in India. *Indian Journal of Public Administration*. 34(4) October-December 1988. pp. 907-32.

Prasad, P.S.V. Judicial activism: its implication for public administration. *Administrator*. 42(2) April-June 1997. pp. 153-56.

Puri, K.K. Bureaucracy and politics in India. *Administrative Change*. 21(12) July 93-June 94. pp. 73-79.

Raitt Bob. Administrative reform in Indonesia. *RIPA Report*. 13(1) Spring 1992.

Raksasataya, Amara. Delivery of public services.: An overview. *Prashasan*. 17(2) March 1986. pp. 8-19.

Ramamurthi, K. Role of civil servants in India. *Nirnay*. 9(4) December 1994. pp. 40-50.

Raman, Sundar. A case for judicial activism. *Politics India*. 1(10) April 1997. pp. 23-24.

Rao, G.R.S. Political populism, administrative careerism and judicial activism: distortions in the process of democratic social transformation. *Politics India*. 1(12) June, 1997. pp. 20-26.

Rao, G.R.S. Structures and systems vis-a-vis work ethic priorities in administrative reforms. *Politics India*. 3(2) August 1998. pp. 12-15.

Rasiah Rajah. Competition and governance: work in Malaysia's textile and garment industries. *Journal of Contemporary Asia* 23(1) 1993.

Ravindra Prasad, D and V. Ganeswar. Reforms in urban governance in Andhra Pradesh: A cosmetic approach. *Nagarlok*. 21(2) April-June 1989. pp. 26-33.

Rawson, Bruce. The responsibilities of the public servant to the public accessibility fairness and efficiency. *Canadian Public Administration*. 27(4) Winter 1984. pp. 601-10.

Reese, Leura A. and Joseph F. Ohren. Decision rules and service delivery in small cities. *International Journal of Public Administration*. 13(3) 1990. pp. 435-58.

Reid, Michael. Local government—service delivery or governance? *Public Sector*. 17(2) June 1994. p. 2.

Reid, Sir William. Public accountability and open government in United Kingdom. *Indian Journal of Public Administration*. 41(3) July-September 1995. pp. 577-83.

Reyes, Danilo. Tensions in the troubled bureaucracy: reform initiatives in public organisations and service delivery systems. *Philippine Journal of Public Administration*. 37(3) July 1993. pp. 239-64.

Reyes, Danilo R. Issues on administrative accountability.: A proposed agenda for a continuing examination of negative bureaucratic behaviour. *Public Administration Journal*. 9-10(2&1) December 1987-May 1988. pp. 30-8.

Risbud, Arvind .C. Performance and accountability in public services. *Indian Journal of Public Administration*. 32(4) October-December 1986. pp. 992-1006.

Rohdewohld, Rainer. Government reforms in developing countries: the case of Indonesia. *Indian Journal of Public Administration*. 43(2) April-June 1997. pp. 181-208.

Romjek, B.S. and H.J. Dubnik. Accountability in the public sector: lessons from the challenger tragedy. *Public Administration Review*. 47(227) 1982. p. 36.

Rothchild, Donald and Michael Foley. The implications of scarcity governance in Africa. *International Political Science Review*. 4(3) July 1983. pp. 311-26.

Roy, Sanjit (Bunker). System for delivery of public services in rural areas. *Management in Government*. 23(2) July-September 1991. pp. 103-08.

Saighal, Vinod. Good governance: reining in the marauders. *Politics India* 1(10) April 1997. pp. 35-36.

Saksena, N.S. Some contradictions in the administrative system in India. *Indian Police Journal*. 30(1) July-September 1983. pp. 12-15.

Salleh, Sirajuddin H. Administrative accountability: the elusive ideal. *Asian Review of Public Administration*. 7(2) July-December 1995. pp. 108-12.

Sanajaoba, N. Judicial activism: politics of power and judicial supremacy. *Administrator*. 42(2) April-June 1997. pp. 157-66.

Sandefur, Gary D. Efficiency in social service organisations. *Administration and Society*. 14(4) February 1983. pp. 449-68.

Sanghvi, Vijay. Government: yes. But governance: No. *Young Indian*. 8(32) 14 March 1998. pp. 3-7.

Sangita, S.N. and Vaidy Vibhavathi. Ethics in superior civil service in India recruitment and training. *Indian Journal of Public Administration*. 42(4) October-December 1996. pp. 665-91.

Sankaran Nair, Chetur. Judicial activism: its relevance. *Administrator*. 42(2) April-June 1997. pp. 141-44.

Sankhdher, M.M. Alternative framework of governance: proposal for a Swadeshi constitution. *Politics India*. 3(2) August 1998. pp. 26-27.

Sanwal, Mukul. Designing training for responsive administration. *Indian Journal of Training and Development*. 18(6) November-December 1988. pp. 1-2.

Sastry, Kuruganty R. and Mukkavilli Seetharam. Participatory elements in structures of self-governance.: An analysis Mandal Praja Parishads in Andhra Pradesh. *Journal of Rural Development*. 8(4) July 1989. pp. 409-13.

Sawant, P.B. Judicial activism: trends and prospects. *Politics India*. 1(10) April 1997. pp. 9-14.

Sayeed, Omer Bin. Job satisfaction and organisational evaluation in a government bureaucracy. *Indian Journal of Industrial Relations*. 23(4) April 1988. pp. 487-97.

Schneider, Mark and Kee Ok Park. Metropolitan countries as service delivery agents.: The still forgotten governments. *Public Administration Review*. 49(4) July-August 1989. pp. 345-52.

Selvaraj, B.V. Making administration responsive in grievances hearing.: a new technique. *Indian Journal of Public Administration*. 43(2) April-June 1997. pp. 232-38.

Sen, S.R. Reforming our system of government. *Economic and Political Weekly.* 26(9&10) 2-9 March. 1991. pp. 485-8.

Sharat Kumar Administrative reforms in the context of political and economic restructuring. *Indian Journal of Public Administration.* 41(4) October-December 1995. pp. 793-98.

Sharma, Arvind K. Reorienting governance for speedy service delivery. *Indian Journal of Public Administration.* 40(3) July-September 1994. pp. 486-96.

Sharma, Keshav C. The capacity, autonomy, and accountability of local government in local-level governance: the case of Botswana. *Regional Development Dialogue.* 18(2) Autumn 1997. pp. 57-80.

Sharma, Shyam Sunder. Civil service accountability in Nepali administration. *Prashasan.* 21(3) July 1990. pp. 75-81.

Sharma, Sudesh Kumar. Delivery of public services in South-East Asia. *Prashasan.* 18(2) March 1987. pp. 1-8.

Shastri, Sandeep. Towards more effective governance. *Mainstream.* 36(5) 24 January 1998. pp. 19-20.

Sherwood, Frank P. Comprehensive government reform in New Zealand. *Public Manager.* 21(1) Spring 1992. pp. 20-24.

Sherwood, Frank P. Maggie the manager: administrative reform in Britain. *Bureaucrat.* 20(2) Summer 1991. pp. 39-42.

Singh, S.S. Administrative lawlessness.: concept and concern. *Indian Journal of Public Administration.* 40(2) April-June 1994. pp. 134-54.

Singh, S.S. In search of ombudsman – comment on Lokpal Bill 1996. *Indian Journal of Public Administration.* 43(2) April-June 1997. pp. 173-80.

Singh, S.S. Liberalisation and public service: agenda for reforms. *Indian Journal of Public Adminisuration.* 42(3) July-September 1996. pp. 383-91.

Singhvi, G.C. District and state administration.: a new leadership role for the IAS. *Indian Journal of Public Administration.* 29(4) October-December 1983. pp. 808-20.

Sinha, Satyabrata. Judicial activism: its evolution and growth. *Administrator.* 42(2) April-June 1997. pp. 51-56.

Sinha, Shivendra K. Fifty years of Indian bureaucracy. *Radical Humanist*. 61(6) September 1997. pp. 16-19.

Smith, Janet. Government reform in Canada. *Public Administration and Development*. 17(1) February 1997. pp. 33-39.

Sofi Ali. Public policy making in India: lessons from rural development programme. *Indian Journal of Public Administration*. 38(2) April-June 1992. pp. 109-21.

Stivers, Camilla. The listening bureaucrat: responsiveness in public administration. *Public Administration Review*. 54(4) July-August 1994. pp. 364-69.

Stone. Bruce. Administrative accountability in the Westminster democracies.: towards a new conceptual framework. *Governance*. 8(4) October 1995. pp. 505-26.

Subramaniam, V. Hindu values and administrative behaviour. *Indian Journal of Public Administration*. 12(3) July-September 1967.

Subramaniam, V. Reducing corruption in administration. *IASSI Quarterly*. 16(2) October-December 1997. pp. 102-05.

Sundaram, P.S.A. Recent initiative for administrative reform in India. *Indian Journal of Public Administration*. 43(3) July-September 1997. pp. 553-59.

Thara, D. Responsiveness of district administration – working of Rajkot collectorate. *Nirnay*. 11(1-4) March-December 1996. pp. 39-42.

Thompson, James R. and D. Jones Verman. Reinventing the federal government: the role of theory in reform implementation. *American Review of Public Administration*. 25(2) June 1995. pp. 183-99.

Toonen, Theo A.J. The unitary state as a system of co-governance: The case of the Netherlands. *Public Administration*. 68(3) Autumn 1990. pp. 281-96.

Tritfer, Jonathan. The citizen's charter.: opportunities for user's perspectives? *The Political Quarterly*. 65(4) October December 1994. pp. 397.

Vajpeyi, Dhirendra. Bureaucratic political culture in India: continuity and change (1976-1981). *Indian Journal of Public Administration*. 29(4) October-December 1983. pp. 783-807.

Valsan, E.H. Democratic decentralisation: selected experiments of India, Egypt and Africa. *Administrative Change.* 23(1-2) July 1995-June 1996. pp. 37-54.

Varma, Hemendra K. The bureaucratic strangle hold: a citizen's view point *Management Review.* 17(3) 1990-91. pp. 17-22.

Vashist, P.D. Reforming services. *Yojana.* 31(9) 16 May 1987. pp. 18-21.

Venkataraman, R. The role of bureaucracy in development administration in India. *Management in Government.* 18(3) October-December 1986. pp. 273-80.

Vijay Kumar, Is judicial review counter-majoritarian constitutional democracy and judicial activism. *Mainstream.* 34 (36) 10 August 1996. pp. 30-32.

Virmani, Arvind. Size and role of government: quality vs. quantity of intervention. *Indian Economic Journal.* 37(4) April-June 1990. pp. 23-42.

Vishwakarma, K.R. Democracy, development and bureaucratic neutrality in India. *Indian Journal of Public Administration.* 43(1) January-March 1997. pp. 66-78.

Wadhwani, M., O.P. Minocha and Arvind K. Sharma. Reforms to improve public sector performance: the Indian experience and perspective. *Asian Review of Public Administration.* 7(2) July-December 1995. pp. 12-20.

Wallace, S. Sayre. Bureaucracies: some contrasts in systems. *Indian Journal of Public Administration.* 10(1) January-March 1964.

Wegelin, Emiel A. New approaches in urban services delivery: A comparison of emerging experience in selected Asian countries. *Cities.* 7(3) August 1990. pp. 244-58.

Wilson, V. Seymour. Public Administration reform and the "new managerialism": a comparative assessment of a fundamental challenge confronting Canadian public administration. *International Journal of Public Administration.* 19(9) 1996. pp. 1509-553.

Wishwakarma, R.K. and Rakesh Gupta. Organisational effectiveness of urban basic services programme in slums of Delhi. *Nagarlok.* 27(4) October-December 1995. pp. 1-13.

Wittrock, Bjorn. Governance crisis and withering of the welfare state: The legacy of the policy sciences. *Policy Sciences.* 15(3) April 1983. pp. 195-203.

Woode, Samuel N. Administrative responsibility and ethics. *Greenhill Journal of Public Administration.* 7(3-4) July-December 1990. pp. 1-30.

Wright, Deil S. and Yasuyoshi Sakurai. Administrative reform in Japan: Politics, policy and public administration in a deliberative Society. *Management in Government.* 19(2-4) July 1987-March 1988. pp. 39-67.

Wunsch, James S. Institutional analysis and decentralisation: developing an analytical framework for effective Third World administrative reform. *Public Administration and Development.* 11(5) September-October 1991. pp. 431-51.

Yeager, Samuel J. State administration and ombudsman: *International Journal of Public Administration.* 6(4) December 1984. pp. 431-49.

Zaidi, S. Akbar. Pakistan: crisis of governance. *Economic and Political Weekly.* 33(11) 14 March 1998. pp. 572-73.